"Do You Know...?"

The Jazz Repertoire in Action

Robert R. Faulkner
Howard S. Becker

16pt

Read How You Want
LARGE PRINT BOOKS, BRAILLE & DAISY

Copyright Page from the Original Book

Robert R. Faulkner is professor of sociology at the University of Massachusetts Amherst. He is the author of *Music on Demand: Composers and Careers in the Hollywood Film Industry*.

Howard S. Becker taught at Northwestern University, the University of Washington, and the University of California, Santa Barbara. He is the author of numerous books, including *Tricks of the Trade* and *Telling about Society*.

The University of Chicago Press, Chicago 60637
The University of Chicago Press, Ltd., London
© 2009 by The University of Chicago
All rights reserved. Published 2009
Printed in the United States of America

18 17 16 15 14 13 12 11 10 09   1 2 3 4 5

ISBN-13: 978-0-226-23921-7 (cloth)
ISBN-10: 0-226-23921-7   (cloth)

Library of Congress Cataloging-in-Publication Data

Faulkner, Robert R.
    Do you know—? : the jazz repertoire in action / Robert R. Faulkner and Howard S. Becker.
        p. cm.
    Includes bibliographical references and index.
    ISBN-13: 978-0-226-23921-7 (cloth : alk. paper)
    ISBN-10: 0-226-23921-7 (cloth : alk. paper)
    1. Jazz—Social aspects. 2. Jazz musicians. 3. Ensemble playing.
4. Performing arts—Repertoire. I. Becker, Howard Saul, 1928– II. Title.
    ML3506 .F38 2009
    781.65′1438—dc22

                                            2008052963

♾ The paper used in this publication meets the minimum requirements of the American National Standard for Information Sciences—Permanence of Paper for Printed Library Materials, ANSI z39.48-1992.

TABLE OF CONTENTS

i

For Laura and Olivia—
RRF

For Dianne—
HSB

Still, there will come a time, here in Brooklyn, and all over America, when nothing will be of more interest than authentic reminiscences of the past. Much of it will be made up of subordinate "memoirs," and of personal chronicles and gossip—but we think every portion of it will always meet a welcome from the large mass of American readers.

WALT WHITMAN

Preface

This project was a long time coming, though the time we spent on it during which we knew that we were "doing a project" was relatively brief. For both of us, the work began when we started studying music, in early adolescence, or maybe when we started playing professionally, in late adolescence. Certainly not later than that. When we grew up and became professional sociologists, we didn't abandon music. On the contrary, music helped support us through school and afterward. And our research focused, now and then, on music as a topic of investigation. Becker's M.A. thesis and Faulkner's Ph.D. dissertation both dealt with the music business and both authors wrote other things about music and the music business throughout their lives as sociologists.

Which means that we owe a big thank you to all the people who worked with us, taught us, gave us jobs when we needed them, and made us feel at home in music during all the years from then until now—too many to name. But Becker would like to acknowledge, posthumously, Lennie Tristano, from whom he learned about piano playing and a lot of other things, and Faulkner is grateful for the opportunity to make music with Adam Kolker, Bill Goodwin, Scott Hamilton, Donn Trenner, Fred Tillis, Jeff Holmes, and the late, great David Pinardi. Each of these musicians taught him something about the moral order of the bandstand.

A little to our surprise, we did receive a grant to do this research from the National Science Foundation (NSF award SBE-0549584, titled "Repertoire in Action among Musicians"), which we gratefully acknowledge. It provided substantial help in getting the work done. We are also grateful to the Social and Demographic Institute (SADRI) at the University of Massachusetts Amherst, which provided all kinds of support far beyond what was strictly required. Karen Mason, administrator there, was especially helpful in dealing with the kinds of things that only people who have worked in universities would believe could happen.

The world of jazz is full of wonderful scholars, and we have relied heavily on the work that preceded ours to fill in what we didn't know, to explain what needs explaining so that we didn't have to, and in general for providing a supportive intellectual community that makes it easy to get work done. The articles and books of Barry Kernfeld, Paul Berliner, Scott Deveaux, Marc Perrenoud, and Ingrid Monson provided especially useful pieces of the puzzle.

Musicians in Massachusetts and California helped us understand what we all were doing by freely sharing their own thoughts and observations, and by taking part in our effort to understand how we all were doing what we did when we played together. Special thanks to Jay Messer, Bob Ferrier, David Shapiro, Emory Austin Smith, Adam Kolker, Dominic Poccia, Paul Lieberman, and Tim Atherton in Massachusetts, and to Don Bennett, Don Asher, and Andrew Epstein in California.

Several people read earlier versions of the manuscript and made very useful comments, of which we have done our best to take advantage. Thanks to Don

Rose, David Grazian, anonymous reviewer #2 (who knows who he or she is, though we don't), and Barry Kernfeld, all of whom made detailed and useful comments. We haven't always done what they suggested but we did take them seriously and are very grateful for the help.

Part of chapter 5 was originally published in French as "Les lieux de jazz," in *Paroles et musique,* ed. Howard S. Becker (Paris: L'Harmattan, 2003), 17–24; and in English as "Jazz Places," in *Music Scenes: Local, Translocal, and Virtual,* ed. Andy Bennett and Richard A. Peterson (Nashville: Vanderbilt University Press, 2004), 17–27. Pieces of the following texts, jointly authored by Faulkner and Becker, have been incorporated into the book here and there:

> "Le répertoire de jazz," in *Énonciation Artistique et Socialité,* ed. Jean-Philippe Uzel (Paris: L'Harmattan. 2006), 243–48

> "'Do You Know...?' The Jazz Repertoire: An Overview,"

OPUS—*Sociologie de l'art* 8 (mars 2006):15–24

"Studying Something You Are Part Of: The View from the Bandstand," *Ethnologie française* XXXV III, no.1 (2008):15–21.

Finally, our deepest thanks to Doug Mitchell, drummer and editor, who stayed with us through thick and thin, and whose endless enthusiasm for what we were doing always cheered us; and to Dianne Hagaman, who read the entire manuscript carefully and provided helpful feedback but, more importantly, who believed in the project, listened to endless versions of the ideas as we developed them without getting bored, and pushed us to keep at it when our spirits were low. For unending and gracious assistance Rob thanks Margaret Ellen Malone, who showed him how to look at the bandstand (and life) for what it is, not what he thought it was nor what he thought it should be.

Robert R. Faulkner and Howard S. Becker

Amherst and San Francisco, July 2008

1
How Musicians Make Music Together

Every night, all over the United States and in many other parts of the world as well, this scene takes place. Several musicians walk into a club, a bar, a restaurant, a place for a party. They get their instruments out, warm up, and then without much discussion begin to play. They play popular songs of some kind—the kind varies and the variation is important—for several hours while the audience dances, drinks, eats, and socializes.

These players might never have met, though, depending on the locale, that's not very likely. It can happen that players in a large city like Chicago or New York haven't met, but in smaller locales, which do not support so vast a world of casual entertainment, and so contain fewer professional musicians, they probably will have met somewhere, sometime. But even players who know each other may not have played together. More likely still, this particular collection of players may never have rehearsed together and, almost surely, have not rehearsed what they will play on this occasion. But they do just fine, performing well enough for the occasion without noticeable difficulties.

How do several people who haven't prepared a musical performance nevertheless give one? How can they play together competently enough to satisfy the manager of a bar or the bride at a wedding or the mother of the bar mitzvah boy?

When we decided to study this phenomenon, we thought we knew the answer to that question. We have, each of us, played professionally for many years. Faulkner is still quite active. Becker plays, but not so much and not so professionally. No matter. Having each been in the situation we just described countless times, we "knew" that the answer to how strangers can play together so well is simple: it's because they all know the same songs. Right? No. Wrong. After our first fieldwork, when we wrote field notes describing what actually happened in such situations, we saw that that wasn't the answer, because it's not true. That isn't how it happens.

What happened more often—not always, but certainly in the extreme case we thought about as exemplifying the phenomenon in its purest form—was that one player turned to another and said, tentatively, "Do you know 'My Romance'?" The person so addressed might say, "In Eb?" or, perhaps not knowing or feeling comfortable with that song, counter with an alternative: "How about 'Let's Fall in Love'?" adding hopefully that it's in the key of Bb. And so on, until they found something they could agree on and began to play.

Incidents like that showed us that everyone doesn't know all the songs, that one player knows songs another player may not know, so that which song (musicians prefer the word "tune" and from now on we'll use the two interchangeably) they play depends on them finding one they both know. Only then can the answer to the question of how they do it be "because everyone knows it," and we can be sure that it won't be everyone, because the next time another player may not know the tune these two have just agreed on.

All this takes place "on the stand," where the musicians assemble and play for an audience. Before we begin a more formal analysis, we want readers to know in more specific detail the kind of place and event we're talking about. To that end, here are three lengthy descriptions of bands at work, two of them in places we know well. Becker describes a scene from the 1950s, a bar in Chicago where he and his colleagues in the Bobby Laine Trio put together nights of music in a way that could then have been found all over the country. Then Faulkner describes a contemporary scene in a New England restaurant and the very different way he and his colleagues did it in the early 2000s. Between the two we've summarized the elegant and detailed description Bruce MacLeod (1993) gave of a typical kind of musical work—the club date—he studied in the New York area in the 1970s and '80s.

(This is as good a place as any to note that we have used masculine pronouns throughout, because all of the people we observed or interviewed, with a few exceptions that we have noted, were men. The music business is overwhelmingly a male business, almost all the women involved being singers [some of whom play piano as well, often accompanying themselves]. An excellent discussion of this phenomenon appears in Buscatto 2007.)

The 504 Club, circa 1951 (Becker)

It sat just off the corner of 63rd Street, one of Chicago's longer business streets, and Normal Boulevard, in what was then a white, working-class neighborhood. Like many such corners in Chicago then, 63rd and Normal was a small neighborhood business community, with a complement of retail stores, a couple of small restaurants, and several bars. The 504 Club was, as its gaudy neon sign let you know, the biggest bar on the corner and the only one whose license let it stay open until four in the morning (five on Saturday night); the others all had to close at two (three on Saturday night).

Figure 1 Howie Becker (piano), Dominic Jaconetti (drums), and Bobby Laine (tenor saxophone), at the 504 Club on Chicago's 63rd Street, circa 1950.

The back room of the bar filled up on busy weekends but otherwise was empty at night. During the day, it housed a thriving handbook, which took bets on horse racing and may have provided a sizeable share of whatever profits the club made. A door at the back led to a storeroom holding the bar's liquor stock, which consisted of twenty or thirty cases of something called "Old Philadelphia." Whatever the customers thought they were drinking, and no matter what the label on the bottle the bartender poured from, they were drinking "Old Philadelphia," which the bosses poured through a funnel into empty bottles of Seagram's Seven Crown and other local favorites.

The big boss, Joe Contino, was a small-time hoodlum who claimed to be the uncle of a well-known accordion-playing pop star (and he might have been). Joe wore expensive suits and had a (sort of) dapper air. His assistant, Ralph, did the dirty work, filling the bottles with Old Philadelphia and taking care of the horse-racing business in the afternoons. Joe had an "arrangement" with the local police. I didn't know the details, but I did on occasion see him quietly handing a police officer a roll of bills.

We played from a revolving bandstand in the middle of the long oval bar in the front room. It was just big enough to hold a small upright piano, a drum set, the saxophonist, a bass player if we had one and, early in my stay with the band, a trumpet player. Long-term, the band was a trio: Bobby Laine, tenor saxophone, singer, and leader; Howie Becker, piano; and a succession of very good drummers. Bob had been a pilot in WWII, and had lost an eye in combat. I was in my early twenties, had just finished a Ph.D. in sociology at the University of Chicago, and was wondering whether I wanted to be a sociologist or keep on playing the piano. I had studied piano with Lennie Tristano, who later became a sort of reclusive jazz legend, but thought, though I was certainly competent, it was unlikely that I would ever be a great jazz pianist.

We played forty minutes out of every hour. The twenty-minute break was long enough for a drink, a cigarette, even a run down to the corner for a quick hamburger.

We never rehearsed during the year and some months Bobby Laine and I worked together. We just got on the stand and played, one tune after another, for forty minutes. Bobby would call a tune, I'd play a four-bar introduction (eight bars if he needed to adjust his reed or something), and we'd start. He'd play a melody chorus and sing the second chorus, I'd play a somewhat more improvisatory chorus, and he'd finish with a last melody chorus. One of us might play two choruses now and then. Sometimes we played medleys: Bob would play a tune, I'd play another one, he'd play a third one, I'd do a fourth, and so on until we got tired of the tempo. Sometimes he snapped his fingers to set the tempo for the next song, sometimes I just started playing at whatever tempo seemed right to me. We did not discuss keys, we just played whatever we were going to play in the key we had played it before.

Sometimes one of us, usually me, wanted to play something we hadn't played before. If I had a written version I'd bring it, but more often I just played it and then taught it to Bob by playing the melody behind him until he had it. When he wanted to play something I didn't know he'd give me some specific indications (key, perhaps the nature of the harmony), but mostly I picked it up by trial and error.

The tunes we played came out of our shared background of songs that "everyone knew," from a more specialized selection of Irish songs and other material that might appeal specially to the crowd in that club, and from various sources of written music that we referred to when we needed to play something we didn't already know. In addition, I used to insist that Bob learn to play and, especially, to sing (he was a better singer than saxophonist) tunes I thought interesting, which I got from records and elsewhere.

Bobby sang, in addition to a variety of popular songs (and unusually for an Irish American of that day), blues, especially when he could work in some dirty lyrics. But he also did well with ballads and show tunes, and I undertook to enlarge his repertoire by teaching him the kinds of less-well-known songs in which I was becoming expert. He liked learning songs from what later came to be called "The Great American Song Book"—the tunes by Gershwin, Porter, Berlin, Arlen, and other composers now greatly admired. And he was also ready to pick up less-known ones, especially if the lyrics were a little suggestive. So, for instance, we often did "Do It Again." But the tunes didn't have to be dirty. I also remember teaching him "Walking My Baby Back Home."

Patrons of the bar sometimes made requests, which we did our best to ignore. They had trouble addressing us up on our revolving bandstand but could catch us during intermissions, asking for songs we usually reflexively decided we didn't want to play, although occasionally one of them redeemed himself by buying us a drink.

Mostly, however, the customers, busy drinking and socializing, ignored us completely. This amused Bobby, who tested his strong conviction that they didn't know what we were doing by making strange announcements from the stand: "We're having a big party here Saturday night and, if you can't come, just send the money," for instance. No one paid any attention to this or any of his other remarks, and for the most part completely ignored the blues lyrics and the changes he made to the lyrics of popular songs

("Little White Lies" became "Little White Thighs" and "I Only Have Eyes for You" turned into "I'll Open My Thighs for You").

There's a practical question here. How could we be playing all this stuff in a bar full of working-class people on Chicago's southwest side? They weren't aficionados of the Great American Song Book. When they made a request it was likely to be one of the standards we didn't much like, pop tunes of the twenties like "Melancholy Baby." We did that and tunes like it, assisted by a singing bartender who had become a fan of ours and used to follow us from job to job, turning up behind the bar in whatever tavern we were playing in, belting old-timers out in an authentic working-class style. He described himself as an "Irish tenor," had a good voice, sang in tune, and knew what key he sang things in, all of which made him pleasant to accompany (and it couldn't hurt to be on good terms with the bartender). His repertoire was limited to old favorites: "Angry," "Jealous," and some Chicago specials like "Back of the Yards" and "Heart of My Heart." We welcomed the diversion that accompanying him provided.

Once in a while someone would look up, puzzled by the more or less sophisticated repertoire we were playing. But mainly we just provided background noise for customers' drinking and socializing. That's how we got away with it.

As the night went on and the crowd got drunker, we tired out. Playing in a bar took a lot of energy, and around one o'clock fatigue competed with boredom to cause our playing to deteriorate (in Bob's case, his drinking contributed to that result). I would find myself falling asleep at the piano, though I never lost my place and continued to play (I sometimes lost my place when I woke unexpectedly and realized I didn't know what I was playing, what key we were in, or where I was in the song).

Playing such long hours, we would start to repeat ourselves, forgetting whether we had played this or that song already that evening. We tried to play without those repetitions, which meant that we played (calculating three minutes per song and 7×40 or 280 minutes a night) something like ninety songs a night. Our constantly changing repertoire was larger than that, but ninety represents the minimum we knew and more or less had to know to get through a night. I can't even guess what the total of different songs we played during a week was, because we didn't repeat ourselves completely from night to night. Even so, we often got bored, playing the same songs over and over (which is how it felt to us), and that led one or the other to suggest new tunes.

Joe, the boss, took an active interest in how well the bar did, and that created some difficulty for us. He often complained that, yes, the people in the bar were all drinking, but look at what they were drinking: "Beer!" When I asked him what he wanted them to drink, he said he wanted to see a bar full of people drinking scotch. That was pure fantasy; he couldn't have sold a case of scotch in that part of Chicago in a year. But he did fire us a few times so that he could try out groups he thought would do better for him: a

Gypsy band one time, and an all-girl band (as they were called then) another time. This wasn't what the customers wanted and, after business fell off enough, he hired us back.

We played at a number of other bars on 63rd Street and elsewhere in Chicago: a bar farther west owned by an inexperienced proprietor who spent his receipts taking people (us among them) out to after-hours joints and got so far in debt that he finally robbed his own bar and the attached liquor store and went to prison; a club on Michigan Avenue across from Al Capone's old headquarters in the New Michigan Hotel; and other places in similar parts of town. We picked tunes to play the same way in all of them.

New York Parties (1978, as Described by Bruce Macleod)

Bruce MacLeod's ethnography of club date musicians (MacLeod 1993, especially 42–86 and 188–200) in the New York area in the 1970s and '80s describes a quite different scene. What follows summarizes (and occasionally quotes from) MacLeod's description of the typical setting in which these players worked, the kind of music they played, and how they played it, especially from his fieldwork in 1978; we'll return in a later chapter to his findings on the changes ten years brought to the business. (Numbers in parentheses refer to pages in MacLeod's book.)

Club date musicians played for private parties: weddings, debutante balls, bar mitzvahs (an important component of the music business in New York City with its large Jewish population), banquets, and parties given by charitable organizations or corporations. They provided background sound and played for dancing. Bands consisted of as few as three or four players to as many as twenty. MacLeod notes two astounding features of their performances: they played continuously for three or four hours, and they played what seemed to be complex multipart arrangements without any written music or rehearsals, even though some, perhaps many, of the players had never played together before. "The actual personnel in a bandleader's ensemble for one night could be quite different from the same bandleader's group on another night" (18).

Leaders watched the party guests, especially the dancers, to see what they liked and danced to, and shaped the evening's music in response. Most songs were played in medleys, which were

rarely prearranged. Without referring to written music, the band members switch from one song to another following signals from the bandleader, and the signal for the next number may come only during the final measures of a song. The musicians learn which songs are part of the medley only as the medley is being played.... The medley format is used for nearly all the repertoire, not just a small portion of it. Generally speaking, if the band begins a song suited to one particular dance style, it will segue to at least one or two similar songs before moving on to another rhythm. (37)

Leaders picked songs guests would recognize, avoiding obscure songs or musical styles and "in the course of a four-hour party, a band will play sixty or more individual songs, covering a wide range of dance styles and musical genres" (39). The leader expected players to know these tunes and play them from memory. Many musicians knew this repertoire because they had played in big bands, in town and on the road, and had learned the songs (often including harmony parts) by playing them from stock arrangements. In addition, standard phrasings came to be widely known (we put it that way because no one seemed to know who was responsible for this development, it "just happened"):

Each song in the repertoire came to be phrased in a style that was more or less standard throughout the club date business, a style reminiscent of the phrasing used by the larger swing bands. Lead trumpet, saxophone, and violin players became responsible for keeping the phrasing as standard as possible so that other musicians in their sections could anticipate the correct phrasing from previous experience. (47)

Musicians didn't always agree on phrasings, producing some rough spots. But, as one player told MacLeod, "Don't forget—we're not making recordings, and we do not need perfection. All we need is about 90 percent. That's enough because people are not listening to the music critically.... If sometimes I might play a phrase differently from another man, it's not that critical. As long as we're together most of the time." In other words, the bands don't need written music because, in the party situation (as in the 504 Club), no one pays that much attention to them (49).

How much music did these players have to know? MacLeod kept a careful list of every tune played at nine events where he made observations, 520 songs in all. Of course, many songs were performed at several of these events, but "to have performed at all the affairs in the sample—not an entirely unlikely occurrence—a musician would have needed to know approximately 292 songs." And, he concludes, "within each area of the business, then, there is a general repertoire with which all experienced players are familiar." The list of tunes played covered seventy years of American popular music, from "Heart of My Heart" (1899) to "Love Me Tonight" (1969) (63).

Musicians bring to the job, in their memories, all these songs, plus a knowledge of each leader's idiosyncrasies and ways of organizing a set and an evening. They know that one leader, having picked a tune made popular by the Glenn Miller orchestra, always follows it with another Glenn Miller tune, or always follows a song from "Hello, Dolly" with a song from "Cabaret." They also bring to the job the ability to improvise harmony parts, so that four saxophone players who don't know each other can improvise chorus after chorus of four-part harmony on tunes in the repertoire. (Pages 72–86 describe what players bring to the job in great and astonishing detail, with excellent written-out musical examples.) MacLeod demystifies this feat:

The harmony parts generally move in parallel motion to the melody throughout the piece. The baritone part does move in contrary motion at times, but according to other horn players whom I interviewed, this is exceptional. Normally, the fourth saxophone part ... doubles the melody at the octave below.... None of the parts strays very far from chord tones.... Sticking to chord tones may produce a very conservative harmonization, but it at least ensures that the harmony will be acceptable and that individual parts will not conflict. (81)

The Egremont Inn, circa 2007 (Faulkner)

The Egremont Inn is, according to Zagat, a "classic New England Colonial inn" with guest rooms and a spacious dining room and bar. The innkeepers, Steve and Karen Waller, take pride in their chefs, food, award-winning wine list, and their music policy. Steve, a jazz fan, hires the best musicians he can to play in the dining room next to the bar, which serves customers waiting for a table, having dinner, or just having a drink while listening to live jazz, a piano-bass or guitar-bass duo, or a piano-bass-trumpet trio. The Wallers are proud of their commitment to jazz.

Figure 2 Rob Faulkner (trumpet), Jay Messer (guitar), and Dave Santoro (bass), at the Egremont Inn, Egremont, Massachusetts, 2008. Photograph by Olivia Faulkner.

The trio I play in consists of Jay Messer (guitar), me on flugelhorn and cornet, and Dave Santoro (bass), who joined the group when the former bass player got sick and couldn't commit to the gigs Jay had scheduled at the Inn, Castle Street, and several other venues in the Berkshires, western Massachusetts, Vermont, and New Hampshire.

We play facing the dining room, with the long bar off to our left. The comfortable, rustic-feeling room, with an oak and walnut floor and a large oriental rug, has a warm sound. Guests pass in front of the band as Steve escorts them into the dining room, to their tables.

Karen Waller, very sensitive to sound levels, worried about hiring a trumpet player as an addition to Jay's guitar-bass duo. I guess some owners, like Karen and Steve, have had bad experiences with trumpet and tenor saxophone players who take the gig, as one of them ruefully told me, "to blow the roof off of my place." The Inn had a history of cozy duos of bass and guitar or bass and piano players. A horn player, and especially a potentially loud trumpet in the bar and dining room, made the Wallers nervous.

The first time I played at the Inn with Jay, Steve assured me that he loved contemporary jazz, including Chet Baker and Tom Harrell (both trumpet players), shattering my stereotype of owners and managers as philistines, and revealing himself to be a knowledgeable jazz fan. He approached his concern in a low-key way: "We have customers who don't like the band playing too loudly. I don't mind an intense band, but you know what I mean." I told him I understood precisely what he meant, that "playing the room" was an art, and that I could see this was "an intimate setting," a quiet dining atmosphere. I told him, only half-joking, that I didn't even *like* to play loud, preferring to keep things in "a quiet Chet Baker range and mood." I said, "You won't be hearing anything tonight above *mp* [medium-soft], no 'double *f*' [very loud]."

Then I turned to Jay, as he was tuning his guitar, and said, "It's as if owners and managers see a dangerous weapon being unsheathed and fear the worst for their customers, their club, their business." Jay said that one trumpet player he worked with at the Egremont Inn played the entire gig with a cup mute in his horn and the Wallers loved him. In the meantime, Dave had tuned his bass, and set up his fancy new state-of-the-art pocket digital recorder on the piano to his right. It was four minutes until seven o'clock.

I had my cornet and flugelhorn stands out of the case at 6:30. Now we got down to business. I pulled the cup mute out of the case, and set up the horns. Jay was adjusting his music stand and I put my folder of music on the right side of his stand; Jay's pocket watch, which we used to keep track of what time it was, sat on the upper left of the stand; and beneath it Jay had put a three-by-five card on which he had handwritten a list of songs he might want to play that night. I'd seen the three or four cards before but had not examined them closely. I was still busy setting up, but I glanced at it and read the top three entries: "East of the Sun," "The Touch of Your Lips," "The End of a Love Affair." Jay, Dave Shapiro, and I did these jazz standards on a regular basis on gigs in the

Berkshires, restaurants and clubs in Vermont and New Hampshire, and ski resorts in the region. We knew Dave Santoro knew the tunes; he's toured, recorded, and played commercial gigs with the top jazz musicians in New York City.

Three dining room tables were already occupied, and several people were sitting at the bar. Some of these folks looked up from their cocktails. Jay looked over at Dave and said, "East of the Sun," Dave said, "Sure," and Jay began playing a sixteen-bar, out-of-tempo introduction, followed by four bars of chord changes and rhythm to establish the tempo of the tune. I played the lead line, quietly. Dave gave me perfect support, with beautiful bass notes, and comforting intonation. I could tell it was going to be a good night. Laughter broke out from the direction of the bar and quickly evaporated, but plenty of conversation came from there too. This wasn't a jazz concert so not everyone was listening. When we finished the tune, I turned to let Jay know he should take the next chorus. He played three choruses, then I played two, and Dave played two. We took the tune out with me finishing the melody, and ended with a brief cadenza on my part as Dave and Jay held chords for the ending. Marcia, who knows something about musicians, applauded, and so did a few people at the bar who had been listening. The couple in the dining room turned away from one another and responded to the end of the tune tepidly. The reigning matriarch of the larger party at the back of the room applauded approvingly, and that encouraged two others at the table to follow.

Jay said to Dave, "'Body and Soul,' we do it as a bossa nova?" Dave said, "Okay." Jay established a rhythmic figure and Dave immediately started laying down the bass line. After an eight-bar introduction, I switched from muted cornet to flugelhorn and entered playing the melody, in a quiet mood and at a medium tempo.

We followed up with a ballad from the 1930s, "Stars Fell on Alabama," me playing open cornet in a quasi – New Orleans style; a medium-up-tempo, Latin-tinged "The End of a Love Affair";

a bluesy jazz classic titled "A Walkin'
Thing"; and Jerome Kern's "Nobody Else
But Me." Jay had heard a recording of
"A Walkin' Thing" done by Phil Woods
and wrote out an arrangement for
flugelhorn, guitar, and bass. He and I
have played this tune on every gig
we've done in the past year. He added
"Nobody Else But Me" to our regular list
of tunes this week. After hearing a
recording by Stan Getz and Gary
Burton, he fell in love with it, copied it
off the CD, and wrote out a part in
concert key for himself and one in Bb
for me. This beautiful and tricky tune
has some unconventional melody lines
and chord progressions. Dave Santoro
had absolutely no trouble playing it and,
in fact, took two beautiful choruses
before Jay and I returned to play the
melody, taking it out. We finished the
set with our "break theme," "Christopher
Columbus," a Fletcher Henderson tune
based on the chord changes to "I Got
Rhythm," eventually incorporated into
Benny Goodman's "Sing, Sing, Sing,"
and played at a very fast tempo. By
7:50, we had played for fifty minutes,

and by eight o'clock the dining room tables were three-quarters occupied.

A dozen people sat at the bar or stood around it. I walked over to a friend of mine, Ronald Oliveira, a lawyer who is very knowledgeable about jazz and has followed Jay and myself to various places we've played in the Pittsfield and Berkshire area. He likes the music of Michel LeGrand and is especially fond of the Miles Davis/Gil Evans recording "Sketches of Spain." He requested a LeGrand tune, "You Must Believe in Spring." I told him I'd heard a wonderful recording of it by Michel LeGrand and Phil Woods, and said we would play it. I asked him if he knew the tune "Estaté." "Estaté" is a new addition to Jay's list and I was still learning it.

After a fifteen-minute break, we returned to our instruments and I asked Jay if we could play "Estaté" and told him that Ron had requested "You Must Believe in Spring." Jay said, "We'll do those later," meaning that we would do them later in the set, because it's important to honor requests by supporters like Ron Oliveira. Jay called the Paul Desmond classic "Wendy" for our first tune. Dave Santoro didn't know the tune that well, so Jay pulled out the sheet music for it and put it on the stand for Dave to read. He counted off the tune, setting the tempo, and we alternated playing the melody line, back and forth. I took the first solo and two choruses. By a quarter to nine we had played two Cole Porter tunes, "Get Out of Town" and the ballad "Every Time We Say Goodbye," followed by Luis Bonfa's "Manhã Do Carnaval" from the film *Black Orpheus.* Jay wanted to play Charlie Parker's "Dewey Square," and he was going to get the music out for Dave, but instead told him what the chords on the bridge were; these were conventional changes, so there was no need to start searching through fake books to find it. I said, "How about the Michel LeGrand tune?" Jay had been working on this tune and pulled it out of a moderately thick folder of tunes sitting in a package by his guitar case. So we were going to play Ron's request, "You Must Believe in Spring," which required music for both Dave and myself. Jay took the first solo and, as he was starting his second chorus, several couples began to dance. So we had people dancing, the bar was full, and we were playing the request of a friend who's also a good customer. No one complained about the band being loud, and some bar patrons had turned their stools around to watch us.

After we finished the LeGrand tune, the question was "What do we play next?" A slow tune was out of the question; we had just played one. I said, "It Never Entered My Mind," but that was another slow tune, though one of my favorites by Rodgers and Hart. Jay thought for thirty seconds while Dave and I waited. He said, "Let's do 'Do You Know What It Means to Miss New Orleans?'" I put the flugelhorn down and picked up the cornet; Jay counted it off, and I played the melody open, in a traditional style. The bar crowd, or at least a few who were listening to us, liked it. After a couple of solo choruses apiece, we ended with a trumpet cadenza, some fast-note flourishes, and a high note. We immediately heard applause. Jay then called a tune he wrote titled

"Concentration," a medium samba over the chord changes of "I Concentrate on You," one of my favorites. Jay pulled out the arrangement—the lead line and chord changes with their alterations—so Dave could see it. We played "Never Let Me Go," followed by "Night and Day" as a fast samba. Jay had been thinking about adding this to his list.

The customers at the bar who were listening seemed to like this one. Others were talking loudly or eating their dinner at the bar, some of them even occasionally seemed to be listening to the band. The band sounded tight and in tune, and it was a good musical moment for everyone. Jay quickly segued into the opening rhythm and chords of the up-tempo "break tune," and we finished our second set. Dave's secure and steady time made playing up tempos remarkably easy.

I sat down at the bar, ordered a Coke, and started a conversation with a psychiatrist I know who plays a little trumpet on the side. We met at Castle Street, the bistro and jazz venue in Great Barrington, Massachusetts, a few years ago. He likes the tunes we play and likes my flugelhorn sound. He especially liked my ballad playing and wanted me to do some ballads in the next set. Then I checked in with Ron to see whether he had heard the Michel LeGrand tune. He had. I told him we might play "Summertime," since he was a fan of the Gil Evans-Miles Davis *Porgy and Bess* album: "I'll check with Jay." About that time Jay motioned me to the stand for the last half-hour set, which would take us to 10:00.

Jay called Vincent Youmans's "Time on My Hands," for which he had written out the lead sheet three months earlier. We played it at a medium tempo, following the same format we had used earlier: melody statement in the flugelhorn, two or three choruses of jazz on the guitar, two flugelhorn choruses, two bass choruses, trading fours between guitar and flugelhorn, and melody to conclude. Then we played Joe Zawinul's "Scotch and Water," which Cannonball Adderley had recorded, a blues with a bridge, Jerome Kern's "I'm Old Fashioned" as a medium-tempo tune, with some trading fours between me and Jay, and Benny Carter's jazz classic "Key Largo."

There was plenty of noise at the bar and a ski crowd had arrived, with two women who shouted and yakked through the entire set. The men they were with arrived and ordered beers. Soon our band was wallpaper to the group at the bar. We continued with Jay calling "When Your Lover Has Gone," which has been in our book for a year or so. Jay had introduced his arrangement of it to me, a double-time Latin beat over a slow melody. Jay said to Dave, "This is a slow form with Latin, I'll set it up," and he proceeded to play a chorus for us to hear how he wanted it to go. There was scattered clapping over the racket of the skiers. Jay thanked the crowd, introduced Dave and myself, and the gig was over. I went to the bar and Karen immediately came over, asked me if I wanted steak or Caesar salad for dinner, and said, about the noisy customers, "They're only here one week out of the year, and they're good paying customers." I responded, "That's a good ratio, one out of fifty-two. I hope they pay their bills."

Karen nodded yes. She was pleased with the band and my sound. "I like to play softly," I told her, "it's a great room." She smiled and told one of the waitresses to start the dinner order for the band. The Egremont Inn treats us very well.

Ordinary Musicians

We've worried over how to describe the kind of musicians we studied (and are and were). Our subtitle, using the word "jazz," might mislead readers into thinking the book is about famous players like Miles Davis or Dizzy Gillespie. It's not. But there's no word in common use outside the music business that accurately describes the people we're writing about. Becker, writing a master's thesis in 1949, called them "dance musicians," but they don't always play for dancing (Becker 1973, 59–100). We can't call them "jazz musicians" and be accurate because, although almost all of them aspire to play jazz and would do it full time if they could, their working situation doesn't allow that luxury. (A few players, of course, can work full time playing nothing but jazz, but that requires traveling around the country to the relatively few venues that hire only jazz players, and probably abroad as well, to hit the international festival circuit.)

The musicians we studied play (to define them by what they do rather than what they don't do) whatever the people who hire them (the owners of bars, the fathers of brides, the promoters of dances) want them to play, within the limits of their knowledge and abilities. Musicians often describe this kind of activity as "jobbing" or "playing club dates" or similar expressions that refer to playing whatever kind of engagement presents itself. Some musicians might turn down an invitation to play a night with a band that plays for audiences who want nothing but polkas (because they only know a few polkas) but most would probably accept the engagement, believing they probably could get through the night one way or another without sounding disastrously incompetent.

Musicians who play club dates, or "job," usually have a checkered musical experience, playing a little of this and a little of that, but often can find a niche where they play in more or less one style with people who play more or less in the same style. Nevertheless, over the years, the variety of their experiences means that they have played (and probably learned) a variety of kinds of music and songs, though it's unlikely that any two of them will have had just the same experiences and know just the same songs.

Having all this in mind, we've decided that we can most accurately describe these players by adopting the term used by the excellent French sociologist of music (and bass player) Marc Perrenoud in his book *Les musicos* (2007), and calling them "ordinary musicians." That is, players competent in a variety of styles, ready to do what is likely to come up in most engagements, interested in jazz and aiming to play it when they can, but in the end doing whatever the world throws their way. And what we have, somewhat inaccurately, called "the jazz repertoire" refers to the mixture of jazz, popular songs, ethnic music, and whatever else ordinary musicians might learn through their experiences playing in public.

2

Repertoire as Activity: The Basic Elements

Musicians playing together in public places create and recreate the jazz repertoire as they play. We'll explain the four basic elements of the phenomenon in this chapter before going on to describe how it all works.

Songs. Songs, which make up the repertoire of jazz players (of working musicians in general), consist of a melody with its accompanying harmonic structure and lyrics. They exist in a variety of places: in written form, in published sheet music and in "fake books" made up from that source and others; in recordings made by players and singers of many different musical persuasions; and in live performances in a great variety of settings. In addition, performers often create them at the time of playing, inventing them on the spot.

Performers. Musicians and singers perform songs in a variety of situations. Some performers are known nationally and even internationally, others are known only to a small circle of people for whom and with whom they perform. Some play in a variety of styles, others play in one or a few. Some are extremely competent, their skills prized by other performers, others less so, and some more or less incompetent.

Performance situations. Musical performances take place in settings characterized by their location, their personnel, and the demands they make on the performers. The chief variants are: parties, where music is played as part of some kind of festive familial, friendly, sociable, or business event, the music being distinctly secondary for the audience; bars and restaurants, where the music serves as entertainment for people who are also there to drink, eat, dance, and socialize; and concerts, where people have paid specifically to hear these players play the music they are going to play. Situations also vary in the power relations that characterize them: the people who pay the musicians want to get what they think they paid for and will do what they can to get it. In some cases, but not many, the musicians have the upper hand.

Working repertoire. Performers choose from available songs and organize their choices so as to create a performance that takes account of the characteristics of the situation and the abilities of the various members of the playing group. When they perform what they have chosen, we might say that they "enact" the repertoire—turn the potential contained in all these resources into a performance that is the repertoire-in-action. The working repertoire is a subset of the possible repertoire made up of all the songs that exist in one of the forms we listed earlier.

"Repertoire" is shorthand for the production of a musical event involving these four elements.

Songs

Songs have a history. Someone composed them, maybe wrote them down, others learned them and passed them on, publishers and librarians stored them in more or less accessible places, and players who needed songs to perform on a particular occasion in a particular setting chose some from that collection and played them.

Musicians distinguish several sources of songs:

- Traditional songs, created by the "folk" and preserved in the memories and activities of nonprofessional performers ("Happy Birthday"), at least until they are acquired by collectors of traditional culture, folklorists, hobbyists, and antiquarians. Eventually, someone writes them down and makes them available in books and sheet-music collections for sale or in libraries.

- Songs written by professional songwriters for popular consumption. Whenever this industry came into existence in the Unites States, maybe around 1900, by the 1910s it was flourishing, producing thousands of songs a year. (James Maher, in his introduction to Alec Wilder's *American Popular Song,* estimates that between 1900 and 1950 the American song publishing business published around 300,000 popular songs.)

- Songs written by jazz players, mainly but not entirely for instrumental performance, and thus mostly without lyrics.
- Songs musicians occasionally invent on the spot, at the time of performance.

All these songs—all the ones ever written or recorded or played anywhere, however they are stored and preserved—constitute a reservoir of songs performers could play if they knew them, and wanted to, and conditions allowed them to.

The short compositions with accompanying lyrics we call songs take one of a few standard forms. Describing them requires a small, but we think necessary, amount of technical musical talk, for which we've interspersed some explanatory sidebars.

The Names of Chords and the Circle of Fifths.

Musicians understand songs as composed of a melody, the associated lyrics (if there are any), and sequences of underlying harmonies, which they usually refer to as "chords" or "changes." Sequences of chords are called "chord progressions" in technical music theory, and a "cadence" is "a melodic or harmonic motion conventionally associated with the ending of a phrase, section, movement, or composition" (*Oxford Companion to Music,* s.v. "cadence"). The dominanttonic progression furnishes the backbone of the popular song, giving songs and their subparts distinctive endings that indicate to the listener whether the piece is over or will keep going. Cadences and cadence-like chord progressions produce a feeling of appropriate "natural" musical movement and, especially, the feeling of closure and completion most of us learned in school to hear as the movement from "sol" to "do." Most listeners understand this fundamental building block of popular music, whether or not they have learned the music-theory way of talking about it.

Musicians routinely use this technical language of chord progressions, expressed in Roman numerals or letters, to describe a tune's harmonic structure, the changes ("modulation") from one chord to the next. They call the chord built on the first note of the scale of a given key "I" and describe chords built on other notes of the scale with Roman numerals indicating the number of scale steps from that note to the tonic, I. So, in the example below, C is I, D is II, and G is V. The tag after each Roman numeral indicates the kind of chord that is built on that scale tone: a "II7" or a "V7" indicates that the chord built on that note of the scale is a dominant seventh chord, the one that leads "naturally" to the tonic and gives a sense of closure; a "ii7" or "v7" indicates that the chord built on that note of the scale is a minor seventh chord. Chords can also be named with letters, which indicate the actual notes involved rather than the more abstract relations indicated by Roman numerals.

The first chord in the illustration below, D7, is built on the second note of the scale of C major. It "resolves," or leads, to G7, a chord built on the fifth note of the C scale, which in turn resolves to a C6 chord, built on the tonic note of the scale. These chords, in these relationships, are called dominant seventh chords (in the key of C, the G7 chord) or tonic chords (in the same key, the C6 chord):

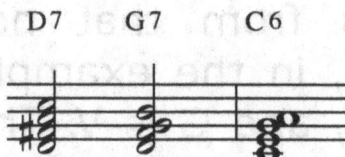

Because the dominant-tonic movement "sounds right" to Western ears, songs use them to move from chord to chord, each tonic chord capable of serving in turn as a dominant chord that leads into another tonic, and the structure sounds and feels natural to players and listeners alike. In the example, the G7 chord resolves to the C chord. Musicians conventionally describe progressions like these as a "II-V-I."

Changing the C6 chord into a C7 after two beats, as in this example, allows it to resolve into an F chord, which creates the effect of a temporary key change.

D m7   G7   C6   C7   F 6

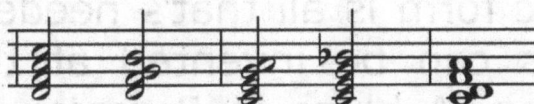

A "turnaround" is "a chord pattern at the end of the final phrase of a chorus, or segment of a chorus, which leads back to the beginning of the theme" (New Grove Dictionary of Jazz, 2nd ed., s.v. "turnaround"). This example shows such a movement—C6 – amin7 – dmin7 – G7 – C6—often named "II-V-I" (or some variation on that, musicians on the job not always being sticklers for terminology) after the last three chords of the sequence:

C6   A min7   D min7   G7   C 6

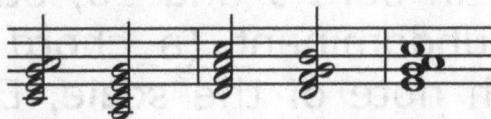

> Play them on a piano and you will recognize them as familiar sounds.

The twelve-bar-long *blues* has a simple harmonic structure: four bars of the tonic chord (I), two bars of the subdominant chord (IV7), two bars of the tonic (I), two bars of the dominant (V7), two bars of the tonic (I). The harmonic form is all that's needed, since melodies can be invented at the time of playing. A blues in B major, with no melody, is often written this way:

$$\text{B}\flat 6////|\text{E}\flat 7////|\text{B}\flat 6////|\text{B}\flat 7////|\text{E}\flat 7////|////|\text{B}\flat 6////|////|\text{Cm}_7////|\text{F}_7////|\text{B}\flat 6////|////$$

The slashes indicate a beat, in this case in 4/4 time. Thus the first bar consists of four beats of a Bb6 chord. Any competent player of popular music can play easily from these spare indications.

Musicians vary this blues structure endlessly. A small example: instead of two bars of the dominant (a chord built on the fifth note of the key, F7 in the example) in bars 9 and 10, bar 10 can be the subdominant (a chord built on the fourth note of the scale, Eb7). The melodies, especially when the blues are sung, are more or less traditional and relatively unimportant. Instrumental versions usually contain short melodies someone has composed over these chords and given a name to (Charlie Parker's "Now's the Time," Duke Ellington's "Things Ain't What They Used to Be"). Musicians traditionally play blues in Bb, as in our example, but can and often do play blues in any key. When players want to suggest that a group play this form, they can describe it adequately by saying "It's a blues in C," or any of the other twelve possible keys (including their counterparts in the related minor keys).

Canonical *popular* *songs,* conventionally known as "standards," and all the might-have-been standards, vary around a common thirty-two-bar form, usually described as an AABA or ABAB' format (B' indicating a variant of the B strain that allows a resolution to the tonic in the first bar of the next chorus). Each letter stands for an eight-bar melodic segment and its accompanying harmonies, with or without a "tag" of four extra bars after the last A segment. A song with an AABA format starts with an eight-bar statement of a melody (A), which is then repeated (A), an eight-bar statement of a different melody (B), and a repetition of the first melody, usually slightly altered to create a sense of closure at the end of the song. In the ABAB' form, the B' strain is a variant of B, altered to bring the song to a conventional end. Popular songs cover a tonal range seldom larger than ten notes (a "tenth"), an octave and a third, and usually less, most of the melody moving scalewise or through arpeggios (the notes of a chord played singly). The eight-bar phrases, the A's, B's, and C's, almost always consist of two-and four-bar subsegments. Well-known examples are, for the AABA form, "Exactly Like You" or "Sunny Side of the Street," and, for the ABAB' form, "Stardust" or "All of Me."

The form took definitive shape in the late teens and early twenties of the twentieth century, and continued to develop and change. In subsequent decades, melodies in some styles incorporated in the ordinary player's repertoire gained complexity, using more notes of the chromatic scale (the second and sixth notes of the scale, the major seventh and ninth, and such altered notes as the flatted fifth and ninth, the raised ninth and eleventh, and so on). Likewise, the canonical ABAB and similar forms experienced many variations as composers experimented with forms, adding more melodic sections, so that a song might have an ABCD structure, as does one of the two songs called "I Never Knew," or changing keys frequently, as does "All the Things You Are," whose first sixteen bars contain four four-bar sections in four different keys. (We should note that none of these descriptions are obvious. It is possible to suggest other analyses of the same songs, though most varieties will agree on the main points; for example, "All the Things You Are" can be read as a series of minor-key progressions, without disputing the central point, that it is a substantial variation on standard practice.) When performers learn a song they ordinarily take this structure as the norm and note variations from it. So they will point out that "Moonlight in Vermont," contrary to what anyone accustomed to the conventional structure would expect, has a six-bar A section (though the final A section has an extra four bars that bring it to ten bars) or that "A Nightingale Sang in Berkeley Square" has an extended (ten-bar) A section.

Ordinary people (nonprofessional musicians) bought these songs in sheet music form in the teens and twenties, to play and sing from at home. Nonprofessionals did not have the training necessary to sing songs with an extended range or songs that contained "difficult" skips (jumping to a note a major seventh above or below, for instance) or the use of nonscale tones in the melody, which accounts for the simple character of the songs written early in the era.

Like structure, harmonies follow a few standard patterns, most commonly II-V-I and its variations. In other variants, the song changes key. Moving up a major or minor third are most common (the second A section of "Long Ago and Far Away" moves from F to Ab), but the song might also rise by a half step ("Body and Soul" moves from Db to D as it goes into the B section); many other variations are possible. Like melodies, harmonies got more complex and varied over the decades.

Because popular songs are formulaic in just this way, a small amount of information serves to orient an experienced player. So Bobby Laine could tell Becker, when he wanted to play his original composition, "Jump, the Water's Fine," which Becker didn't know: "It's 'I Got Rhythm' with a 'Honeysuckle' bridge." The description means that the A section has the same harmonic format as Gershwin's "I Got Rhythm" and the B (middle) section, the "bridge," has the same chord progressions as the bridge of Fats Waller's "Honeysuckle Rose." With that information, a competent player can hear and learn the melody when it's first played by someone else and improvise a succeeding chorus on the harmonies so described.

A common variant from the canonical format is a twenty-bar song made up of five four-bar phrases ("Life Is Just a Bowl of Cherries," "Keepin'

Out of Mischief Now," "I've Grown Accustomed to Her Face"). Greater variation occurred in the less restricted world of the Broadway musical, where a song might contain extended interludes made up of new themes ("Little Boy Blue") or have a second melody independent of the first ("The Trolley Song"). In the last years of the musicals that provided a home for so many of these tunes, Rodgers and Hammerstein, Leonard Bernstein, Frank Loesser, and other composers experimented with arias of greater length and complexity—the "Soliloquy" from *Carousel,* the opening aria, "I Feel Like I'm Not Out of Bed Yet" from *On the Town,* the "Fugue for Tinhorns" from *Guys and Dolls*—but these were seldom performed outside their dramatic context. Adventurous composers began to use notes increasingly far from a song's tonal base (the flatted fifth of a II chord in the fourth bar of "We'll Be Together Again," or the flatted fifth of a chord even more distant from the tonal home in the thirteenth bar of "Laura").

The greatest departures from the standard formats appear in jazz compositions, songs written by jazz composers to be played by jazz groups, which have increasingly departed from conventional formats in number of bars, harmonic patterns (e.g., the introduction of the "Giant Steps" harmonic progression as a formulaic element, discussed later in the book), and melodic construction (unusual skips, nonscale tones, etc.). Jazz composers also began to experiment with time signatures other than the customary 4/4—the 5/4 of Brubeck's "Take Five" and the adaptation of the traditional 3/4 waltz to jazz themes and rhythmic patterns. Composers and arrangers (not always an easy distinction to make) for the large dance bands of the period sometimes wrote extended multipart compositions: Duke Ellington's early "Rockin' in Rhythm" and later multimovement suites like "Black, Brown and Beige," Ralph Burns's four-movement "Summer Sequence" written for the Woody Herman orchestra, Eddie Sauter's "Benny Rides

Again" and "Superman" written for Benny Goodman.

The songs of the jazz repertoire, to summarize, are, for the most part, formulaic, elaborate variations on a small number of templates. Someone who knows the basic forms can play thousands of songs in this great reservoir without much work.

Storage and Preservation

Songs have always circulated, though never exclusively, in printed and published form. When Alec Wilder wrote his book on American popular song he played through several thousand printed songs. Printed songs exist in multiple copies stored in public and private collections, usually easily accessible, and almost always available somewhere (musicians can often tell you the name of a music store in town that has "all the old sheet music"). Published songs have a long life, because so many copies exist and so many people save them.

On occasion, someone writes a song down but it isn't published. The composer may make photocopies so that more than one exists; Becker has the music to some Tommy Wolf songs that may survive only in this form. Or an archive collects someone's unpublished songs, like the Ira Gershwin archive of songs by Ira and George to which only the singer Michael Feinstein has had access. Sometimes only one copy exists. Legend has it that Alec Wilder wrote songs for Marian MacPartland on cocktail napkins, as he listened to her playing piano in bars, and these unique songs would have disappeared definitively had she not kept the manuscript copies and recorded them.

In another version, big bands (and small groups too) play "head arrangements," composed individually or collectively, often during a performance, and never written down. The composer teaches the song to the other players, who remember their parts. The Count Basie and Woody Herman bands were especially known for this.

In what we might call the *Fahrenheit 451* version, musicians simply remember a collection of songs played over and over on the radio or records during their childhood and adolescence. These collections vary with the age and opportunities for radio listening children had. Becker remembers and plays popular hits of the thirties that Faulkner, some years younger, didn't have available to learn. Just as the rebels of Ray Bradbury's novel, living in a society which systematically burned books, preserved them by memorizing them, songs are preserved when, where, and if someone memorizes them and keeps the memory alive by playing them. No one intentionally burns old music, but relics no one has any use for eventually get thrown out as trash, and music disappears unless someone, just as intentionally, preserves written copies and makes them available.

Finally, and increasingly importantly, recordings preserve songs for those who hear them and can learn to play them by listening (more about this later). H. Stith Bennett (1980, 140–45) suggested that some players use recordings as the functional equivalents of a written score.

Different methods of storage require different skills in the person who wants to acquire certain songs. Anyone can buy printed versions of songs or consult and copy sheet music available in libraries. But you can only acquire some songs by learning them face-to-face from someone who already knows them. You have to be able to read music to learn a song from a printed score, you have to have trained your ear to be able to reproduce a song from hearing it performed live or on a recording (musicians refer to this as "taking a tune off the record"). Not all performers have these skills, and we will discuss them at length later.

Performers

Many people perform songs in many places: lay people in the privacy of their homes, amateurs in a variety of settings, and the professionals with which we are concerned perform songs repeatedly in public places, generally for pay.

Where performers learn songs

Individual performers acquire their working repertoire in several ways, all attested to in our field notes and memories. They learn songs by reading them from sheet music on which they are recorded. They may have learned to translate songs they hear into playable notes they can reproduce when needed. Some jazz players learn this invaluable skill in ear-training classes but most probably teach themselves.

Performers hear songs in a variety of places, but mainly by listening to public performances (including those of the groups they play with) and listening to the radio and records. What you can learn from public performances depends on what kinds of performances are available where you are, whether you are old enough to be in the places where the performances occur, and your ability to learn by hearing something just once. What you can learn from the radio depends on what's available on the radio stations to which you have access. This has varied over the years, as we'll see later. In the 1930s and '40s, big bands played for hours every night over local stations tied to one of the three big networks, but by the 1950s that source had disappeared. Some contemporary radio stations specialize in jazz or in music of particular eras, and many of these stations are available via Internet radio, so that young performers, even those out of reach of broadcast radio, can hear almost anything if they have the patience to search for it.

Recordings, available to anyone who can buy or borrow and copy them, let the listener hear the same song repeatedly, making it easier to learn. Almost anything that was ever recorded is available today somewhere. Jazz players typically treat the recordings of well-known players and singers as privileged sources of material (a song recorded by Chet Baker has a better chance of being heard by players learning new tunes than one recorded only by commercial dance bands of the song's vintage).

What Is Improvisation?

Barry Kernfeld (*Grove Online,* s.v. "improvisation") gives a clear and concise definition:

The creation of a musical work, or the final form of a musical work, as it is being performed. It may involve the work's immediate composition by its performers, or the elaboration or adjustment of an existing framework, or anything in between. To some extent every performance involves elements of improvisation, although its degree varies according to period and place, and to some extent every improvisation rests on a series of conventions or implicit rules. The term "extemporization" is used more or less interchangeably with "improvisation." By its very nature—in that improvisation is essentially evanescent—it is one of the subjects least amenable to historical research.

Many years ago Becker appeared with the well-known jazz writer Ralph Gleason (then a regular columnist for the San Francisco Chronicle) on a panel in Berkeley, California, discussing jazz. They each gave their prepared talk and then jointly answered questions from the audience. As Becker tells the story:

The first question came from a sociologist who asked us to explain the relation of jazz to the concept of the mass society. We struggled with that. The second question, from a young man withfire in his eye, was directed to Gleason and went something like this: "Man, I mean, you know, I read your review of Charlie Mingus and, man, I mean, I'm sorry, you were just wrong, man." I let Ralph deal with that one. But the one that threw both of us came from an elderly woman with a strong Viennese accent: "Both of you have used this word improvisation. Could you please explain to me what this means?" At that point, we knew the difficulty of talking to the multiple audiences a lecture on jazz might interest.

And we have realized all along that we would have this problem in this book, nowhere more than in trying to describe the multiple meanings attached to the word "improvisation."

Paul Berliner's book, Thinking in Jazz: The Infinite Art of Improvisation (1994) provides the most complete exploration of the idea we know of. Berliner takes more than eight hundred pages of text, musical examples, and notes to give readers a comprehensive understanding of what the term encompasses, and no short explanation will do justice to that complexity. A (very) short version of what he has to say there would be that jazz players routinely play versions of songs they already know or whose form they can guess at, substituting melodies composed on the spot for the original, but always keeping in mind that those melodies ought to sound good against the (more or less) original harmonies of the song, which the other players will be (more or less) expecting to be the foundation of what they play together. Jazz improvisation, then, (more or less) combines spontaneity and conformity to some sort of already given format. The parenthetical qualifications indicate that none of these things is always true all the time or, maybe, not even most of the time. Improvised solos are spontaneous, yes. But the people who play them have often worked long and hard to become familiar with the harmonic and melodic "bones" of the tune they will later improvise on in public (Faulkner 2006). The solos they perform do conform to those basic structures but cannot be predicted from a knowledge of what the players have learned and practiced beforehand. The limits within which melodies and harmonies and rhythms can be altered and transformed vary from one playing situation to another, from one group to another, from one era to another. What "sounds good" against the basic chords of the original song varies from player to player and time to time. And players often disagree on what's allowable in an improvisation, as do audiences.

So "improvisation" is one of those words of which we can say that everyone who knows what it means knows what it means but no one who uses it can define it in a way that will satisfy even the definer, and certainly not the rest of the interested community.

Learning a song, knowing a song, and improvising on a song

When musicians answer a colleague's question by saying that they "know" a song, what do they know? The most complete knowing of a song includes knowing the melody as written and/or played by the composer and/or an admired performer; the underlying harmonies players typically use as a basis for accompaniment and improvisation; any well-known or quasi-traditional background figures, additions, or substitutions to the melody or harmony; any solos well enough known to have become canonical; and the lyrics. Many jazz players insist that to improvise on a song properly you should know the lyrics. Lester Young said: "A musician should know the lyrics of the songs he plays too.... Then you can go for yourself and you know what you're doing" (Berliner 1994, 791, quoting Hentoff 1956, 10).

In the ideal case, every player would know all of these things about every song they might play. But not every player has all that knowledge. Sometimes a performer knows the melody but not the harmonies or, just as common, knows the harmonies but not the melody. Or knows the melody and harmony but not the well-known (to some other performers) variations on the melody or harmony, or the background or counter figures that might be used when playing that tune.

Certain variations are critical, depending on the situation. If someone else in the band can play the tune when it's called for, the player who doesn't know it won't suffer. If all you have to play is the melody, you will not suffer because you don't know the harmony. Not knowing the lyrics usually harms only a singer.

Performers "learn" a song by first learning the melody and then practicing improvising on the harmony, finding melodic lines that fit the harmonies and feel comfortable while sounding original, looking for transitions between chords and parts of the song they can use as they work their way through a chorus. They want to become familiar enough with the song not to get lost or sound awkward, ideally so familiar that they can make the most of the possibilities it might contain. (Berliner 1994 goes into all of these processes in great, and interesting, detail.)

That's what they'd like to do but, on the job, performers often have to play songs they don't know well, and even songs they don't know at all. When the bar owner or someone in the audience asks a group to play a song they may not all know, the players first ask among themselves if anyone knows it. If at least one player knows it, the others can learn it by listening to him play the first chorus, which will give them a clear enough idea of the melody to be able to play something like it for the second chorus, or at least a clear enough idea of the harmony to be able to improvise a second chorus. The piano player can usually deduce the harmony from the melody he hears.

That these seemingly difficult things can be done at all results from the formulaic nature of popular and jazz tunes referred to earlier. A player who knows at least a phrase of the melody can guess that the succeeding phrases will repeat it, perhaps on a different degree of the scale, and that the harmonies will go through certain regular patterns. Players who know the tune can indicate well-known patterns in a few words ("It's 'I Got Rhythm' chords").

These workarounds for problematic situations don't always work. Some songs, especially in the later years of the format, moved far enough beyond these simple formulae to require more knowledge and superior skills of listening and translating. Still, the departures could often (but not always) be communicated as variations on a standard pattern.

Songs have a "standard" key, the one the composer originally wrote them in. Players often have to play the song in a different key (perhaps to accommodate a singer whose range differs from the one in which the song was written). Transposing is simplified by the formulaic character of songs, and further simplified by the practice routine of some players, who often practice whatever they learn in all twelve keys.

Individual repertoires

Performers create their personal repertoire over the time of their musical activity and experience. They learn songs with increasing degrees of detail, ranging from a mere acquaintance with the name, key, and general outline of the melody and harmony to a deep knowledge based on extensive playing and exploration of its possibilities. What they have learned, what they know and can play at a particular moment, constitutes their repertoire, which may well resemble the repertoires of many other players of the same age who have had some of the same experiences. But no two individual repertoires are identical. No two players have had exactly the same experiences, listened to the same radio programs and records, and played with the same bands, and so they haven't learned exactly the same songs. That's why even players with similar musical backgrounds and experience have to ask each other, "Do you know...?" when they propose a song to play. They will know a lot in common but almost surely not everything.

Players' experiences of specific songs have a history. At first acquaintance a song will perhaps "interest" me, offer suggestions of novelty and possibilities for improvisation. But because I don't yet know it, it's also potentially dangerous. Maybe my lack of familiarity with it will lead me to make mistakes and play a bad solo, give a bad performance. Later on, when I have played it a few times, practiced it at home, I may feel more at ease and will play it and improvise on it without worry. Still later, I may arrive at a kind of stable improvised solo which will not vary much from performance to performance. Finally, I may feel that I've exhausted the song's possibilities and start to think of it as "boring." I might then drop it from my active repertoire. I can play it if someone else wants to but won't suggest it myself (unless, in a moment of panicked necessity to play something, anything, it comes to mind and I grab it).

That suggests one possible history of a given song's participation in the working repertoire of a single musician. Chapter 4 contains a detailed account of the way Becker's repertoire developed over many years. The jazz repertoire, as a generalized phenomenon characterizing some collection of musicians, gets built up from their combined knowledge of songs. A musical community's repertoire consists of all the songs that at least one member of that community knows and can, if necessary, play and teach to others, and thus the collection of songs potentially available to that community for performance. "The jazz repertoire" as a single entity (which is what phrases like "The Great American Song Book" suggest the repertoire is) doesn't really exist, except insofar as some collection of players, singers, and listeners agree on its contents. Since they never do, we should think of "the repertoire" as a useful fiction, which refers to a more complex continuing process of learning, selection, playing, discarding, and forgetting. We'll return to this problem later.

Performing Situations

The places musicians work and perform in have their own "demand characteristics": requirements for what can be played, what should be played, and what mustn't be played. When situations confront them with these demand characteristics, performers learn songs they might otherwise not have learned and learn to play them in ways they might never otherwise have played them (as in the situations Bruce MacLeod describes of players who can play the full scores of current Broadway shows in close harmony just as though they had written music in front of them).

Conversely, players who don't learn the necessary songs and ways of playing them make themselves ineligible for jobs that require that knowledge and those skills. A good jazz player who nevertheless does not know the well-known standards of the past might (although this depends on a lot of other things) thus not be hired for jobs that require that knowledge. A player who can't play polkas won't be hired to play at Polish weddings.

In commercially organized events, an audience pays, by buying tickets or drinks, to hear the music played and perhaps to dance to it. At private events, hosts invite guests whom they will entertain with music, food, and other amusements. The music is incidental to the event. In concerts, a producer sells tickets to people who want to hear specific performers do what they are known for. Either way, someone hires the musicians to play what they want played. In the best case, from the musicians' point of view, they're hired to play their own choice of music. Otherwise, they play what they have been hired to play or deal with consequences, which range from minor unpleasantness to being fired.

Commercial situations

The owner or manager of a club or ballroom, whose business depends in part on an audience being satisfied with the music, hires a band. He thinks he knows what kind of music will help his business. Watching the cash register and the crowd, he makes more or less informed judgments about the music's effect and issues orders accordingly. His personal musical tastes help shape his decision about what kinds of music he wants his employees to play and what, therefore, they should have in their repertoire, but usually do not override his business judgment.

What the clientele of such establishments likes and wants to hear varies widely. "All-around" musicians can play "Does Your Mother Come from Ireland?" or "O Sole Mio," "My Yiddishe Momme," or tarantellas or freilachs, if ethnic dances are needed. They can play working-class ballads or gamblers' songs. In some establishments, an audience might want to hear classical American standards, while in others they would be looking for the more contemporary songs of Steven Sondheim or Andrew Lloyd Webber. Some crowds want to dance to Latin American music. Some want to hear up-to-the-minute jazz. Each establishment finds its place in the competitive world of entertainment spots, and what music the players need to know and play results from the spot's niche, the clientele that goes with that, and their tastes.

As audiences change, what's necessary to know changes too. There are probably not so many ethnic Italians who want a tarantella played at the wedding party as there once were. And the sentimental working-class songs Becker played for the appreciative patrons of the 504 Club—"Wedding Bells Are Breaking Up That Old Gang of Mine" and "Heart of My Heart"—have probably lost their audience as well.

Owners and managers usually simply refuse to rehire groups who don't do what they're told. Since performers usually want to keep their jobs, bosses generally get their way about what's played. This is a strong external constraint.

Private parties

The demands of these situations come either from the leader who has booked the job and wants to continue to book jobs like it (MacLeod gives a good description of these pressures) or from the person throwing the party who has hired the band. In either case, whoever is in charge of the party usually wants to see people on the floor dancing.

Musician-only events

Strictly speaking, these rehearsals or sessions aren't jobs, since the musicians are not playing for an audience of nonmusicians in a public place. Instead, on occasion, performers get together to play with one another and for one another. Other people are present, if at all, on the understanding that no one is interested in their opinions or desires. At these events, musicians need not worry about the opinions of nonmusicians, need not tailor what they play to what they have been told or guessed about what someone else wants, and need not worry about what will happen if they ignore the opinions of nonmusicians.

As a result, these situations provide a place where players can try things out: something new to them individually, though not necessarily new to others, maybe a new harmonic or rhythmic possibility they have been exploring in their practice periods. They may try something collectively that they have all done before individually, but not together. Or they may experiment collectively with something none of them is familiar with.

These events provide opportunities for players to add to their repertoires, experimenting with new possibilities, and creating some new possibilities of collective work.

Situations in which the musicians playing constitute the only audience create the conditions under which players can make the choices that form their repertoires. Commercial playing situations limit what they can choose to play from the larger pool of available material.

Working Repertoire

So *performers,* who have learned some but not all of the possible *songs* they might have learned, work in *situations,* one or more of them playing for a certain amount of time for whoever is there. The payoff of this way of thinking does not lie in that general statement, but rather in the results you get when you specify the character of each of these inputs. This specific group of players playing in this specific place with its specific demands and using the specific repertoire that is, one way or another and at one level or another, available to them individually and collectively, will create, on the spot and perhaps for this one time only, a *working repertoire*—this working repertoire being the specific list of songs they play on this occasion.

A working repertoire may well not exist beyond the specific occasion in which players created it. Consider the situation Becker found himself in when he was asked to perform at a jazz club in Copenhagen.

I asked my hosts to hire a bass player for the occasion, and they went far beyond my modest requirements, hiring Mads Vinding, one of the best bass players in Denmark and an internationally known player. Vinding, with whom I was going to perform in Copenhagen, e-mailed to ask what I had in mind to play, and I wrote back: "Judging by the record with Fischer, you know all the tunes. But it's true that I like to play some things that aren't so well known so I thought I'd suggest some things I will perhaps want to play and, if they're unfamiliar, I can send you a chart. Here are some of the things I might be playing—if you'd like a lead sheet on any of them let me know: 'I'll Remember Suzanne,' 'Suddenly It's Spring,' 'What Can I Say after I Say I'm Sorry,' 'No Moon At All,' 'Keeping Out of Mischief Now,' 'When Somebody Thinks You're Wonderful,' 'En Dag i Augusti' (the Monica Zetterlund tune). Probably some others too."

And got this reply: "I don't know how you did it, but you managed to pick 7 tunes I don't know!—(and I do know a lot). Anyway, if you bring lead sheets it shouldn't be a problem. No need to send them unless there's a lot of difficult bass notes."

That list of songs is what the two did play that night in Copenhagen. But this never became a working repertoire because these two players have not played together since, nor is it likely they will.

(For those who, like this great bass player, don't know these songs, "Suzanne" and "Spring" are pop tunes of the forties; "What Can I Say" is from the twenties; "No Moon" was played by Page Cavanaugh, the pianist-leader of a jazz trio; "Mischief" and "Wonderful" are Fats Waller specialties; and "Augusti" is a Scandinavian tune in the American pop style, recorded by the Swedish jazz singer Monika Zetterlund.)

Though this kind of situation happens from time to tine, especially in larger urban musical communities, the same performers often do work together in the same situation (or the same kind of situation) for long periods of time, and the working repertoire they develop becomes a resource they can and do call on again and again. They've worked out what they jointly know, what the situations demand and/or tolerate, and they have a list of playable tunes from which they only need select some tunes and decide what order to play them in to produce an evening's performance.

Repertoire as process

What process produces a working repertoire? We will consider this at length in chapter 7, but for now will just suggest some of the basic steps, some of them foreshadowed by the vignettes in chapter 1:

One of the performers recognizes that it's time to start playing, and suggests that they decide on something so that they can meet that situational need.

Someone proposes something for the group to consider, drawing on his own repertoire to find something he thinks suits the occasion and the group. He might make the proposal verbally or (this is something piano players have the chance to do, and many take it) start playing something (for instance, a few bars recognizable—by some players, at least—as Charlie Parker's introduction to "Star Eyes") and see if anyone accepts his nonverbal suggestion.

The others consider the proposal, checking to see whether the tune is in their individual repertoire. If it is, do they like it and feel like playing it at that moment? If it isn't in their repertoire, are they willing to take a chance on it if someone else knows it? They usually do a little negotiating at this point: proposals, counterproposals, questions, and clarifications. A suggestion might be met with a question about what key the tune is in, or the proposer may clarify an ambiguous suggestion ("It's 'I Got Rhythm'" or "It's a blues") until the others have a clear enough idea of what the suggestion will entail for them to decide whether to accept it or not. The questions, answers, and discussions reflect dimensions of what performers think has to be considered in this situation. If they reject the suggestion, they start all over again. These negotiations, as we'll see later, take place in a few seconds but are no less complicated for all that.

Once players agree on a tune, they play it and deal with such problems as might arise if it turns out that everyone, after all, doesn't know it well enough to play it credibly.

Stable repertoires

When, as we said earlier, a group plays together for a while—many nights over many weeks—the individual players learn what the others know, what tunes they know in common, and where the overlaps fail. They also learn what others are willing to do, how much trouble they are willing to take to learn something new, and how willing they are to take chances with a tune they don't know well or at all. They teach other songs or ask that others learn them. This kind of repertoire construction results from a process too. One member of the group may be the de facto finder of new things he then proposes that the others learn and play on the job (or several players might share that work). They also consider the "outside influences," especially the people who have hired them and what they may insist on. The players who go through this process develop a repertoire from which they can draw repeatedly, night after night, to put together a musical performance.

In the chapters that follow, we take up each of these elements in turn, exploring what's involved in greater detail, explaining variations, and showing how musical performances both result from and produce the phenomenon of a repertoire.

We think that our research has something to say to social scientists who have found the idea of repertoire a compelling and useful way to talk about culture. We have put that discussion in the appendix, so that people mainly interested in the music will not be distracted by it.

3

Learning Songs and Building an Individual Repertoire: Sources

Remember that the U.S. popular-music industry published something like three hundred thousand popular songs between 1900 and 1950. Those songs, plus an unknown but probably sizeable number of jazz compositions, which were never "popular" but were and are known in the player community, plus the equally unknown (but also probably large) number of songs written since 1950, and a similarly unknown number of traditional and ethnic songs, constitute a reservoir out of which jazz and dance musicians construct a repertoire: for themselves as individual players, for a group playing together for a night or for a longer period (a "steady gig"), and for a local community of players from whose members leaders make up bands for specific engagements. The songs exist in many forms, and players have many kinds of access to them. When they play a job—when they perform for the public somewhere—they typically play a sequence of tunes, taking turns playing the melody or variations on it, improvising backgrounds. If you are going to play with other musicians on a job like that, you have to know tunes the other players know.

Players find the songs that come to constitute their repertoires in the many places and forms they have been stored, depending on what the organization of music in their time and place makes available (available sources vary historically): from printed music, from the radio, from recordings, and from other players they encounter on the job. They pick and learn tunes from this reservoir of possibilities in idiosyncratic ways so that, while everyone of necessity learns tunes that "everyone knows," they also learn tunes that not everyone knows, and that variation in what players know makes continuous repertoire change and exchange among them possible. The repertoire keeps changing as players meet and play together.

Lead Sheets, Fake Books and Other Written Sources

Most simply, players can read songs from printed or written music they bring to work with them. The leader usually assumes that responsibility but other players likely have some music in their instrument cases too. Just as often, they rely on the collection of songs they carry around in their heads, hundreds (sometimes thousands) of songs "everyone" (or almost everyone) knows or knows well enough to at least try to play. (We'll take up the not-so-simple question of what it means to "know a tune" in the next chapter.) The songs they know in common and can thus use to put together a night's performance comprise what we mean by the jazz repertoire. Not everyone knows every tune, no tune is known by everyone, but enough players know enough tunes in common to make the night possible.

How does that happen? Where do the tunes that make up the repertoire come from? Where is the repertoire stored? How do players learn its contents? Note that not all the tunes in the reservoir are jazz, on any construction of that word. We have used it as shorthand for the popular music with which and from which most ordinary musicians know and work.

First, some definitions. Popular songs were originally published, and still are published, as "sheet music," two or more printed pages containing the melody written on a separate staff, the lyrics printed beneath the melody notes, and a piano accompaniment; the publication almost always includes the harmony accompanying the melody, in the form of tablature for guitar and the names of the chords written out in a shorthand familiar to most professionals and many amateurs, especially but not only pianists. Many pianists ignore the written accompaniments, which are sometimes interesting but usually not, relying instead on the melody line and the chord names. So songs are often presented with just those things, plus the lyrics, in what is called a "lead sheet."

A lead sheet, more compact and easier to carry around than several pages of printed sheet music, summarizes the parts of the song players need in order to play it in an ordinary playing situation. Looking at the lead sheet, a pianist can perform a complete version of the song. Any other instrumentalist, looking over the pianist's shoulder, can do the same. If the pianist is playing in a bar or cocktail lounge, a collection of lead sheets gives him what he needs to fill an evening with music. If a trio or larger group is playing for a party or dance, the same collection lets them play for dancing until the wee hours.

Lead sheets were, until the developments about to be described, often handwritten, sometimes (for tunes published by the major publishers) printed. But, in 1942, a radio-station director named George Goodwin recognized the need for lead sheets in a compact form that players could easily carry around, and created Tunedex. Subscribers to Tunedex paid $15 a year for which, every month, they got one hundred 3×5-inch index cards, printed on heavy stock that would withstand constant use, each card containing the melody, chords, and lyrics of a song, plus copyright information, which confirmed that this was a legitimate enterprise paying royalties to ASCAP and BMI. They also got a small box to hold the alphabetized cards; they might even have received cards with letter tabs to assist in the alphabetizing (the sources aren't clear on this, but some people remember such amenities). Tunedex ads suggested that, with this little box on the piano, you could quickly find any tune an audience member requested. (Kernfeld 2003, 2006 tells the whole story, which we have summarized here.)

The songs Tunedex sent out covered a wide range: standards; tunes from the '20s and '30s, even a few from the teens and before; waltzes; a variety of ethnic music (Irish and Italian were well represented, and the collection included some polkas, which could be played for Polish audiences); Latin American (rumbas, tangos, a few sambas and cha-chas); patriotic; etc. These cards prepared you for pretty much anything.

We don't know how many people subscribed to the Tunedex service. Kernfeld (2006, 51) points out that, as the number of cards increased, the ease of use went down. Most musicians eventually acquired its contents, in a more portable and practical form, from less legal sources (the FBI tried unsuccessfully to put them out of business), who sold spiral-bound photocopied books with the cards printed on 8.5×11-inch paper, as Becker recalls:

> One night, when I was playing at the 504 Club, a car pulled up to the curb as we were standing outside the club on the sidewalk. A guy jumped out, and wanted to know if we were musicians. When we admitted it, he opened the trunk of his car, lifted up a blanket, pulled out an 8.5×11-inch spiral-bound book, showed us what it contained, and offered it to us. I looked it over, saw that it was some kind of photocopy of the Tunedex cards, and bought it on

the spot, even though it cost $25, a lot of money then. I don't know if Bob did or not (he could read off mine), and the drummer didn't need it at all. I knew without being told that it was illegal—if it was legal they would have had it in the music stores—but I bought it anyway. Divided into fast tunes, slow tunes, waltzes, Latin, Irish, etc., it was always useful to me and still is today.

The book Becker bought contains, roughly, six hundred to seven hundred tunes. (We could have bought the whole Tunedex library, we learned from an eBay ad, for $2,500: "There is also a 15,000 card file Tunedex.... 3×5 cards that are lead sheets of music that was being released or rereleased. It is virtually complete, in alphabetical order and in metal file cabinets. I am asking $2,500.00 plus shipping for this.")

Becker says he found the book useful. Useful for what? If, like the Bobby Laine Trio, you played in a bar forty hours a week, forty minutes out of every hour, you might often find it difficult to think of a tune to play next.

At which point you could open up the book, flip through the pages, and come up with something.

We often played medleys, the saxophonist and I taking turns playing one song after another, usually medium-tempo ballads, and the book was great for finding something to play when your mind went blank, as often happened at two in the morning. It was also great for relieving boredom, which could arise from playing the same old things all the time. So I (more than Bob, whose drinking interfered with his musicianship some) constantly tried out things we had never played before.

The fake book Becker bought came out in new editions often. The publishers added songs from newly issued cards, or by photocopying melody lines from sheet music or handwriting them, and pasting the results into the lead-sheet format.

The original fake book had no name and no publisher and was sold by crooks out of the trunks of cars and in other clandestine ways but, eventually, it wasn't the only fake book. In 1975 (Kernfeld 2006, 129–43), students at the jazz-oriented Berklee School of Music in Boston collected the more accurate and better-harmonized versions of standard tunes advanced musicians were then playing, as well as new compositions by jazz artists and composers, and put them out as *The Real Book.* In the end, they produced three *Real Books,* others produced three further *New Real Books,* and these collections (and still others with a variety of names) became standard reference works players brought to the job and from which they learned repertoire.

As we write, you can now buy, via the Internet, a CD-ROM containing fifteen fake books of differing ages and contents. Some resemble the original Becker bought long ago. But most contain two kinds of additions. They now include more of the same, more popular tunes of the kind jazz players like to play or might have to play on occasion. Comparing the later books with the original, just looking at the songs whose titles begin with the letter

A, we find such additions as "Alone Together," "Amapola," "Almost Like Being in Love," and "Angel Eyes." But the newer books also contain, and some are almost completely made up of, jazz compositions, songs composed and recorded by well-known modern jazz players like Thelonius Monk, Wayne Shorter, John Coltrane, and Charles Mingus. For instance, again from the letter *A,* Benny Golson's "Along Came Betty," Sonny Rollins's "Airegin," Wayne Shorter's "Ana Maria," and the variation on the chords of "I Got Rhythm" that Dizzy Gillespie and Charlie Parker called "Anthropology." Songs like these are usually identified as coming from the recordings from which they were transcribed.

According to guitarist Pat Metheny, who was then teaching at the Berklee School:

> Honestly, at the time, neither I nor probably anyone else considered that *The Real Book* would ever have much of a life beyond the few interested parties who were around the scene. No one knew that it would ever become an almost

biblical reference work to young musicians. (Quoted from Kernfeld, 2006, 135–36)

The books became the standard reference. Players carried them everywhere and consulted them, propped open on the bandstand, for "correct" chord changes and melody lines. Steve Swallow, a bass player who taught at Berklee at the same time, described the change:

In order to walk to the rooms where I taught my ensembles in Berklee, I had to run the gamut of dozens of rehearsal rooms, down a corridor. On either side of this corridor I would hear twenty or thirty guys playing standards and a month after *The Real Book* was published, all of a sudden I was hearing the right changes to tunes that had been butchered. It used to be a hilarious journey down the corridor, to hear the flagrant harmonic violations just spewing out of these rooms. It's not to say that all of a sudden everything sounded great and it was Bill Evans at every turn, but there was a huge improvement. These particular 400 tunes were canonized at the expense, obviously, of what they left out, and they left out plenty. But I'm not complaining too loudly, because to a large extent I think they were accurately reflecting what college jazz people were listening to at that time, and were skimming the cream of that repertoire. (Quoted from Kernfeld 2003, 6)

Musicians also learned standard tunes from available books of songs by particular composers, which often include not-so-well-known songs by, say, Harold Arlen or Richard Whiting, Gershwin or Cole Porter. Becker, for instance, learned Hoagy Carmichael's "Memphis in June," which he had heard a few times and liked, but had not bothered to memorize, after he bought a book of Carmichael compositions and found it there alongside the better-known "Stardust," "Rockin' Chair," "Skylark," and "Two Sleepy People."

Written music thus provides a commonly available source of material that any player can produce so that a tune can be played by and learned by others.

Records

Players also learn tunes from records, from ten-and twelve-inch 78 rpm discs, then from the 33 rpm LPs and, finally, from the CDs and mp3 files of the 2000s. All players collect recordings by jazz artists, big bands, and small bands alike. Becker continues his memoir of how he learned tunes this way:

> These songs I was learning and playing weren't all in the fake book I had bought, not at all. I learned a lot of them, especially the more esoteric standards, by listening to my ever-growing record collection.

> I learned most of what I came to know from records. "Fine and Dandy," an up-tempo staple for jazz players but also useful as background music to get vaudeville "acts" on and off stage, was in my fake book. But "My Old Flame," a complex tune with harmonies that moved far from the original key,

changing every few beats, was not (but it is now in *The Real Book 2).* I learned that one from the Count Basie recording, which featured a beautiful solo by trumpeter Buck Clayton. I listened to it over and over, sang it to myself until I had the melody surely in place, then worked out what the harmonies were likely to be (back then I would have said, I'm sure, "had to be") and tried them out until I had the tune down. Then I could teach it to Bobby Laine or whoever I could get to give it a try on the job. (I almost invariably learned the words as well, I'm not sure why. But many jazz players do that.)

Berliner (1994, 171) quotes Max Roach: "The old-timers always used to tell horn players to learn the lyrics just like a singer does, so that they know the meaning of the piece." We've deferred description of the technique of "taking a tune off the record" this way, and other skills necessary for acquiring repertoire, to the next chapter. Berliner devotes more than two hundred pages (1994, 63–285) to the topic.

Many jazz players learn new tunes from the recordings of more or less jazz-oriented singers who make a specialty of searching out little-known, or almost completely unknown, songs by well-known composers: songs from musical shows that never became popular or, what made them even less known, were dropped from the shows they had been written for before the shows opened, or songs that had never been published but continue to exist in an archive to which the singer has gained access. The singer/researcher Michael Feinstein, for example, became friendly with Ira Gershwin and thus got access to his collection of unpublished George Gershwin material.

Singers don't confine their searches to the Gershwins and Berlins. They also prize lesser-known composers who have left traces in sheet music and on recordings. Tommy Wolf, a St. Louis pianist, composed many interesting songs ("interesting" in having clever melodies and unusual harmonic patterns or structures) that he performed himself and recorded on at least one LP. He's recognized for one song most players know and like to play: "Spring Can Really Hang You Up the Most." But his other songs were also known and performed by the well-known duo of Jackie Cain and Roy Kral (e.g., "You Smell So Good" and "Season in the Sun") on some of their early LPs, as well as by others. And Wolf also composed the score for a not very successful Broadway show, *The Nervous Set.*

Players who discover one good tune by a songwriter may search out more of his work. Becker liked Hugh Martin's songs from the movie *Meet Me in St. Louis,* ("The Boy Next Door," "The Trolley Song," among others) and found some others he liked just as well, particularly a song from the show *Best Foot Forward* called "Ev'ry Time," which he learned from a CD by the singer Jeri Southern. A Web search reveals that Hugh Martin wrote 132 songs, none or almost none of which appear in fake books, but do continue to exist on recordings. Pianist-singers like Dave Frishberg and Bob Dorough write and record their own material, songs in a sort of elaborated Great American Song

Book style (examples are Frishberg's "Do You Miss New York?" and Dorough's "Love Came on Stealthy Fingers"). Few jazz players or players on ordinary jobbing dates know these songs.

Remember that tunes often become standards not because players think they are especially good, but because someone musicians respect recorded them for some possibly quite accidental reason. Many tunes would have vanished long ago if they hadn't profited from such an accident. Would anyone be playing "Surrey with the Fringe on the Top" today if Miles Davis hadn't recorded it? Or "Mean To Me" or "What A Little Moonlight Can Do" if Billie Holiday hadn't recorded them because the Brunswick recording company, in the 1930s, had hired her and Teddy Wilson to turn out four sides a month of currently popular tunes? Wilson hired the best musicians around, Holiday developed her classic style in the course of this long series of sessions, and today the recordings are jazz classics, part of the storehouse of available music players have learned from.

Many contemporary players owe their knowledge of pop tunes of the forties to the idiosyncratic choices of Chet Baker, a respected trumpet player. When he began singing, he specialized in tunes from the '40s that earlier generations had learned as pop tunes of the day, like "Let's Get Lost" or "This Time the Dream's on Me." Some fake books identify tunes (even standard pop tunes) by referring to a particular recording by a well-known player. (We needn't suppose that players learn a tune *because* Mr. Famous played it, but rather that they hear him play it, see its possibilities in the way he develops it, and then decide to learn it themselves.)

Bossa nova, a Brazilian invention, became part of the American jazz repertoire through recordings. Brazilian groups had been playing in the United States and some players knew their recordings, but bossa nova became a quasi-required genre of music after guitarist Charlie Byrd came back from Brazil with a collection of tunes by some of the best young composers (Antonio Carlos Jobim, Dorival Caymi, and others) and recorded them with Stan Getz. Their recordings, especially those with vocals by João and Astrud Gilberto, taught a generation of players a new body of repertoire, a new rhythm to use on all kinds of songs, and some distinctive harmonic patterns and variations. Jobbing musicians learned to play "Wave" and "Girl from Ipanema" and "Chega de Saudade" (which Dizzy Gillespie turned into "No More Blues"). More adventurous types discovered other composers and performers (e.g., Chico Buarque, Gal Costa, and Caetano Veloso) whose work could be played successfully in the U.S. Some of these songs from another country and another (though related) popular music tradition became part of the repertoire in the United States.

Recorded music, like printed music, stores songs in a retrievable form. So long as the physical object (score or recording) exists, an enterprising player can find it, learn it, play it, and teach it to others. So stored, it can always enter someone's active repertoire.

Air Shots (Sometimes Called "Remotes")

In the '30s and '40s, maybe into the early '50s, players also learned music from the radio. The radio played popular music all the time. *Your Hit Parade* played the Top Ten songs every week. "Air shots" or "remotes" broadcast from clubs and ballrooms all over the country presented dozens of the popular big bands playing more or less randomly chosen selections from their current book. Becker describes how his repertoire grew from these sources:

I heard them on the radio. That's where I learned most of the currently popular tunes, the ones that occupied a spot for a while on *Your Hit Parade,* the radio show that spotlighted the Top Ten of the week, however they arrived at that.

I learned many tunes by hearing the famous big bands of the day on the radio (and occasionally seeing them in person). Since I was only maybe thirteen or so, I couldn't go to hear jazz played by small groups in places that served liquor, which was where almost all of that kind of playing took place. The big bands played in ballrooms, which I was also too young to go to, and in the "big rooms," sort of nightclubs, in the major hotels. In Chicago, that meant the Panther Room of the Hotel Sherman on Randolph Street, the Boulevard Room of the Stevens Hotel, and, a similar kind of place, the Blackhawk on Wabash Avenue. Once in a great while I could persuade my parents to take me to such a place that otherwise would never have let me in and that I couldn't have paid for anyway. I once actually persuaded my father to take me to hear the Basie band playing in a ballroom called "White City," which I believe was in a black part of town (it was what remained of an amusement park that had been built for the 1893 World's Fair).

Outside of those few excursions into the actual places where music was played, my connection to the music I wanted to hear was through records and, better yet because it didn't cost anything, the radio. At that time—I don't know exactly how old I was or what the year was, but it was probably the very late '30s and early '40s, including the war years—most big network-affiliated radio stations broadcast until midnight or 1:00 a.m. They had no paying programs (supported by advertisers) in the late hours (from maybe 10:30 until they signed off) and filled the time with what were called "air shots" or "remotes," broadcasts from places where big bands played: ballrooms like the Aragon and Trianon in Chicago (which specialized in commercial bands I considered corny and beneath contempt, like Eddie Howard, Dick Jurgens, or Lawrence Welk), and hotel rooms like the ones I mentioned above, where bands I liked (Goodman, Krupa, Woody Herman, the Dorseys, Les Brown, Ellington, and many lesser-known groups) played two-week dates before going out on the road for one-nighters and landing again in another hotel or ballroom for an extended stay.

Of the four major networks in those days—CBS (the Chicago outlet was WBBM), NBC-Red (WMAQ), NBC-Blue (WLS), and Mutual (WGN)—at least three would be playing music from local spots during the late evening hours. As a result, I didn't miss out on what I might have heard had I been old enough to go to these places legally. These stations, affiliated with national networks, also carried music from places elsewhere in the country where a local affiliate had arranged a remote broadcast. That meant that I not only got the local venues, but also heard music from the eastern time zone, which in practice meant New York and environs. These places typically brought the same bands in once or twice every year, so in the course of a year I would hear Benny Goodman from the Hotel New Yorker, Glenn Miller from the Pennsylvania Hotel, Tommy Dorsey from the Starlight Roof of the Hotel Astor, Hal MacIntyre from the Glen Island Casino, Claude Thornhill from Frank Dailey's Meadowbrook, and bands like Jerry Wald, Jimmy Dorsey, Artie Shaw, and many others from a variety of places.

As if that weren't enough, there was the phenomenon of the "clear channel station." The FCC allocated wavelengths to stations on a sliding scale, depending on who knows what. Some stations could not broadcast at full strength and could only be heard in the local area but not, say, a hundred miles away. Others had a stronger signal and could be heard at greater distance. Two or more stations in different parts of the country often shared the same wavelength, the limited strength of the signal preventing interference. A few stations here and there, however, had a wavelength to themselves for the entire country. WGN, in Chicago, was such a clear channel station and could be heard pretty much all over the country (barring the interference of mountains and other natural obstacles). Others were WWL in New Orleans and WLW in Cincinnati. After local stations went off the air at midnight, I could hear these stations from elsewhere and so got to hear music from the West Coast, which came on too late for the local stations to carry.

That was how I heard the Gene Krupa band play "Rockin' Chair," with Roy Eldridge playing the same solo he later recorded note for note one night from the Palladium Ballroom in Los Angeles. He brought down the house and there was an ovation from the dancers that went on for a long time.

That wasn't typical. Mostly the dancers in these places danced and you could hear, behind the music, people talking, silverware and dishes clattering, and all the other noises of a busy club. But you could hear the band, introduced by an announcer who went out to the club to announce the show, and who offered tidbits of information about the band, who had been featured playing a solo on the last tune, who was going to sing the next tune—things a thirteen-year-old jazz fan would want to know.

Faulkner has similar recollections:

I used to listen to Charlie Spivak from Lakeside or the Gardens in Denver and listen to the tunes his big band played. Then I went down to hear him in person with my mother. They had air checks [broadcasts], the big band. He was a good trumpet player. What was his theme song, "Star Dreams?" Met him when I was ten years old.

A bass player recalled a similar experience from his childhood:

I was there in this small town in Oklahoma, we'd get these stations at night from all over, from Chicago, from St. Louis, me too, I'd be in bed listening to them when I was supposed to be sleeping, so I'd hear all these tunes.

(Although books on jazz ordinarily give the names of the players they quote, books reporting sociological research just as routinely don't. We've explained our choice in this matter in the appendix.)

We shouldn't misunderstand what these programs contained, reading into them contemporary notions of jazz performance. Benny Goodman had played a "jazz concert" in Carnegie Hall in 1936 and others occasionally did something similar, but it wasn't common. (See DeVeaux 1989 on the history of jazz concerts.) The bands heard in air shots played for dancing and entertainment. Songs rarely exceeded the three-minute length of the ten-inch records of the time, and (rather than being jazz favorites) came from the continual output of Tin Pan Alley. They included the tunes known in later years as the Great American Songbook, and many more songs not very different but not usually glorified that way. Air shots publicized the bands' records, perhaps increasing sales but surely making them more attractive to the audiences they played for in person when on tour, and simultaneously publicized the venue, perhaps increasing the club's business. The stations filled their airtime at the minimal cost of sending an engineer and announcer out to the club. All of it promoted the pop tunes.

And young people, musicians-to-be like Becker and Faulkner, put their lights out, kept the music low, and heard their favorite bands. In the process, they heard, over and over, popular tunes of the day, and acquired, without forethought or effort, a sizeable repertoire. Some of those songs would later become part of the standard repertoire and others could remain candidates for inclusion in that group because so many players had learned them from the radio.

In the heyday of that version of the popular-music machine, bands didn't record and play a collection of agreed-on musical gems. So these young would-be musicians heard the tunes the machine produced played by bands of varying quality. Most bands, in addition, had their own well-known specialties: theme songs and special arrangements of songs that had become hits on records and thus had been played in homes and on jukeboxes and radio everywhere.

You can get a good idea of what these bands played by seeing what they recorded: large numbers of forgettable pop tunes which have in fact since been forgotten, as well as some pop tunes contemporary players might well think worth reviving if they knew they existed. Big black bands, as well as the big white bands, recorded this repertoire (Count Basie's recorded repertoire, for instance, contains a large number of pop tunes). Black people lived in the same world of radio as everyone else and, though they also had "race" favorites not popular among white listeners, the two repertoires overlapped substantially.

So young would-be musicians everywhere in the United States had the output of Tin Pan Alley available to them to learn at no cost. They would have had trouble avoiding it, since it was on the radios and jukeboxes as well as the records they bought. They heard this musical material over and over, night after night. Becker recalls:

When Peggy Lee, then an unknown kid from the upper Midwest, joined Goodman's band, I heard her sing "Somebody Else Is Takin' My Place," a not particularly terrific pop tune, night after night. Having heard it enough times, and without any effort or in fact any desire to do so, I "knew" it.

In which of the many possible senses of "know a tune" did these young listeners "know" these songs? Remember that they were, quite often, literally listening in the dark, so they couldn't notate the song musically and, in any event, may well not have had the necessary transcription skills. What they could do was sing the song along with the radio and then to themselves afterward. When they began to study instruments and to play, they began listening harder for, and trying to reproduce, the actual intervals of the tune and then, later still, to figure out the harmonies that went with the melody they had learned. Without thinking about it, they learned the words as well.

They especially prized the "instrumentals" that allowed the star jazz players who worked in some of these bands some room for improvised solos. Becker recalls:

> If you heard Goodman you heard (at one period) Cootie Williams, and on a rare night Goodman might play, in the middle of a hotel dance set, a special number like "Superman," the original composition Eddie Sauter had written for Williams; or "Bennie Rides Again," another Sauter composition; or one of Mel Powell's originals, like "Clarinet à la King." And similarly with the other players (Chu Berry with Cab Calloway, Buck Clayton with Basie, any of the several famous soloists with Duke Ellington). But those were the exceptions. We were more likely to hear pop tunes, even though they were in good charts by people like Sauter.

In addition to these unsponsored air shots, many bands appeared on commercially sponsored shows. Glenn Miller had a fifteen-minute show five times a week around six o'clock, where he gave a good workout to his formula of "something old, something new, something borrowed [another leader's theme song], something blue." Woody Herman had a half-hour weekly program for a year or two sponsored by Wildroot Cream Oil, a hair preparation that must have had a jazz-loving executive (this sponsorship is reflected in tunes Herman recorded like "Wildroot").

These kids got a continuous exposure, night after night, to all the output of the commercial-music machine, and absorbed a lot of it, good and bad, usable for jazz or not, through a constant repetition which gave them the raw material for endless exercises in ear training. They learned lots of tunes, and the skills of transforming heard music into music they could play, as the result of a historical conjunction of circumstances—radio stations needing to fill the time, bands willing to fill it, in return for some publicity, with songs they were recording because that was what people danced to, and youngsters who had no other way to hear this material over and over again taking advantage of all the repetition to learn songs.

The resulting repertoire consists, as we've noted, of tunes that became known to another generation of jazz players because Chet Baker or Charlie Parker or Billie Holiday recorded them, or because they furnished the underlying harmonic structure for a bebop tune (as "Whispering" furnished the harmonies for "Groovin' High"). But the repertoire learned this way also contains tunes that didn't have that good fortune and that might reasonably be called "could have beens"—tunes that share the musical characteristics of better-known songs but never were recorded by the right people or turned into a bebop anthem. Or even when they were recorded by the right people, as were "The Lady's in Love with You," "Sleigh Ride in July," or "You're Looking at Me," were then for unknown reasons forgotten, though occasionally revived by an appreciative soloist or singer. In addition, this radio-transmitted repertoire includes tunes no musician has ever, then or now, thought worth playing, but which people who learned from the radio in that era still know ("Three Little

Fishes," "Hold Tight," and other novelty songs).

Music heard on the radio doesn't exist in permanent form and thus isn't as easily retrievable as music printed or recorded. But it penetrates many players' consciousnesses, through sheer repetition, and some of them will remember a tune for a long time, so that it can always reenter someone's active repertoire and, through them, others' repertoires as well.

Later Developments

Two things especially important for our story happened in the era that began after World War II and culminated in the age of digital communication: the rise of television and FM radio and the development of the Internet and new systems of distributing musical materials.

FM radio

When television replaced radio as the major vehicle of mass entertainment, radio lost its hold on the country's musical experience. It no longer provided the major pathway for the distribution of popular music, and the kinds of programming described above almost entirely disappeared. No more *Hit Parade* and, especially, no more remote broadcasts from places where musicians were playing their ordinary repertoire for live audiences.

Although invented in the 1930s, FM radio did not become commercially important until the 1960s, when hundreds of local FM stations began to compete successfully with network-affiliated AM stations for listeners. To summarize a very complicated story, FM made possible niche broadcasting, programming aimed at audiences with very specific tastes: country and western, the emerging genre of rock and roll, ethnic and racial groups with specialized musical tastes, religious music, and, in general, anything anyone could find listeners for. As a result, listeners had much more freedom to restrict their listening to just what they wanted to hear. While popular hits of whatever kind continued to dominate record sales, they no longer dominated the airwaves monopolistically as they once had. Stations that catered to a particular audience might play the same recordings incessantly but there were many other stations available that played other songs and other genres.

This had several consequences for musicians who played for dances, in bars, and in all the places that someone who accepted whatever work might come along would find themselves playing. Some of the new music was music they didn't know and, for the most part, didn't want to know or play. They weren't prepared, either technically or by virtue of their restricted tastes, to play country and western or rock and roll, two of the most important genres that gradually became major vehicles of popular entertainment.

Perhaps more to the point, the kinds of tunes musicians liked to play, that fit into the formulaic patterns they felt at home with and prized, no longer informed the average listener's emotional life and audio experience as they once had. Composers continued to write such songs and play and record them, but you could no longer expect "everyone" to recognize and enjoy them.

The taste for songs like these became restricted to people who had developed a taste for them.

Jazz-oriented players and listeners, however, also benefited from these developments. The specialized audiences FM made possible included jazz audiences. Many cities had full-time jazz stations (some of them broadcasting twenty-four hours a day) that played a wide variety of music from traditional New Orleans style through the big bands of the 1930s–1950s to the most advanced contemporary players whose music was available on recordings. Elsewhere, community stations often made room for substantial jazz programming, which played the role that "air shots" had played for players in earlier decades.

An FM license allows broadcasters to send, in addition to their regular programming, several other signals that they use to provide "background music" programs for public establishments of all kinds—restaurants, bars, hotel lobbies, even elevators. "Elevator music" once meant bland arrangements of innocuous music, designed to make a little sound without offending or annoying customers. Recorded background music, as we write, consists very largely of contemporary jazz arrangements of the formulaic songs of the American song book.

New distribution systems

The development of digital audio recording and, somewhat later, electronic instruments and the Internet, made it possible for any imaginable kind of music to be recorded, edited and manipulated, and distributed. Musicians could now create their own recordings (which were, to be sure, of varying technical quality) and distribute them as CDs or over the Internet, where interested listeners could download them, for a fee, from merchants or music services like iTunes, or at no cost at all, via various file-sharing programs.

The resulting proliferation of available music means that musicians interested in any particular style of playing need not rely on the local presence of someone who plays that music to learn it, or even on a local merchant who sells it. If it isn't played on local radio stations, interested players can find it on the Internet, hear it, perhaps download it, and study it at length and at their leisure. They also have, easily available, a great variety of educational aids: instruction manuals and music-minus-one recordings, which provide accompaniments to players who want to practice playing tunes without rounding up other players to do that for them.

As a result, listeners, no longer at the mercy of the programmers who decide what radio stations will play, can go to either of two extremes. On the one hand, they can restrict what they hear to one or a few specialized musical genres; hearing only what they want, no matter how special their tastes, means that they need not know, if they don't want to or find it necessary, anything other than what their own taste dictates. On the other hand, they can get, any time they want to or find it necessary, music of any kind to listen to and, if they want or need to, to "take off the record."

This means that contemporary musicians have the option of narrowing what they play to very specialized genres or of building repertoires that cover a great variety of possibilities. If they know how to learn a song from a recording, then everything is available to them. But if they find only a narrow selection of kinds of music interesting, they will never have to listen to the variety of musical material some of the people we quoted earlier listened to and almost inevitably learned, whether they wanted to or not, from the radio.

We don't think that technical developments in some way determined what happened to musicians' repertoires. The underlying processes of learning didn't change much, although the technical means by which they were implemented did.

Learning on the Job

Perhaps the most important storehouse of musical material, then, exists in the memories of active and formerly active players. Musicians learn much of the repertoire they know on the job. They go to work and one of the other players wants to play a song they don't know. They agree to play it even so, maybe from music the other person provides, maybe by hearing someone else play it first and picking it up that way. (We'll explore the dynamics of this on-the-bandstand construction of working repertoires later.) How does learning on the job contribute to the repertoire players carry with them in their heads from job to job? The bass player we quoted earlier talks about players from whom he learned songs:

> Well, the one that I learned a tremendous amount from was Norma Teagarden. You know, she played for years at the Washington Square Bar and Grill. I learned a lot of the older tunes from her, tunes from the forties. Another person I learned a lot from was Joe Dodge, who was the drummer with Brubeck in the beginning, in the old band with Ron Crotty, he'd been in the army with Desmond. Then another one I learned a lot from was Bob Bissell. He was an

arranger, he really taught me a lot about the logic of music, how you could make things logically connected.

Becker gives more specific details of learning tunes on the job, giving us some sense of how specific kinds of work provided different learning situations and results:

> I learned a lot of other tunes from "stock arrangements," printed arrangements you could buy for bands from five to twelve or more pieces, of popular tunes or of recorded hits by the good big bands we admired. So you could buy Les Brown's "Bizet Has His Day," Count Basie's "920 Special," or many charts recorded by Count Basie or Benny Goodman or Glenn Miller, and learn those songs that way. I remember learning "In the Mood" from such a stock arrangement.

Musicians learn on the job when the leader (or someone else who is calling the tunes) doesn't wait to hear whether everyone knows a particular song. A twenty-eight-year-old percussionist who is assiduous about learning tunes from the Great American Song Book as well as older jazz standards told us:

That's one of the good things about playing with Tim. When he calls a tune, we'll just play it. He'll just call a tune, and almost be counting off the tempo, so the piano player or bass player doesn't have a choice but to find it in their book. He'll just—you know how he does it! You know, "Broadway," two flats. Because a lot of times when you do make a set list, you can run into "Well, I'd have to read that tune," or "I don't really know that tune, let's do something else." So the repertoire doesn't really get passed on, do you know what I mean? It's so easy to fall in the loop of the same tunes.

Faulkner describes how a not very well-known Jerome Kern tune, "Nobody Else But Me," entered his personal repertoire as a result of an extended process of learning it on the job initiated by the leader on one of the jobs he was working regularly:

"Nobody Else But Me." This is the newest tune for our group.

Three gigs back, probably at the Egremont Inn, Jay [the guitarist-leader] brought in the music to this Jerome Kern gem. He had a Bb part for me so I didn't have to transpose. This was a sign of his seriousness. Beautiful chord changes, especially bars 5–7, the last twelve bars are pure heaven. Introducing tunes is serious business. At Egremont, I found this to be a difficult tune to play on but loved it immediately. We continued to play it on every gig thereafter. On the way home from the Castle Street gig, Jay played the Stan Getz recording of this tune with Gary Burton. Getz's conception of the tune is unusual and presents a highly personal approach to rhythm and timbre. It was a revelation. At any rate, aside from my attachment to the tune, I asked Jay if this CD is where he learned the tune and got the idea to bring it into the group and teach it to me. The answer was yes. So there you have a direct pathway from Getz to Jay to Rob to group.

Jay's remarks on the same song:

And that new tune we've been working on, "Nobody Else But Me," the way it moves harmonically is really hip for 1927. I heard the Getz recording and started working on it. It's swinging and of course he changes the rhythm of the melody in a lot of places and the notes sometimes, makes it into Stan Getz's version of "Nobody Else But Me," makes it his own that way. I like it when people do that. Some people think they have to stay exactly on the melody, but especially if you hear the words to the song, I think that to improvise the melody and embellish the melody in ways that you can still hear the lyric, I don't know if Stan does that through the whole thing, I think he improvises totally toward the end section there, sort of a cadence, or an extension at the end.

Leaders can provoke learning through idiosyncratic ways of introducing new repertoire. A guitar player and leader in his late forties describes this process in his work within a group with a trumpet player and leader, Dave Pinardi, in the Amherst area:

> I owe my knowing a lot of tunes to Dave Pinardi, because of his style of doing things, bringing in a lead sheet and playing a new tune one week, then not playing it again, maybe ever again, bringing in another tune, another lead sheet. This got me to learn a lot more standards than I would have on my own. Sometimes [new tunes were introduced] right on the bandstand, sometimes with *no charts.* Pinardi would play a melody and nobody would have the music for it. Somebody would half know the tune a little bit. We would get through it, we'd find the right harmonies ... all of a sudden we have a new tune. This would improve your skills as far as listening and hearing, hearing a bass line, trying to hear what the chord was without having any music.

Many players pride themselves on the breadth of their knowledge of tunes. But they can still be stumped by someone who has made a specialty of digging up good tunes few players know.

The resulting spotty distribution of repertoire among players makes it likely that players will be learning new songs from the people they work with. Some know a lot of tunes, others know fewer; some know more of this kind of song, others more of that kind of song. It doesn't take much overlap to get through an evening, but it can be annoying to play with people who don't know what you know and feel like playing. That provides motivation to pass tunes on and motivation to learn them when someone else on the stand suggests them.

Several things contribute to this uneven distribution of knowledge of tunes. Differences in the ages of players produce differences in what they know. Younger and older players know different songs. Older players will have learned, as in the case of Becker's repertoire, discussed above, a lot of popular tunes just by virtue of growing up when those songs were popular. Becker didn't have to "learn" "Deep

Purple." It was popular when he was a teenager, played constantly on the radio, often requested on the job, and he couldn't have avoided knowing it. But someone half his age will only know it, if they do, because some well-known jazz player recorded it. Only a few did and none of those recordings became well known, so younger players don't know it. On the other hand, many players know "It Could Happen to You," a similar though "more interesting" tune, because many jazz greats liked to play it. Faulkner, for example, learned it from the recording by one of his idols as a trumpet player, Don Fagerquist.

Younger players thus often don't know the full range of old pop tunes and other esoterica older players know. This disparity in repertoire sometimes provokes older players to rant about how kids today are no damn good, they don't know any tunes, a topic we will explore more deeply in the chapter on generational change. Becker gives the example of a pianist in his twenties with whom he occasionally met.

When we played four hands, we immediately ran into this problem, because he had a very limited repertoire, maybe knew twenty tunes. Perhaps as a result of this, he wasn't very good at playing tunes he didn't already know, because he hadn't had enough experience playing different tunes to recognize the common patterns underlying them. He eventually confessed that the older jazz pianist he had been taking lessons from had bawled him out and told him he had to learn more tunes.

Similarly, younger players will probably know more of the compositions of well-known later jazz figures like Thelonius Monk, Charles Mingus, John Coltrane, and Wayne Shorter (let Coltrane's "Giant Steps" stand for this branch of the repertoire). They will probably be ready to improvise, in the style of some of the Miles Davis recordings, on modal harmonies, which some older players find difficult or even incomprehensible.

As individual leaders and players introduce tunes, casually, on the stand during a job, tunes move around in a musical community, and become widely known, the kind of tune "everyone knows" and which therefore can be "called" without fear that someone won't know it. A leader/player describes this process in an interview with Faulkner:

I asked him about the tune "Estaté" and its history in our playing together. He had brought it to one of our duo gigs and asked, "Do you know this?" I didn't, we played it, I loved it, and we continued to play it, at the next gig and then the next. I worked on it at home. We added it to our repertoire. He was introduced to the tune by another musician, in this case a trumpet player with a reputation as a "tunehound," someone who knows a large number of tunes, can play them with assurance, and is constantly searching for new material:

"That tune came to me from working with Dave Pinardi. Dave's way of playing is that if he has a steady gig week to week, he seldom will play the same tune that he played the week before—all night. Occasionally, there were certain tunes he would lean on, a few tunes. He would always be searching for new material for the next night. You'd see him thumbing through a book, and that's how he arrived at 'Estaté.' He had heard the song, I think a Lena Horne recording of it. It was a very slow, seductive, Brazilian piece. So he brought it into the group. We played it. The harmonies were beautiful, it kind of took some different turns, and I liked the tune immediately and put it in my own book, that is, the book for my band. I also started playing it solo, when I have my solo-guitar jobs. And I brought it to a gig with you. I introduced it to you. After that time, I heard a version of it with Jon Hendricks singing it, it was very beautiful."

As the tune moves around in a musical community, both groups and players through whose hands it passes experiment with it and change it to suit their own needs:

We recorded that tune with Dave and we had some trouble with keys. What we did was play as an introduction the bridge section, the bridge as an introduction in a different key, and that led us to think about the range of the song and possibly a different key, because the range of that song is vast. The middle section goes up pretty high. Finding that particular key that works well. On solo guitar we look for keys that are advantageous to open strings on the guitar. I would think of a key that might be a half step below the key I might play with you on trumpet. So that way I can take advantage of the open sounds on the guitar. But finding the right range for a horn player, or any instrument, is important. Finding the best place it would fall for the horn is important, and I guess that is why we arrived at some key changes for that song. To me, the bridge on that piece is climactic and to drop it down an octave brings the dynamic of the song down, so

I felt to build up to the bridge, which goes into a higher register, like we had to find the lower register for the first section to give the horn a good sound without being too low.

I asked him about "Get Out of Town," a recent addition to our repertoire.

"Get Out of Town" came to me from a couple of places. I heard it before I played it, it might have been a guitar player I heard play it on a CD, and the guitar player played it at a bossa nova tempo. And the tune came from Pinardi also, because he brought it into a group that we played in together. I was attracted to the tune because of the minor-major thing. "Get Out of Town" is in a major key, Bb, but it starts off in the relative minor, it is very melancholy, the words are very melancholy. The second section of the tune, you will recall, goes to major. To me it was very melancholy the first section; the second section went to G major instead of G minor, it gives you this happy feeling. So I was attracted to the song. You have dark and happy in the same piece. When you get to the cadence at the end of the song it kind of resolves. It kind of closes the door. It resolves. Those qualities attracted me to the piece. So I heard the tune and wrote a chart for it. I heard it in a trio, from a guitar player, learned it from hearing it, wrote it down, and started playing it in my own group. I changed it around a little bit. And then one time, strangely enough, Pinardi brought it in to another band we were in and he wanted to play it as a bossa nova also, after never having played it together with him. Maybe it's been played over the years, in socials, and has kind of gravitated to a bossa. Originally it was more of a ballad. But you can't go wrong with Cole Porter.

It's great bringing new tunes to the book. It brings excitement to the players. It's fun. It's new. It's not playing all the tunes exactly the ones you did at the last gig.

Faulkner goes on to describe one of his own initiatives in introducing tunes on the job:

I heard "Prelude to a Kiss" on the local radio jazz show one night. Steve Kuhn, a piano player, did it as a bossa with his trio. I started thinking about the tune and how it would fit into our repertoire. I wanted to expand our selection of medium-tempo bossa tunes, and this tune done in this way seemed to be a new approach. I thought it would be a good idea to work on it and then ask the guitar player if he would like to do it. Shortly thereafter we had a gig at the Egremont Inn in the Berkshires and I asked Jay if he would like to do "Prelude" as a bossa. He thought for a moment about the chord changes, silently working out the opening A section. He asked me what tempo I would like this at and I counted it off and we played it. Early into the tune I knew this was a winner. The tune is beautiful, has a beautiful line with a nice intervallic leap at the bridge. When approached in a relaxed and quiet fashion with an open, dark tone, it sounded perfect for the dining room and adjoining bar where our trio (flugelhorn, guitar, and bass) first played it. The dinner crowd and bar crowd seemed to like it too. In this case, thinking about this tune, done in this way, for this crowd, paid off. You have to know your colleagues and what they like to play, the setting you are going to play a tune in, and the audience you're playing it for.

Becker learned a variety of tunes in a variety of playing situations when he first started playing. (See the sidebar.)

The Development of an Individual Repertoire (Becker)

I began playing piano when I was about twelve by teaching myself to play transcriptions of boogie-woogie piano solos by the classic artists of the genre, Meade Lux Lewis and Albert Ammons. They required more technique than I then had, but I learned the standard blues progressions in several keys from the effort.

Then I took jazz piano lessons from a teacher who taught me some of the old standards from the 1920s: "I Ain't Got Nobody," "Sugar," "Sweet Lorraine," and "Someday Sweetheart," among others.

Shortly afterward, when my playing had improved sufficiently, I joined a band of other teenagers that played high school dances and learned, by playing stock arrangements, a number of popular tunes and some big band classics that I continued to play for years, Count Basie's "One O'Clock Jump" and "920 Special," among others. I also learned Les Brown's "Bizet Has His Day," adapted from one of Bizet's "L'Arlésienne Suites," which was more difficult, since it began with afigure for bass and piano that had to be played "as written," a restriction I hadn't encountered before.

These experiences gave me a grounding in the conventional circle-of-fifths harmonic progressions that underlay almost all popular music and jazz of the period. As a result, I knew enough to take the bare bones of a stock arrangement piano part and play something based on it that would work. And that meant that I knew enough to play behind soloists when we "jammed" or just played without written music.

During the war I played for several months at McGovern's Liberty Inn, a striptease joint on Chicago's Clark Street. (I was hired for this job because so many more experienced players had been called for military service. Only sixteen, I was still available.) I learned a lot of older, less jazz-oriented tunes on this job, such as "Ain't She Sweet" and "Barney Google."

When I was a little older I joined the hundreds of players who frequented the musician's union hall on Monday and Saturday afternoons, where players looked for jobs and leaders looked for players for jobs. As a result, I found myself playing with polka bands for Polish weddings and parties, and with a variety of other groups at Italian, Jewish, Irish, Syrian, and German parties (these are the ones I remember), adding to my repertoire a mélange of tunes like "Beer Barrel Polka," "O Sole Mio," and "Does Your Mother Come from Ireland?"

I played with a campus band at Northwestern University, just outside Chicago, where I played popular tunes of the day like "I Wish I Knew" (which became a sort of jazz standard due to recordings by players like Chet Baker, Lester Young, and John Coltrane) and "I'll Remember Suzanne" (which was recorded only by Gene Krupa's big band and never became part of the standard repertoire).

I played with a (then quite rare) multiracial band led by Harold Fox, a Chicago tailor who claimed to have invented the zoot suit (see his obituary by Robert McG. Thomas Jr. 1996). We played dances and parties for all-black audiences (white employers were not yet "ready" for racially mixed bands), everything from the big ballrooms like the Parkway and Savoy to very exclusive formal parties for the black upper class of the city. The younger audiences demanded, and Harold required me to learn and play, note for note, several well-known piano solo pieces with orchestral accompaniment: Avery Parrish's solo on the Erskine Hawkins recording of "After Hours," Eddie Heywood's "Begin the Beguine," and Stan Kenton's "Concerto to End All Concertos." These didn't have a permanent place in my repertoire since Harold was apparently the only person who really wanted to hear them.

My piano teacher, Lennie Tristano, introduced me to the playing of Lester Young, Art Tatum, and others, and I listened to and learned songs they had made well-known recordings of, among them "Laughing at Life," "Easy Living," and "Mean to Me," which in turn led me to similar tunes that they hadn't recorded, like "I May Be Wrong" and "Do It Again." Lenny also taught me to use altered notes in the chords I played: flatted and raisedfifths and ninths, augmented elevenths.

By the time I worked with Bobby Laine, I was a confirmed "tune-hound," and found interesting tunes in the recordings of Mel Tormé (e.g., his own composition "Born to Be Blue"), Dave Brubeck ("As Long As There's Music" and his composition "In Your Own Sweet Way"), and Alec Wilder ("I'll Be Around" and "It's So Peaceful in the Country"). My investigations led me to many other tunes that, as I discovered, I would have to teach other musicians to play: Vernon Duke's "Autumn in New York," Hugh Martin's "Ev'ry Time," Matt Dennis's "Violets for Your Furs" and "Will You Still Be Mine?" Fats Waller's "Keepin' Out of Mischief Now," Hoagy Carmichael's "One Morning in May." I learned some songs from singers I accompanied, as I learned "Day In, Day Out" when I accompanied Patty Tucker singing it in Kansas City. (My ability to transpose made it easy for me to work with singers.) In later years, I stopped playing professionally and had less occasion and reason to learn new songs. As a result, I did not learn, until years later and still do not have complete mastery of, an entire repertoire of post-bebop tunes by Thelonius Monk, Wayne Shorter, Chick Corea, and other jazz players of a later period. But I had developed an active interest in Brazilian popular music just at the time the bossa nova became part of the American repertoire and I added to my knowledge during a trip to Brazil, collecting recordings and sheet music of songs associated with Brazilian singers and players—Gal Costa, Chico Buarque, Dorival Caymi, Baden-Powell—not then available in the U.S., as well as the work of people more well known in North America, like Jobim and João Gilberto.

For grownup players, learning on the job is perhaps the major way they learn new material and add to their repertoires. What they learn depends on who they play with and under what circumstances they play. But every job is a potential learning situation and has a potential for adding to a player's repertoire.

Where the Songs Are

Players construct repertoires to play on specific occasions out of musical materials they find stored in print, on recordings, and in their own and other's memories. What their musical environment makes available to them to learn depends on when and where they do their learning, a point we return to later. Songs have a long life, continuing to be at least potential members of someone's repertoire as long as they still exist in printed or recorded form or, failing that, as long as someone remembers them and can bring them to life again, teaching them to others and relaunching their careers. Players who know a song can teach it to others, encourage them to try it, even force it on them if they're in a position to do that, as a leader can simply require band members to play something.

Histories of the recording and music-publishing industries shed light on what gets into these forms of storage, although even casual observation shows that the reserves are enormous. We have more difficulty reconstructing what people carried in their memories and passed on in a musical analogue of the oral tradition analyzed by folklore scholars. What we have seen in this chapter is how players learn, teach, and pass around the reservoir's contents.

4

The Skills You Need to Play the Contents of the Song Reservoir

Individual players, musical groups performing together for one or many nights, and local and national communities of players put together their performances by picking material from the large reservoir of available songs. It can seem that players need only access this reservoir and use the results. That sounds easy, and sometimes, for some players, it is. But everything looks easy once you know how to do it; learning how musicians do it and the difficulties they experience will show how much there really is to learn. What skills do players need in order to read printed music, "take a tune" off a record, or learn it by hearing someone else play it? How do they learn those skills? And what does knowing the answers to those questions tell us about making music together? (Here again, we cover ground Paul Berliner [1994] goes over at great length, and readers who want to know more should consult that book. Our own emphasis differs from his, in concentrating on the way all these materials and skills contribute to performances on the job.)

Learning to Read Music

As we've seen, musicians learn many tunes by reading the melody from a printed or handwritten "lead sheet" containing it and its accompanying chords. We can't take the ability to do that as a given, a skill musicians just naturally have, since no one starts life knowing how to do that, and many musicians in various traditions don't learn to do it, because they have no need for such a skill.

The musicians we studied live in a world that expects them to have a substantial amount of musical knowledge. They have usually learned, by the time they begin to play with others for dances and parties, to read at least well enough to play an orchestral part more or less correctly or to decipher the basic information contained in a lead sheet. Most schoolchildren learn the rudiments of singing from printed musical scores in grammar school, and most brass (trumpet and trombone) and reed (saxophone and clarinet) players begin their musical lives playing in high school (if not elementary school) bands or orchestras where they acquire rudimentary reading skills. They know that the placement of notes on the staff indicates pitch, and the shape of the note indicates how long to hold the note.

They know the meanings of the manuscript or print markings that tell you when to repeat measures; the double bars and dots that mean you repeat the section you've just played; the lines that indicate first and second endings to these repeats; a line over one or several bars with the number 1 underneath, indicating that when you reach this point you return to a previous double bar with two dots and play from there again until you reach the beginning of "1," at which point you jump to the section under a similar line marked with a 2, and continue from there. They have learned more complicated signs, indicating that you return to a special sign inserted earlier in the score and play from there until you reach a second special sign from which you jump to a later section similarly marked.

They have similarly learned the rules defining keys and key signatures, and those governing the assignment of flats and sharps. They know that a key signature showing three flats indicates the key of Eb, and that they should "flat" (that is, play a half step lower than otherwise) every occurrence of the notes B, E, and A (Bb instead of B-natural, for instance) and, similarly, that a key signature with two sharps, indicating the key of D, means that you "sharp" all instances of the notes F and

C, playing them a half step higher than the note you would ordinarily play (F# instead of F). They know that a sharp next to a note indicates that, whatever the key signature, the player should raise that note a half step and a flat means the note is lowered a half step. They know, too, that such a change persists for the duration of the bar, and that a natural sign undoes the instruction. They know that a dot beside a note means they should lengthen the note's duration by half of its original value: if a quarter note gets one beat, a quarter note with a dot beside it gets a beat and a half.

Players with this basic knowledge can look at a lead sheet or an orchestral part, see what key the song is in, and know what notes they should play in what order and how long they should hold them, whether what they're playing is the melody line of a tune or a harmony part in a brass or saxophone section.

The rhythm instruments—piano, bass, drums, guitar—call for different reading skills. Jazz pianists and guitarists seldom play, note for note, anything that appears on the printed page, though they may occasionally find that they have to play a part "as written." More often, they work from the notations of harmony on the page, the names of chords or diagrams that give guitar players similar information. Bass players may read the notes from the written part, but quite often play notes they select themselves that they think will provide a proper musical foundation for what the others play. While drummers even less often read from a sheet of music, those playing with a "big band," with full brass and reed sections, may have to provide backing for rhythmic phrases played by the whole band, and communicated to them via a written part. And all rhythm players have to know when to "lay out"—not play at all during a break for an instrumental soloist or for a special effect the arranger wants.

Where the Chords on Lead Sheets Came From

Kernfeld (2006, 43–50) explains how the chord symbols musicians came to take for granted appeared on sheet music and lead sheets:

[A] mid-1920s craze for the ukulele led to the addition of four-string ukulele tablature to some published sheet music.... This tablature was situated above the vocal line, so that performers might realize the song with ukulele and voice, rather than piano and voice—or alternatively with all three together. The purpose of ukulele tablature was to provide, via graphic illustration, blow-by-blow instructions for an instrumentalist to place his or her fingers on the appropriate frets of the appropriate strings. Withfingers pressing down in the proper position, the ukulele player would then strum across the strings, producing a succession of chords that were meant to provide a suitable accompaniment to the melody line and to be reasonably in accord with the notated piano music. In general, ukulele tablature represented the simplest possible chords, intended for amateur performance. Alternatively, four-string tablature in pop-song sheet music might specify tuning andfinger positioning for the banjo, rather than for the ukulele, or for a hybrid of the two instruments, the banjulele.

Then ... in 1930 "harmonic symbols" [as he calls them], "chord symbols" [as they are also known], "chord changes," or "the changes" [as in jazz parlance] began to be inserted above the tablature. The original intent of these symbols seems to have been an entirely pragmatic one: to avoid the potential confusion of having two different sets of tablature running across the page. If four-string tablature for ukulele, banjo, or banjulele appeared above the vocal line, then chord symbols for the six-string guitar would appear in conjunction with that tablature. The six-string instrumentalist was expected tofigure out string tuning andfinger positioning from some source other than the sheet music itself. And vice versa—if the sheet music presented six-string tablature for guitar, then the ukulele player, banjoist, or banjulele player would get chord symbols only and be left on his or her own tofigure out string tuning andfinger positioning for a four-string instrument. In some publications of sheet music, the tablature dropped out altogether, while the chord symbols remained....

In the culture of faking it, the transition from piano music to string tablature and then to chord symbols represented an absolutely crucial move from the specific to the abstract. At the first stage, the piano part in a piece of sheet music specified how the music should be played—insofar, of course, as it was possible to make such representation on paper. (Any thinking musician should be aware of the immense roles that personal interpretation and physical circumstances play in the conversion from notation to sound.) This piano part invariably included accompanimentalfigures which operated in ornamentation of or in counterpoint to, the vocal melody. At the second stage, string tablature told an instrumentalist how to form chords, specifying exactly which notes to play, but otherwise it did nothing other than to make direct connection between particular chords and particular notes of the melody. If an accompanist were to do something more than strumming simple chords beat by beat, then it was up to that player to invent the ideas. At the third stage, chord symbols carried this task into the realm of abstraction. Chord symbols tied the name of a particular chord to a particular note of a given melody, but otherwise these symbols said nothing about how that was to be realized or about the further step of breathing musical life into that realization.

This was a tremendously important development in the realm of pop music (and jazz). However simple and practical the original intent may have been in adding tablature and then chord symbols to sheet music to provide a mechanical guide to string players, these additions soon thereafter took on a life of their own, for anyone who cared to make use of them. Indeed an accomplished pianist, rather than trying to play the specified piano part as it was written, might now take another route and make up an accompaniment. A trumpeter or a saxophonist could use the symbols as guidelines for inventing new melodies that fit a song's harmonic structure. Indeed, with chord symbols available, it was no longer necessary or even expected that a pianist would follow the notated piano part. In fact, on Tunedex cards, there was no piano part. That aspect of the sheet music had dropped away, and only melody, lyrics, and chord symbols remained. It was a new game. Make your own version of a song. Fake it.

The harmonic indications above the melody line on lead sheets give horn players knowledge they can use when they play from the printed page. Competent players know what notes a dominant seventh chord contains, what notes make up a minor, augmented or diminished chord, and how to understand and use these indications to improvise alternate melodies that will "sound right" with what others are doing.

Horn players must also know how to transpose. Lead sheets notate the song in the "standard" (often called the "concert") key, the one in which the composer originally wrote or in which it's conventionally played. But the trumpet and tenor saxophones are "Bb instruments." When the lead sheet indicates Bb as a melody note, these players have to play one note higher, C, to be playing the same note. And the alto and baritone saxophones are "Eb instruments." When a lead sheet in concert key indicates an Eb, they have to play the note three half steps lower, C. Trumpeters and saxophonists thus have to be able to look at the lead sheet and play, without thinking about it, not the notes written, but the notes on their instrument that produce the same sound.

Pianists often have to transpose too, because a horn player wants to play a song in a key other than the conventional one or singers want a song in a different key because the key in which it's written covers a span of notes that goes beyond their accustomed or possible range. In general, lead sheets are written in keys comfortable for the average male voice. As a result, female singers frequently want a song transposed to accommodate their range, and a competent piano player makes that change automatically and instantaneously.

The players we studied have all these skills. If they didn't, the people they usually play with would think they weren't fully competent.

Taking A Song off the Record and Learning on the Bandstand

Experienced players often learn songs by hearing them, either on a recording or by hearing someone play the tune on the job. After one or a few hearings they can play the melody and, making good guesses about the underlying harmonic pattern, can improvise in a way that fits with what the rhythm section provides as background harmony. That's why a frequent bandstand conversation goes like this: "Do you know [name of a song that another player may not be familiar with]?" "No, you play the first chorus and I'll take the second one," meaning that, after one hearing, the second player will know the tune well enough to play it.

Players do this in a way that anyone who has had ear-training exercises will recognize: by learning to identify and reproduce the intervals between a melody's notes. The relatively simple melodic and harmonic structures that underlay most older popular music of the day—not as simple as early blues, but simple compared to contemporary jazz or classical compositions—make doing this relatively easy. Players train themselves to pick out melodies by recognizing intervals, learning to recognize what schoolchildren learn as do re mi, through repetition, hearing when note 2 is so many notes away from note 1 in the diatonic or chromatic scale. You know how to sing do-sol (C-G in the key of C), and learn that that interval is called a fifth, and then that do-mi (C-E) is a third, do-re (C-D) a second, and so on. With those sounds drilled into your aural recognition equipment, you progress to chromatic notes and larger skips, learning to recognize and reproduce minor thirds (C-Eb) and flatted fifths (C-Gb) and skips of a major seventh (C-B) when the melody moves to them.

With this knowledge, you can hear a melody, memorize the tune, and then identify its notes one at a time. Beginners have trouble doing this and may need several minutes of trial and error and comparison with a recording to identify an interval correctly, and considerably longer to get the entire tune's notes right. You can do this work at the piano, testing what you heard and can sing against the piano keys, or by just singing to yourself. Children in many other countries learn the skills of singing from written music and taking musical dictation in solfeggio classes (see the description of French elementary school training in solfège in Hennion 1988).

Once beginners learn the rudiments of keyboard harmony—the I-VI-II-V turnaround and the concept and practice of the circle of fifths, described briefly in chapter 2, and about which more later—they can find the chords underlying the melody they have worked out. With those two elements, they have the tune.

The rudimentary structure of most popular tunes, also described earlier, makes learning new ones simple. Sixteen bars of melody and harmony, with repetitions, make up most songs, and the relatively few variants are likewise made up of repeating four-and eight-bar phrases.

For many years, jazz compositions (those not based on the blues) had the same thirty-two-bar structure as popular songs, and often the same harmonic structure. Musicians knew many chord sequences by the name of the tune in which they might first have appeared or in which, in any case, they did appear prominently. So a "new" jazz song might be explained as "really being" some other song on whose chords it was based. Many first-generation bebop compositions were built on the chords of well-known popular songs jazz players already knew and played. Thus, "Groovin' High," one of the first recordings by Dizzy Gillespie and Charlie Parker, was (as players said) "really" an old pop tune of the 1920s, "Whispering." And "Ornithology," named in honor of Charlie "[Yard]Bird" Parker, was "really" a tune from the 1930s that jazz players liked because it changed key frequently and thus was "interesting," "How High the Moon."

All these skills work well when players learn a tune from a recording and can compare what they hear and what they play until they get it right. After some period of intense practice, players need hear a tune only once (others might need more)—played on the stand by a colleague or even from recorded background music—to be able to reproduce the melody and improvise on it. And after some years of doing this they can play a large number of songs with little or no difficulty, and can play many others they don't know at all after one hearing. That accumulation prepares them to perform creditably with others who may be strangers to them or at least people they have never played with before, who have accumulated a similar stock of intervals, harmonic structures, and tunes.

A thirty-eight-year-old tenor saxophone player active on the New York scene put these modes of learning in a narrative perspective, describing how confused he was when he began playing standard tunes. (Needless to say, he isn't confused this way any more. The semi-incoherence of this account results from his trying to reproduce his earlier confusion, which he does in part by using the present tense throughout, as though describing a current state of knowledge. Compare it with the discussion in chapter 7 of similar difficulties with the same few bars of "Smoke Gets in Your Eyes.")

I was a good reader, which in some ways can be a hindrance to developing as a musician because you rely on those skills rather than those skills that are important which is your ears, and learning music by ear, which is slower, harder, but much more true and beneficial, especially for a jazz musician.

He describes how he taught himself the skills of solfeggio, though he doesn't use the term and might not even know it:

> First of all, you need to know the melody. I want to train my ear to hear a note, to hear a pitch, and to hear that pitch within a harmony. And what I mean by that is when I was trying to figure out "Smoke Gets in Your Eyes" and where that bridge modulates to, the fact that I knew, and again I may be wrong, but I think it modulates down a major third, B major, the ii-V is Dbm7-Gb7, that may be wrong and, if that's not it, it means I have to do more work. Anyway, I hear that note and the way I figured out, if in fact I figured out what key it went to, was that I heard that note within a melody, a lick that I know.

Still speaking in the present tense about this past experience, he explains how he found this transition confusing to do without the music in front of him:

> That's a weird one, because if you don't know the melody goes on the bridge.... [He started singing

the melody, and sang the last note of the A section with a questioning look on his face. The note is potentially confusing, because it is the last note of the A section—an Eb, the tonic note in the key of Eb, the key the song is in at that point—and simultaneously the first note of the B section, which is in the key of B, so that the note becomes D#, the third in that key.] So how would you learn that, would that be a memorization issue? I mean you memorize it by knowing that the bridge, the melody, starts on the same note?

He learned tunes he didn't know when he played them on jobs:

I didn't learn a lot of tunes until after college, playing weddings. I had to go play weddings to make a living. A majority of the tunes we had to learn was dance music from the forties and *that* whole group of jazz standards. You know, Cole Porter, the Great American Songbook, plus the big band standards too.

[So you would learn those?] Well, I would *not* know them and then after the gig, if I was doing what I should be doing, I would go home and try to learn them. I don't think I was as conscientious as I should have been. We had books of standards. There is one called *The Real Book.* And it is *really bad.* But I didn't know better, or maybe I knew better but didn't care. That's funny, this is not exactly something we're talking about, but I never really dealt with the harmony as much as I should have when I was younger. I never really, really understood chord changes and, you know, play them on piano, that's the way to learn tunes if you are not a piano player. [You] organize them, understand how the harmony moves, how harmony works, and really investigate. But anyway, so I had *The Real Book* and I was pretty much limited to reading tunes that were in *The Real Book* or if I was on a gig and they had music, then I would read the tune, read the [chord] changes.

And not through singers, and not knowing them through lyrics. I don't know any lyrics to any tunes. I don't know any of the right changes. I know the changes that they played. [He is talking about the groups with Miles Davis, John Coltrane, and Hank Mobley.] I don't know, I mean, a lot of times they were playing changes that were different [from those in *The Real Book*]. I know I shouldn't say this because it is probably through my uneducated years that I didn't ... that a lot of the songs and the harmonies of the songs were probably distilled down to very basic II-V-Is, and not knowing and really getting deeply into the *real* chord changes, the passing diminished chords, whatever.

Ways of Knowing a Song

Players distinguish basic minimal knowledge of melody and harmony from deeper kinds of familiarity with a song, each level making a different kind of performance possible and creating a different potential for working with other players. They learn, in part, when they set aside time:

> to practice scales, to work on and work up exercises, to learn new tunes, to play solo motifs, to even pre-compose a solo or part of a solo to a tune, [and] to prepare for the transition into ensemble work, playing chord progressions with another in a duo, or with several others such as a rhythm section, or even such larger ensembles as big bands. (Faulkner 2006, 94)

When asked about learning tunes, the saxophone player quoted earlier makes some important and basic distinctions:

> [You are learning tunes.] I am *being exposed* to tunes. I was learning them but then that brings up this whole issue of what it means to learn a tune, I mean *really learn* a tune. And how to learn the tunes, like at what level do I know the tune? One of the issues I am still trying to deal with is how do we process learning music? For example, the example I

always use that spurs my thought processes on is when somebody says to me, "Let's play 'Woody 'n' You,' whatever." And I, like, wow, say I used to know that tune, but I don't know it now, I can't remember it, I know how the melody goes, which is important, obviously, or maybe not, but in this case I know it, maybe, but I might get stuck on the bridge, what key it modulates to or where the bridge starts, but "we're going to play this tune."

Now I might know this tune because I remember the changes, the chord changes. But if I were an actor, for example, and I memorized my lines, and say for example we're doing this show and I go up on my lines and I forget what my next line is, do I know the play at that level where if I go up on my lines am I screwed or do I know the play at a level where I know what's going on, I know where we are, I know the meaning of what I'm talking about, and if we screw up we can get out of it because I can improvise because I know where we are, and know what we're talking about. I'm not just spewing lines. I'm not just playing licks. So how do you *learn* a tune? So if someone calls a tune I'm working on today five years from now, and I'm like ... you know, I used to play that tune all the time but now I can't, I don't, I couldn't play the chord changes to it on the piano right now, but I think I could play the tune, I think I could improvise on it, and I could hear my way through it. So what skills do I have to develop to be able to do that? Because I think that's kind of important, or more important, being able to know what the tune sounds like in my head so I can sit down and play it.

I'm pretty good at being able to hear something and being able to play it back, but if I heard somebody playing changes at me, I couldn't play them back. I could blow over them [improvise on them]. I have a melodic sense of it, but I don't have a harmonic sense. And I don't know how to get that, just through playing a lot of piano, understanding how harmony works, organizing tunes in a certain way, really being diligent about seeing root movements and voice leadings.

[What about "Giant Steps," the John Coltrane classic?] I can blow over it but with set routines that I have thought about and memorized. I always practiced it, you know, but I practiced it by rote, practicing a lick over every dominant chord, every tonic chord, just memorizing exactly. But at *some point,* at some point, the more I played it I could play it the way I play a blues. At some point it started to work. It worked, it got to that level in my subconscious, like when you play a blues now you don't have to think, I mean you can [think] but, if we do, it usually screws us up. But we could play a blues without thinking, we could play rhythm ["I Got Rhythm"] changes probably without thinking, a lot of standards without thinking. "Stablemates," I'd have to think. I'd have to think, but you know it would be a great exercise playing "Stablemates" and not thinking or playing "Stablemates" in another key, Try playing "Stella [by Starlight]" in another key, without accompaniment and see if you can. Without trying to intellectualize the chord changes, OK, I'm not going to play "Stella" in Bb, I'm going to play it in E. I'm not going to try to transpose every chord change up a tritone or something, I'm just going to try to blow through. "Stella" is complicated because it goes through a lot of changes in a lot of ways, you can end up somewhere else, because you have weird resolutions. That's when you really know a tune, when someone says, "Let's play Stella in B" and you just blow on it, and [you] don't think about the chord changes.

We have quoted this player at such length because he makes a crucial point. Players can know a tune in many ways. You can know the melody as written. You can know the melody well enough to be able to play it in other keys than the "original" key. You can know the harmony as well, in the original key or in other keys as well or in any key at all, relying on a deep familiarity born of lengthy practicing. For him, and many others, the deepest knowledge lies in knowing the tune and its underlying harmonic structure so well that you needn't be conscious of what you are doing.

Through repetitive practicing, playing it becomes in some ways automatic, freeing you from mundane considerations of what the key and the harmony are and leaving you open to improvise, secure in knowing that what you play will not be in the wrong key and will not conflict with the harmony others are playing, and also in knowing that you will not get lost and not know what part of the song you should be playing at that moment.

[What kind of practicing?] You know what a two, five, one sounds like [II-V-I (for instance Dm7, G7, C) is the standard cadence that ends a song segment, described earlier], I know what a two, five, one sounds like, but that's why I like to practice a lot of random two, five, ones. [Just like the changes in "Giant Steps"?] In another key, play the bridge to "Have You Met Miss Jones?" in another key, whatever. I mean you are going to screw up, inevitably, but it's an exercise, you're training your ear. Screwing up is inevitable and screwing up is welcome. That's what we are training ourselves to do.... A lot of times we can hear the changes in our head but we don't know what they are, and we couldn't say "that's going up a third" or something, but we know what it sounds like. You know what I mean? ... That takes a lot of nuts-and-bolts training, ear training, and playing repetition. And, for me, it's not a straight line in terms of our learning process, it's very forward-back, forward-back, we go back and pick up what we missed, forward, go back and pick up what we missed, you know. I know 60 percent of this tune but 40 percent I don't know.

Players needn't engage in this kind of analytic practicing for every song, because so many songs are so formulaic, as we have seen earlier, that you only need know which of several basic patterns they rely on to be able to play them, the blues serving as the model for such learning.

A jazz piano player and theory teacher whom Faulkner has known and played with since 1978 explained how he familiarizes students with these formulae:

> I was teaching my class how to analyze "The Devil and the Deep Blue Sea": sing the major third of the key you start in, that's A in the key of F, and then you hear that that's the root of the first chord of the bridge, which is A major. Then you can hear how the root of the second key that the tune moves to in the second four of the bridge, which is C in the key of C major, becomes the root of the V (C7) in the original key, so they can check, you know, verify what they heard. They learn those three tones. Then they can hear it.

For this kind of analytic practicing, reading from the sheet music becomes an impediment, as the tenor player quoted earlier told us:

I'm going to have to start taking these tunes off the record instead of trying to learn them from the book.... I don't want to learn them by sight. I want to learn them by ear, because that's the only way that you remember it, that it gets into your brain.... We have to get away from reading. You really have to get your ear working if you are going to be a jazz player. Once it becomes subconscious, then you're *playing,* you're singing, you know? You can have your saxophone and you know the chord is a C altered and you know the scale but you are not singing, and that is the thing: the ability to sing on your horn. And to sing something convincing is hard. Miles [Davis] is the perfect example: something simple but profound. He's hearing every note he's playing.

An example of practicing and how it pays off comes from Faulkner's field notes:

I had a fake book with "Smoke [Gets in Your Eyes]" in it, along with "Bebop" on another page and I wanted to go slow and learn both tunes in detail. With "Smoke" that meant: first, I played the A section several times, working on the intervals, the leaps, slurring them, playing the interval in another key, playing the A section in another key just to return to the original key with a huge comfort factor.

The II-V-I from the A section into the bridge took forty-five minutes, because I turned it into an exercise on how to get from the A section to the bridge. The bridge has a nice set of intervals that have to be mastered and become part of your blood stream. The bridge has two parts with the second part differing from the first by using some new and highly inventive notes, such as the last two or three that lead back into the A section. The II-V-I leading to the bridge is a Eb7-Ab7-Db and I worked on that chord progression along with getting from the end of the bridge's last two notes to the start of the last A section.

Once I learned the melody, I ran scale passages tightly linked to the chords, such as descending diminished, like riffs for the bridge.

Then, rethinking the piece as played by Don Fagerquist, I spent another hour or so imitating his chorus. I found the solo he took on the CD, and then looked to see if the Fagerquist solo had been transcribed by someone. I located the Web site that had the transcription. I made a copy and checked out what he was playing but didn't feel compelled to imitate his notes, having reached a satisfactory approach of my own to the tune. I did steal some leaps to high C on the last A section, and worked on imitating his vibrato.

When I played this tune on the gig, I called it off too fast and it didn't work. I decided to play it as a ballad, play it slow, and practice it at a slower tempo.

Later, describing another gig where he played the tune and harvested the fruits of this hard work: "I signaled to the piano player to do 'Smoke Gets in Your Eyes.' He nailed the first change and I did a Don Fagerquist imitation. I was in heaven, frankly." (See the more detailed analysis of practice routines in Faulkner 2006.)

Players who learn tunes from well-known recordings typically learn not only the melody and harmony, but also more specialized and detailed ways of playing it that occur on the specific record from which they learn it. As Faulkner explains, "When you learn a tune from a recording you admire, you learn not only the tune but how it was played by those people on that occasion":

> I first heard "Nica's Dream" on one of the first Jazz Messengers albums with Hank Mobley, Donald Byrd, Art Farmer, and Horace Silver. I listened to that track and "The End of a Love Affair" over and over, and then "took the tunes off

the album" (transcribed them) and then I taught them to a bass player and drummer I was playing with at the time. They had listened to the album too. We knew it was what we called a "Latin, swing, Latin" tune, meaning that there was a rumba or Latin A section and then, at the bridge, the B section, it went into 4/4 swing tempo, then back into Latin when you returned to the A theme. On the solos we knew we should retain this pattern—Latin, swing, Latin. That was how you played the tune.

When I learned "There Will Never Be Another You," it was straight ahead 4/4, no Latin-swing-Latin pattern. Learning a tune meant learning how others (for instance, the Jazz Messengers) played it. Learning "Split Kick," a tune written on the chord changes of "There Will Never Be Another You," was another matter. That was like "Nica's Dream," Latin, swing, Latin (Latin for eight bars of the A section and then swing in the second eight bars, alternating back and forth between Latin and swing). I first heard "Split Kick" on a Verve recording made in Los Angeles with Stan Getz and Conte Candoli, one of my favorite trumpet players who I heard at the Lighthouse in Hermosa Beach.

When most players on a job or in a session know the same recording (especially when that interpretation is widely admired locally or nationally), they can treat such details as variations in rhythmic patterns (as above) or background figures to be played behind soloists and similar matters as though they were part of the tune.

Feeling Comfortable

Players who have mastered all these skills know how to acquire tunes and add them to their repertoires. But there's still more to know. Players also look for an ideal state of familiarity with a tune, what they sometimes call "feeling comfortable." What do they mean?

Players feel comfortable with a tune when they know it well enough that they can play whatever the situation calls for them to play when it is "called." For many players in many playing situations, this means knowing the tune well enough to improvise on it with fluency and ease. They don't want to feel uneasy, unsure of what to do next, unsure of whether they will know what to play. They want, rather, to feel sure that they can play what others expect them to play. This kind of ease depends on having the underlying knowledge we've already described.

Feeling comfortable, while not quite the same as the feeling of freedom and intuitiveness described by the saxophone player quoted at length above, is related to it. Feeling completely at home and at ease with a tune in any key in the way he describes, for instance, is not something many players experience, though some do. But players can achieve a similarly comfortable feeling at points along the way to that kind of comprehensive mastery of a tune. More commonly, playing situations call for players to have the kinds of basic knowledge we're going to describe now.

The II-V-I Progression

Becker remembers learning one of these basic building blocks that promotes feeling comfortable during his lessons with Lennie Tristano.

One of the first things Lennie taught me wasn't anything spectacular, but it served me well for years, still does, and gave me a solid basis for feeling comfortable with all kinds of tunes.

People who play popular music are all familiar with the II-V-I progression, the movement from, say, D7 to G7 to Cmaj. These days people call it a II-V-I, but I learned to call it a "circle-of-fifths" progression. This particular arrangement of chords, this cadence, is the more formal musical term, comes up repeatedly in popular music (and in all kinds of tonal music), so that feeling comfortable with it, knowing it to the point that it's almost automatic, takes you a long way toward being comfortable and at home with many kinds of music.

What Lennie showed me was several alternative ways of voicing that progression of chords. Here are some examples. First, a simple one: Gm7 with a ninth added, C7 with a raised fifth and an added ninth, and F with an added sixth and ninth (re-sol-do, for people who learned those terms in school):

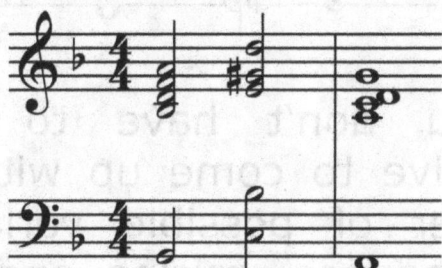

He insisted that I play that over and over, until I could do it in my sleep, and learn it that well in all twelve keys.

When you know that in your sleep, you can add variations. Lennie showed me how to substitute the chord a tritone (six half steps) away for any dominant seventh chord, getting the same effect of a cadence but with a more modern sound. So, for the C7 chord with its little additions, you could play something like this, substituting a

Gb7 chord with an added ninth and augmented eleventh for the C7 chord (and making similar additions to the other two chords):

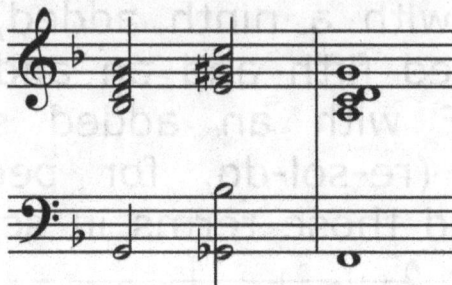

You don't have to be very inventive to come up with a large number of possible variations on this cadence, raising and lowering fifths and ninths, voicing the notes differently (spread out or bunched up, with different notes at the top of the chord because they were the melody notes), and so forth. I practiced lots of them, always in every key. As a result, I always had under my fingers a variety of ways of negotiating important parts of any song I might be asked to play.

Cadences, Scales and Similar Patterns as Building Blocks

Most popular songs of the kind that were the bedrock of the older jazz repertoire were constructed of sequences like this, sometimes ending on a tonic chord, signaling finality, but often ending on another dominant seventh (in the above example, instead of ending on an Fmaj chord, ending on an F7, which could then, with the same formula, take you to a Bb chord, either tonic, dominant seventh, or some variety of a minor chord). You could easily go through most of the harmonic changes in any tune with combinations of cadences like this, picking the chords and voicings so as to put, for instance, the melody note on top. (See the description in Sudnow 1978, 3–8.)

Faulkner explains the practice routine that familiarizes him with these fundamental building blocks:

> I work on the dominant cadences, any II (or ii or bVI) chord resolving to any V, which in

turn resolves to any I. [This is the harmonic pattern Tristano had Becker practice.] Of the hundreds of possible dominant progressions, I usually restrict my practicing to a few. For instance: II-V-I. In the key of F that's G7-C7-Fmaj7. Here are a few that I practice to get to a minor tonic chord: G diminished-C7-b5-Fm7 or even an Fm chord with a raised seventh and an added ninth (F Ab C E G). This is Latin flavored and you can hear it on *Sex and the City*. More fancy would be: Dbmaj7-Gbmaj7-Fm with a major 7.

This builds a foundation and is the slowest and often the most painful part of practicing. You have to listen, have the chops to do these over and over again, and be patient.

With a few such patterns at your fingertips, you can play almost any combination of chords that appears in a song. You have no reason to wonder how you will get from one bar to the next because you can use one of these formulae to do it. This explains one of the more mysterious abilities players display, being able to play a tune they don't know and have never heard before, as in the following example taken from Becker's field notes:

> Don [a San Francisco bass player in his seventies with whom Becker occasionally plays] and I were discussing what tunes he knew and where he had learned them. He has an enormous repertoire, ranging from traditional and pop tunes of the twenties to a lot of contemporary compositions, so this was a lengthy discussion. Then I asked him if he had ever had to play a tune he didn't know at all. He said that of course he had, everyone had to do that sometimes. I asked how he did it, and he looked sort of puzzled and finally said that he wasn't sure. "But, I'll tell you what, let's try it and see what happens. Play something I don't know and I'll follow you and tell you what's going on."
>
> I thought for a minute and picked a very obscure tune from the 1940s (I had probably learned

it from hearing the Glenn Miller orchestra play it on the radio), "I'm Stepping Out with a Memory Tonight." No jazz great ever recorded it, so it was not likely it would be known because of that. (It was, however, recorded by Glenn Miller and several other big bands of the 1940s, as well as by the singer Jeri Southern). I told Don the name and he said he had never heard it. I started to play it, in the key of F. Don, like any bass player would, watched my left hand closely, to see what bass notes I was playing that he could pick up on. He had no trouble with the first four bars, a standard I-VI-II-V progression. The fifth bar goes from the major chord on the tonic—in this case, Fmaj7—on the first two beats, to the same chord with an E in the bass. As soon as I played the E, Don said, "Stop right there. That's a clue." I said, "What's a clue?" "That E. When you play that, I know almost for sure that the next note is going to be an Eb going down eventually to a D. And that means the harmony is almost surely going to be F7 going to Bbmaj7, maybe a Gm7. Then I'm home free."

As soon as he said this, I knew exactly what he was talking about, knew that I would have made essentially the same analysis of the possibilities that he had made, and would have come to the same conclusion. And thus would have been able to play at least that part of the tune as he was able to do it. (Although, being a bass player, he did not have to be able to play the melody.)

He added, "You know, there are clues to things like not only what the next chord will be but when you're going to play a big Las Vegas ending."

Many other patterns, similarly familiar, can serve as clues to harmonic patterns for experienced players: the "Honeysuckle Bridge" we've referred to before, where the third eight-bar segment of a song (the "B" strain) begins on the tonic note, this time harmonized as a dominant seventh chord, which then moves to its tonic a fourth above, and the similar movement at other points in a song; the less common but also familiar change of key to the key based on the note a minor third above (as in the second eight bars of "Long Ago and Far Away"); or the move to a minor chord a third above the tonic.

When players "analyze" a tune (they may not use that word but they often engage in that action), they look for these underlying patterns. We've put together remarks scattered throughout an interview with a veteran piano player who has worked in various parts of the country to make this clear:

> I love that tune [Cedar Walton's "Bolivia"], and I always felt that I was, ah, a slave to the sheet music with that tune, because it's got some what at first seem like arbitrary chord changes. Then after you investigate it with a little bit of analysis you realize that this tune is quite logical and very beautifully created, it's very ingenious.
>
> [Talking about "Hot House," a melody composed by Tadd

Dameron:] It's over [based on] the chord changes of "What Is This Thing Called Love?" Right? It tends to use a minor two-five-one chord-change pattern and that's something I've been working on a lot with my students and the melodic minor scale and its different applications. For example, it starts with a G half-diminished chord, right? And so what scale goes along with that? It's actually the Bb melodic minor. And then there's the C altered which is the same as the Db *melodic minor,* right? And it resolves to the F minor which is the F melodic minor.

[Learning this tune then is learning a series of bebop patterns?] Right, but I think of it as a little bit more, rather than patterns, I think of it as getting familiar with the scale, and that scale is something I've been working on a lot and being really facile in that particular scale and trying to think of its many uses. So that's why I choose that tune.

[Speaking about Thelonius Monk's "Round Midnight":] One of the things that I found with that tune that is really nice is to *remove* [chord] changes from it rather than *add them* to it or play what was written in the fake book, because when you take out [changes], there can be some static harmony in that piece, like just stay on the Eb minor until you go to the two-five to Gb, you can just kind of stay in Eb minor there instead of doing the descending line, you know?

The same kinds of familiarity grow up around time signatures and rhythmic patterns. For a very long time, jazz players played almost nothing but 4/4 time, and the indefinable feeling of "swing" served as a major marker of a player's skill. Players felt at home in 4/4 and uneasy in other time signatures, which, for many years, they had no need to do (other than play an occasional waltz for old-timers who liked dancing to that meter).

Sociologists find the best clues to the social organization of any kind of work in the problems and discomforts workers experience. When workers complain, we can be sure that something interesting is happening. (We take up the changes that took place in the music business starting after WWII and their impact on what players had to know, and on their feelings of comfort on the stand, in a later chapter on generational change.)

Do Players Really Have to Know All That?

People, sociologists among them, often speak of this or that skill or resource being necessary for people to be able to work together efficiently, or at all. And we have been intimating that players must have a collection of tunes as a resource, and a collection of skills those resources require, at their fingertips in order to play with others competently.

Dick Hyman, the virtuoso jazz pianist who plays in all styles with equal facility, says as much, insisting that a competent jazz player must have a minimum repertoire of three hundred songs. We infer this from the titles of two articles he wrote in a magazine for piano players: "150 Standard Tunes Everyone Ought to Know" and "150 More Tunes Everyone Ought to Know" (Hyman 1982a and 1982b). But he probably meant an even larger number.

In fact, the world provides more flexibility than that. Players don't inevitably and necessarily have to know all these things. They must know whatever it takes to play with the people they play with. That tautology makes an important point. Repertoire makes playing together possible. What a player must know depends on what the group is going to play. Conversely, the group will play whatever its members know and can play. We learned, during this research, just how little a player can get away with knowing. Some jobs require a lot less than the large repertoires most of the people we talked to had, and leaders, who do the hiring for a job, needn't know any more than it takes to satisfy whoever has hired their band, which may be quite a bit less than Dick Hyman thought.

David Grazian, a fellow sociologist, studied blues clubs in Chicago. We mean no disrespect to him or his research when we use it as an example of how little knowledge players sometimes actually need. The clubs he studied catered to blues fans from all over the world who wanted an authentic "blues experience." The working definition of that experience was a list of twenty or so songs made famous on classic blues records by traditional blues artists. The musicians who performed in these clubs needed a repertoire of no more than those songs to get through their evening's work. They may have had more available, but it wasn't necessary to what they were doing. (They hated playing this list of blues over and over again, and referred to it as "the set list from hell.")

But Grazian himself provides an even better example, a kind of limiting case, of how little a player needs to know to perform in public. A graduate student, he wanted to play blues but didn't know how, and wanted to write a thesis that would simultaneously indulge his musical desires. He started hanging around blues bars. He had an alto saxophone (he describes it as a "beginner's horn," meaning that it was the kind of cheap model a beginner might own, but perhaps also that he had not progressed beyond being a beginner before he put it away in his closet). He knew how to assemble the horn and read music but not much more. When he went to blues clubs and tried to sit in, he really didn't know what he was doing, what key the other players were playing in, or what notes he could play that would sound like anything anyone else was doing. (Grazian 2003, 107, 113–15, and 2008, 51).

He had found a "blues scale" —or, in the key of —written out somewhere, which he could read and play. He had written it out on what he called his "cheat sheet," in all twelve keys. He seems not to have learned the idea of chords, so that his playing consisted of variations on the blues scales on his cheat sheet. Once he figured out what key others were playing in (which he describes as a major difficulty), he could play these notes in various combinations and more or less fit into what was going on. From his description of "the set list from hell," he might even have been able to work a job, if he had to, in any of fifteen or twenty blues clubs in Chicago. This may be exaggerating what would have been available to him had he chosen to abandon sociology for music. Perhaps not, as this description of one of his adventures makes clear:

> At half-past two in the morning, Jack, a local bandleader, invites me up to the stage with my saxophone to take a solo during the last song of his final set. I slowly approach the bandstand while Jack points to me and whispers, *"Dave, just play off a shuffle in F major."* But, as he awaits my improvised solo, I suddenly freeze. Most blues instruments are tuned to the key of C, but the alto saxophone is always tuned to the key of Eb. Consequently, when a bandleader requests a solo in a particular key, I always have to mentally transpose that key into the appropriate equivalent for the saxophone, which in this case would be D major. Most

professional musicians either have the formula for this transposition committed to memory, or the talent and experience to enable them to figure it out immediately, playing by ear after listening for a few seconds. But for someone like me, who at the time possessed *neither* of these abilities, this process takes a little bit longer. And so, amidst all the excitement, I forget the notes, and after running through the possible combinations in my head for what must seem like an eternity, I begin slowly fumbling through *all* the keys on my horn, evading the microphone as I hunt in vain for the appropriate sound.

Jack's face reveals concern as he mistakes my technical incompetence for stage fright—as does his guitarist, who leaves his post to lower the microphone into the bell of my horn. So, not wanting to disappoint, I start honking and squeaking out random notes as I search in noisy, out-of-time desperation for the correct key. After another half a minute of poking around, I eventually stumble upon the appropriate blues scale, and finish out the song barely in tune. Surprisingly, Jack the bandleader announces, *"Let's hear it for Dave!"* and the audience generously proffers its enthusiastic applause. As I leave the bandstand ... the German tourists at my cocktail table shake my hand, and seem unusually impressed. (Grazian 2008, 54–55)

When we heard Grazian play at the sociological conference where he presented the paper we have been quoting from, he played simple rhythmic variations of the blues scale he had by then memorized, and it sounded more or less like a blues chorus—not a particularly good blues chorus, but nevertheless a recognizable blues chorus. His performance constituted an existence proof that all it takes is seven notes and you can be a working musician. Not one that can do all the things it would be good for a working musician to know how to do, but someone who could in principle play a whole night in a club and get paid for it.

What he can't do with this minimal knowledge, however, is play anything but blues. He not only can't play "All the Things You Are," he can't play anything that requires an understanding of II-V-I sequences, which means he can't play any of the standard repertoire. He could only play in a club catering to a very selected clientele, as the Chicago blues clubs do. But he could do that, and that might be enough for some kind of career.

Players who lead their own groups needn't have all the knowledge we have described in such detail. A piano player told us what it means to be the leader: "If it's my gig I'm *not* going to call tunes that I don't know." That means a leader can avoid situations where he has to play what he doesn't know. As long as you can get the jobs and hire the others, they play what you know.

We will see, in later chapters, how groups negotiate what they play, taking into account what the players do know or can play without knowing. Those two conditions limit the working repertoire.

Now we turn to something that has lurked in what we have written up to now, something that transformed our own thinking substantially: the historical shifts in the conditions of listening, learning, and playing, and the way they have affected the content and use of the repertoire.

5

Things Change: The Organization of Musical Life

We've written as though jazz existed in an unchanging world, where composers wrote songs, musicians learned them (having first acquired the necessary skills), and then formed groups and worked out how to play the songs they had learned collectively, in duos, trios, and big bands as large as eighteen or more pieces. As working musicians ourselves, often confronted with the need to learn things we hadn't known before, we knew better than that.

The world of popular music and the world of jazz associated with it change all the time. After a short overview of changes over the last 150 years or so, we will take up in detail the major change that's affected the people we're writing about: from a music based on popular songs known to "everyone" to a more esoteric music based on original jazz compositions far removed from the musical experience of the general listening public. This change took place in three areas, and the three occurred simultaneously, each creating the conditions for the others. Changes in venues—from bars, nightclubs, and dance halls to jazz clubs and concert halls—resulted from changes in audiences and what they wanted to hear, but also created new kinds of audiences for new kinds of music. Changes in venues and audiences created the conditions for changes in what musicians learned on the job: more and more players got their formative training in schools, rather than on the job. All these changes produced a great change in the repertoire—in the tunes players knew and were ready to play, in the tunes they had to learn and play on jobs—from music based on tunes known and loved by the general public to music created by musicians for themselves, following its own inner dynamic of aesthetic development. And all that led to troubles for players when they had to get it together on the bandstand, the trouble fueled by a moral interpretation of repertoire. We'll take these matters up one at a time, and so will occasionally ask readers to wait until a little later for the explanation of something and the complications and exceptions that also exist.

Some Historical Background

We can conveniently begin the story of American popular music with the parlor music of the post–Civil War, what we might call the Stephen Foster period, sentimental songs in styles that resembled those being played in European cities but also incorporated elements of American folk music. (There are, of course, other possible beginning points, but the exact point is not crucial for what we have to say.) As the expression "parlor music" indicates, amateurs performed these pieces at home, in their parlors, for themselves and their guests, not in public places or for audiences of strangers. The traditional picture of the family gathered around the piano, singing while someone played the piano accompaniment from the sheet music, captures the idea. Other family members might have joined in, playing flute or violin. Some people performed in town bands, playing the horns and reed instruments that made up those contingents, in holiday parades and in park band shells. None of the songs of this period became part of the contemporary repertoire. Musicians no longer play them as part of an evening's entertainment, though the songs are still known and often sung in school music classes and choruses.

Around 1900, what for a while was called Dixieland, and eventually acquired the label of "traditional jazz," appeared. Jelly Roll Morton surely did not invent jazz in 1902, as he sometimes claimed, and it's not completely clear where it came from or if that's even a sensible question to ask. Certainly jazz had roots in the marching-band music so many young men learned to play in school, and the New Orleans tradition of parades and funeral marches gave them venues in which to perform it. So did the New Orleans tradition of whorehouses and nightclubs, where the music served as entertainment and background to more lucrative activities.

The music eventually came to the larger cities—St. Louis, Kansas City, Chicago, Detroit, Philadelphia, New York, and others—of the upper South, the Midwest, and the East, as well as eventually arriving on the West Coast in Los Angeles, San Francisco, and even as far north as Seattle.

Some members of the general public heard this music in person in the nightclubs and speakeasies that became popular places of entertainment in the teens and twenties, in the heyday of Prohibition. Many more heard it on records they bought and played at home.

Simultaneously, from the mid-1920s on, "big bands" of twelve or more players began playing, for dancing, in ballrooms all over the country. Thanks to the automobile and the developing system of roads, bands could make a living touring, playing one-nighters—a night in this ballroom, the next night in another ballroom some miles away, and an occasional longer stay of one or two weeks in a ballroom or nightclub in a larger city. The more or less improvised small band jazz of the teens and twenties turned into big band popular music. Some bands played the swing that had grown out of that earlier music—early swing arrangements were often of such old favorites as "Muskat Ramble"—while others played "sweet music." They all played the pop tunes the composers who worked for music publishers collectively known as "Tin Pan Alley" produced in an unending stream. Commercial radio spread across the country, and people heard music, broadcast live at first and eventually recorded, over local radio stations.

The songs of this era, some written directly for bands and singers to perform in person and on the radio, and some written for more special uses, mainly in musical comedies on the Broadway stage and for films, make up what's now often called the Great American Song Book, though, as we've said earlier, many more songs no one ever inducted into that hall of fame shared enough of their characteristics to be recognizably part of the same genre.

This popular-music machine collapsed in the post-WWII years, killed off by the rise of competing forms of popular music, the arrival of television, and other major shifts in American popular culture. Rock and roll, acid rock, the other offshoots of that root, and other varieties of generic pop music took over popular culture, becoming the Top Forty. As the fifties turned into the sixties and beyond, the kinds of songs that had characterized the standard repertoire became less widely known and ceased to be the basis for people's emotional life.

Composers continued to write "popular music," more or less in the style of the older songs, for a variety of purposes. Composers like Marilyn and Alan Bergman ("The Windmills of Your Mind"), Jimmy Van Heusen (who did many big songs for Frank Sinatra in the fifties and sixties, including "Come Fly with Me" and "I Guess I'll Hang My Tears Out to Dry"), and Mel Tormé ("The Christmas Song" and "Born to Be

Blue") wrote songs many musicians learned and liked to play.

Many of these songs, which had the characteristic features we described earlier (the thirty-two-bar format, for instance), began to depart from it in ways that made them less interesting to players who took the older songs as the standard: lengthier formats, with more differing parts; less harmonic variation, more repetitive melodies; and songs written by singers (ranging from Joni Mitchell to Bob Dylan), who used as subject matter their own lives and feelings. Still, the songs of performers like Stevie Wonder, Billy Joel, and the singers associated with the Motown tradition, among others, entered the musical consciousness of audiences as did, massively, the songs associated with the Beatles, the Rolling Stones, Jefferson Airplane, the Grateful Dead, and other rock groups, along with such "tamer" groups as the Mamas and the Papas. Younger people had grown up on these songs and wanted to hear them when they went out for fun.

Composers continued to write for the Broadway stage and for films, and while many of their songs followed the older formats, many more departed from them. A sampling of these shows would include Schmidt and Jones's *The Fantasticks* and its hit songs, "Try to Remember" and "Soon It's Goin' to Rain"; Kander and Ebb's *Cabaret,* from which few individual songs stood out; Bock and Harnick's *Fiddler on the Roof,* with songs like "Matchmaker" and "If I Were a Rich Man"; Strouse's *Bye Bye Birdie,* which featured "Put on a Happy Face"; Frank Loesser's *Where's Charlie?* and the song, "Once in Love with Amy"; and many more. (A comprehensive guide to this music, as well as to more esoteric material from the world of cabaret is Jenness and Velsey 2006, which we have drawn on in the next several paragraphs.)

Some of the songs from these sources resembled what musicians routinely played on jobs and they easily incorporated them into their working repertoires when that was necessary. Many songs, however, lost their interest—for audiences and players alike—when they weren't done by the original performers or when they were divorced from their dramatic setting: Frank Loesser's "Fugue for Tinhorns" (from the show *Guys and Dolls),* the Master of Ceremonies's "Willkommen" (from *Cabaret),* or "Make a Miracle," the duet for the two leads in *Where's Charlie?*

The players we studied—and presumably others like them elsewhere— didn't, as a rule, know this material or use it on jobs unless they had to, unless audience members or someone who had hired them requested or insisted on it. Faulkner describes this coming up in conversation on the job between Paul, a piano player in his early fifties and Erik, a saxophonist in his forties who has played in big bands in the New York area:

> Paul and I were on a gig nine months ago, a wedding at Old Deerfield Inn, and in the last set Paul called a Stevie Wonder tune with a descending chord sequence, "Don't You Worry 'bout a Thing." I was talking to Erik and mentioned this gig and the tune, saying to Paul and Erik that I didn't know it. "Where did that tune come from,

the Stevie Wonder tune you called?"
I asked. "We covered it in a band
I played in in the seventies," Paul
said. Erik added, "That's another
genre that you have to know, the
Stevie Wonder tunes, the Roberta
Flack tunes. Freddie Hubbard was
covering those tunes, you had to
know them to do weddings at that
time. 'Too High' was pretty hip for
jazz players. 'You Are the Sunshine
of My Life' is one, 'Don't You Worry
about a Thing' is another, it's a
little bit more complicated."
"You play with instrumentalists who
know that?" I asked Paul. "Very few,
very few," he said. Erik overheard
this, and announced with some pride,
"I know *every* Stevie Wonder tune
ever written, just about." "Why?" I
asked, incredulously. "Because I'm a
big Stevie Wonder fan." I asked Erik
if he calls the "Stevie Wonder
repertoire" that he "had down" on
gigs and, if so, which ones. "If I
think people know it, yeah. There's
a piano player I work with. We'll sit
down and play a cocktail hour or a
wedding, something like that, we will

play every tune off of *Songs in the Key of Life."*

"Which is an album?" I asked. "Which is a two-record set, twenty tunes," he said. I guess I got told. He had considerable pride in knowing all the tunes on a two-record set and being able to sit down and play them professionally for a wedding or cocktail hour. I turned to Paul and asked him if he knew the album and its twenty or more tunes. Paul said, "No, no, I know very few of those tunes actually." I then asked George [a bass player oriented toward postbop music and particularly the Miles Davis recordings with Tony Williams and Ron Carter] if he knew "that," meaning the two-record set of twenty Stevie Wonder tunes Erik knew. "I probably know a couple of tunes I could do." Erik then inserted, "'Sir Duke' is probably the most famous." Somebody had written a big band chart on the latter tune, Paul said; he learned the tune from that chart.

This proliferation and increased variation of tunes has meant that fewer and fewer songs are widely known among players. Musicians who play for Jewish weddings will know the songs from *Fiddler on the Roof,* but not everyone plays those jobs. Musicians who play for crowds of baby boomers, born in the fifties and sixties, who grew up on the Beatles, Stevie Wonder, and Motown will know those songs but may not know *Fiddler.* And the songs are less easily learned in the casual and informal way we described in the last chapter, because they aren't built on the well-known formulas of earlier songs.

Even so, some songs from later periods do find a secure home in almost every player's repertoire. "Everyone" knows "Hello Dolly" and everyone knows a song with a different provenance, the cabaret favorite which is also a jazz favorite, Tommy Wolff 's "Spring Can Really Hang You Up the Most." So the repertoire does incorporate new popular song material.

But performed jazz, and the repertoire it is based on, have

definitively changed. No longer a widespread form of popular culture, jazz and its songs have become, to put it extremely, a form of art music, played in places specially designed for music to be listened to (not danced to or ignored as background to sociable activities) by people who have come specially to just that place to hear just that music. Somewhat paradoxically, musicians now have many fewer jobs to play and many more records to listen to. The jazz concert and the jazz club have become the major public venues for the music, both for jazz in its "purer" forms and for the songs that have come to constitute its repertoire.

Of course, people still have parties, and the music that had formed the basis for jazz continues to be played, and people still go to bars and restaurants where music serves as background for their socializing. As a result, the general public still recognizes the older music, even if it is not what they grew up with, and musicians can still play it on jobs for audiences whose musical tastes may well lie elsewhere.

In this major historical shift, new kinds of music replaced what musicians and public alike had known as the "standards." The large audiences targeted by the commercial-music industry having chosen rock and other forms of what is now called "pop" music, while people who liked jazz were increasingly exposed to a music far more esoteric, far less dependent on the "classical" song models than what they had grown up with. As musicians developed radically new styles, fans layered themselves in generational niches, from diehard fans of traditional jazz through lovers of bebop and West Coast jazz of the fifties, and then an increasingly more diverse array of choices, many difficult to listen to without some familiarity and training.

Musicians had once learned jazz primarily on the job, but now they went to school to learn it, taking classes in jazz and performing in school orchestras and bands in high school and college, and even getting Ph.D.s in what an earlier generation had learned far less formally.

Songs, venues, forms of storage and distribution of songs, and ways of learning to play exist in a kind of symbiosis. What follows takes up, in turn, the historical changes in where popular music was played, where it was stored and how musicians learned it, the kinds of music involved at different periods, and the kinds of problems of musical coordination these changes entailed for the working musicians we studied. We concentrate, as we said earlier, on the shift from a widely popular music to the esoteric forms now more common, roughly from the late thirties and forties, when the oldest musicians we talked to (as well as the two authors) began their careers, until the late 2000s. Within these general types many variations occur, and we'll pay attention to those as well, particularly to the phenomenon of minigenerations, cohorts of musicians separated by as little as ten years—a short time, but long enough to produce important changes in what people hear, know, and can play.

The Places Musicians Play

Every art work has to be *someplace.* Physical works, like paintings and sculptures, have to be housed someplace: a museum, a gallery, a home, a public square. Music, dance, and theater have to be performed *someplace:* a court, a theater or concert hall, a private home, a public square or street. Books and similar materials take up space too—in bookstores and distributors' warehouses and people's homes. What places have musicians had to perform in? Who owns and runs them? How does the organization of places constrain the work done in them? What opportunities does it make available?

Jazz has always been very dependent on the availability of venues where you could play it. For much of its history, musicians played jazz in bars, nightclubs, and dance halls, places where the money to support the entire enterprise came mostly from the sale of alcohol and secondarily from admission charges of various kinds (mainly so-called cover charges in nightclubs). So the availability of places for the performance of jazz depended on the viability and profitability of such places. Thus, one of the great centers of jazz development—Kansas City in the 1920s and '30s—drew its vitality from the political corruption that made night life profitable:

Kansas City jazz prospered while most of America suffered the catastrophe of the Great Depression, largely because of the corrupt but economically stimulating administration of Boss Tom Pendergast. Through a combination of labor-intensive public works programs (many of which closely resembled later New Deal programs), deficit spending, and the tacit sanction of massive corruption, Pendergast created an economic oasis in Kansas City. Vice was a major part of this system and gave a strong, steady cash flow to the city. Jazz was the popular social music of the time, and the centers of vice—nightclubs and gambling halls—usually hired musicians to attract customers. The serendipitous result was plentiful, if low-paying, jobs for jazz musicians from throughout the Midwest and an outpouring of great new music. (Pearson 1987, xvii)

Pearson, a historian of Kansas City jazz, says that "over three hundred Kansas City clubs featured live music, and many also included floor shows." And he explains the consequence: "the constant jam sessions and warm socializing that thrived in nightclubs. K.C. in the thirties enjoyed a remarkable musical community that largely existed in and around its clubs" (107). He quotes Count Basie:

> Oh my, marvelous town. Clubs, clubs, clubs, clubs, clubs, clubs, clubs, clubs. As a matter of fact, I thought that was all Kansas City was made up of, was clubs at one time.... I mean, the cats just played. They played all day and tomorrow morning they went home and went to bed. The next day, the same thing. We'd go to one job we'd play on, then go jamming until seven, eight in the morning. (108)

In a setting like that, musical innovation flourished. The jam sessions allowed an experimentation with new forms and ideas, and the chance to improvise at length, to play far beyond the time allowed by a disc or a dance set. There was no audience other than the musicians themselves. Or, if the public wasn't paying much attention, perhaps too drunk to care, their indifference to the music allowed many visiting players to sit in and turn an otherwise commercial job into a sort of session.

The setting for Kansas City jazz changed radically in later years. Boss Pendergast went to prison for corruption, a cleaned-up municipal government closed down the wide-open town and, by the 1950s, the thriving jazz scene was comparatively dead. Similar changes took place in cities across the United States, perhaps not so much in response to this kind of scandal and its aftermath but rather as the result of multiple changes in urban structure, the replacement of live entertainment in bars by big television screens, and changing musical tastes.

Music didn't die. But it now lived in a different world than the one that supported the kind of work and content that dominated the thirties and forties. Substantial changes in performance venues led to new playing opportunities, as musical innovation began to move out of clubs. Jazz began turning into an art music, no longer an accompaniment for dancing and drinking, but rather a music people listened to attentively in the (relatively) quieter settings of jazz clubs, also supported by entrance charges and the sale of drinks, and of the concert hall, supported entirely by the synergistic sale of recordings and tickets, where people came to hear the groups they had learned to appreciate from recordings. Dave Brubeck's biographer traces the development of the "college tour," in which a small musical group could travel around the United States performing on college campuses, to Brubeck's wife's desire to see more of him at home. He may exaggerate her influence, but the change happened and had remarkable results for the top layer of jazz players:

Iola [Brubeck's wife] one day came up with an entirely new concept that quite incidentally revolutionized the old one-nighter, road-trip concept. She searched the list of colleges and universities in the *World Almanac* for every institution on the West Coast, and personally wrote to more than one hundred of them, suggesting the Brubeck Quartet as a great entertainment for campus concerts, citing their recordings and reviews. So successful did these events become that they spread nationwide and opened an entirely new avenue for expression and income for jazz groups everywhere. Before that, many bands had played college dances and fraternity parties, but very few concerts. (Hall 1996, 50)

College campuses contained large numbers of bored young people, most of whom had an interest in popular music and some of whom were jazz fans. Between the two, you could sell enough tickets to fill a mediumsized auditorium and thus pay the expenses and salaries of such a traveling operation. Students came to the concerts to hear Brubeck play the kind of jazz they had become familiar with through his recordings. The records created an audience for live performance, and the live performances created an audience for the records. In university concert halls, Brubeck could play music people couldn't easily dance to, like his experiments with unconventional (for jazz) time signatures like 5/4 ("Take Five"). The quartet could play as they felt like, as long as they liked, and experiment with forms of expression the public had never heard before. The ticket buyers had come to hear them do just that. The place—the concert hall—created the musical opportunity.

That's how the world of employment, of possible jobs, changed for working musicians. For a more detailed picture of this change as it showed up in the lives of working players, one which makes room for the persistence of earlier kinds of places and work into the present, we'll turn to the memories of musicians whose careers began in that earlier time.

Let's first define a "place": a building (or part of one), or an enclosed space in the open air. But, also, a place socially defined by its expected uses, by shared expectations about what kinds of people will be there to take part in those activities, and by the underlying financial arrangements. And defined further by a larger social context that provides opportunities and sets limits to what can happen. A place, so defined, can be as large as a city (as large as Kansas City) or as small as a nightclub or concert hall. Places change more or less continuously, and what musicians can play in them varies as well.

Any large American city contained, in the 1940s and '50s, a great variety of musical venues. Working musicians did not make a living by specializing in one particular kind of place, but rather by taking what employment was available when it came their way. Becker describes his situation as a working musician in Chicago in the '40s and early '50s. The organization of musical life he describes, of course, no longer exists and much of what we now think "natural"—the only possible way things could be done—didn't exist then.

Professional players, paid for their services, played popular music in hundreds of public places. The entrepreneurs who owned and managed these places had a variety of motives for hiring musicians. Entertainment might simply cover up other, more profitable activities, such as booking bets on horse races. Or a factory worker who had saved up some money might decide that running a tavern with a band was his chance to be his own boss. But they all presented music as part of their business activity, intending to make a profit. To be profitable, the place had to attract patrons, who would pay something to hear the music played, directly or, more usually, by buying liquor. So the music my colleagues and I played had to be acceptable to the bosses we worked for and their customers. If it wasn't, they fired us, or didn't hire us again, bringing in someone who played more acceptably to replace us.

Few places with live musical entertainment presented jazz without apology or disguise, advertising themselves as "jazz clubs," to which customers went to hear some kind of jazz played. There were almost no "jazz concerts." A few clubs presented traditional jazz (which we called "Dixieland"), and one or two clubs in the Loop (the city center), such as the Blue Note, presented small jazz groups. Several large clubs, most of them in the major hotels, presented big bands, many (but not all) of whom played one or another version of big band jazz, although always for dancing as well as listening. In the late '40s and early '50s, a number of bars presented well-known players fronting small groups of five or six players—Miles Davis at the Crown Propeller Lounge on 63rd Street, Charlie Parker at the Argyle Show Lounge. These groups did play for people who paid especially to hear them play some form of jazz. All these places, however, featured performers from outside Chicago, groups known to the relatively small group of Chicago jazz fans, many of whom were themselves working musicians.

I didn't play in any of the places that presented jazz, nor did most other Chicago musicians. We worked in a variety of commercial entertainment venues. We played for "private parties," entertainments presented by private persons or groups for the pleasure of their members and guests, most commonly weddings, bar mitzvah parties, and parties given by organizations for their members. These events typically took place in places rented for the occasion: a country club, a hotel ballroom, an ethnic meeting hall, a church social hall. The hosts usually provided food, usually prepared by a commercial caterer, and music, provided by a small band made up (though our employers usually didn't know this) of musicians hired for the occasion, who might never have worked together before.

We called these performances "jobbing dates." Or, more simply, "jobs."(The term varied from city to city; in other cities they might have been called "casuals" or "club dates.") The bandleader [like those described by MacLeod in chapter 1] wanted to provide suitable entertainment because he hoped the hosts would recommend him to other party givers. But the musicians themselves (the "sidemen") only wanted to do a good enough job that the bandleader would hire them again or recommend them to some other leader. There were many more jobs for small groups than for large ones. Since bands almost invariably had a piano player, I got more work than many of my friends who played instruments more easily done without.

What we played on such occasions varied with the class, age, and ethnicity of the group attending the party. The wedding customs of ethnic groups varied substantially, often requiring special music. If we played for an Italian wedding, we had to be ready to play "Come Back to Sorrento," "O Sole Mio," and maybe a tarantella (a southern Italian folk dance in 6/8 time) to which the older people danced enthusiastically. A Polish wedding called for polkas. Some ethnic groups' musical requirements were too exotic for the average player, and a special ethnic band might be hired in addition. So, one night when I played for a Syrian wedding, a Syrian band made up of a tenor banjo and a tambourine alternated with us; we played for "American" dancing and they played for the more traditional dance. Greek music was too difficult for most of us too, since most of it was played in unfamiliar—to us—time signatures like 5/4, 7/4, and 9/8 (which we learned to do years later when Dave Brubeck recorded "Blue Rondo à La Turk").

Some bands came together only for the one occasion, that night's job. The personnel were often assembled ad hoc, perhaps even, in those days, at the local union hall, where musicians would assemble to look for work and leaders for players. Some more established groups used much the same personnel night after night to play the same material.

A party usually lasted three hours, although a lively party might provoke the host into splurging on an extra hour or so. We played forty-five minutes or more out of every hour, music that people could dance to (not too fast), a mixture of currently popular songs from the *Hit Parade* and older standards. We almost never played jazz tunes not known to the general public. ("Satin Doll," yes; "Lester Leaps In," no.) We seldom played more than three choruses of anything, varying the tempos, but of course never played the very fast tempos a lot of jazz players liked to play. And we usually played the melody or something that didn't depart too much from it.

I worked for a year with the Jimmy Dale band, a racially mixed big band that only played for black dances and parties (in those segregated days). The leader, a tailor named Harold Fox, made uniforms for many well-known bands and got their arrangements in return. So we played, essentially, the jazzoriented arrangements of bands like Basie, Woody Herman, and Stan Kenton. Similarly, playing for Jewish audiences allowed us to play the more swinging Latin American rhythms that were becoming popular.

Musicians like me also played "steady jobs" in bars and clubs. Chicago had hundreds of bars and, at the time, before television provided the major form of entertainment, many had live music, usually a trio or quartet. No one who played in these neighborhood bars had enough of a reputation to attract people who wanted to hear them play jazz. These bars catered to a local trade, and we provided background noise.

Bars had their plusses for young, would-be jazz players.

People in the bar usually paid very little attention to the band or to what we played. Since they weren't dancing, tempos didn't matter and we could play as fast as we could play, if we wanted to. Some owners didn't mind if our friends sat in, which led to jam sessions on the job. When no one cared, we played whatever we wanted.

Playing long hours gave young players hours of paid practice time, crucial for the development of their technical and improvising skills. They played the songs of the basic jazz repertoire over and over, hundreds of times in a year, until improvising on their chords became effortless. They had time to experiment with melody, harmony, and rhythm.

Some clubs we played had "entertainment," usually striptease dancers. Others had real entertainment: singers, dancers, magicians, jugglers, comedians. These acts sometimes had written or printed scores we played more or less as written, without rehearsal. Since their music was quite conventional, that was never difficult, except when the music was so faded we couldn't read it. There was seldom room for anything resembling jazz.

A few venues featured well-known jazz players from elsewhere, but those jobs were never available to people like me. I studied jazz piano with Lennie Tristano, a Chicagoan who soon moved to New York, where the opportunities were somewhat better, and even he never worked more than a few nights anywhere in Chicago.

Our repertoire and playing were completely dictated by the circumstances of the places we played in. We knew what we wanted to do, which was to play like our heroes—in my day, big bands like Basie or Herman, small bands like those of Gillespie, Parker, and Getz. But we seldom could do that. Most of the time we played what the "place"—the combination of physical space and social and financial arrangements—made possible.

This situation has some obvious consequences, common in the experience of older players and not foreign to the experience of contemporary musicians.

Big cities and many smaller extended communities as well house a variety of venues, each providing its own combination of circumstances affecting what the musicians playing there can and must do. Most will be neither totally hospitable to jazz nor completely devoid of possibilities for occasionally playing it. Most musicians, playing in the full range of places available, learn to play in a complex and varied repertoire of styles: music for strippers to dance to, polkas for Polish weddings, Latin American music for people who want to dance those dances, popular tunes of whatever kind are then popular, standards for the minority that will probably request them, and so on.

This constraint continues to operate in all kinds of specialized milieus. A bass player gave us the example of the swing-dance crowd, people who (in the 2000s) dance in 1930s swing style, doing dances like the Lindy Hop, and compared them to other kinds of audiences with other requirements:

Your tempos [for the swing dancers] are probably from 120 to 180 [metronome marking], in that range, and you're going to play those tunes all night long. Those people who come to that particular dance know how to dance that particular type of dance and you can't assume they know how to dance other styles such as bossa nova. The swing dancers are not really there to listen a whole lot closely to the music because they're doing something else. It's not a listening crowd. They basically want to dance the same dance over and over again with as many different people as possible. They want to keep it short, not longer than three minutes. And then they can dance with someone else. It is totally opposite than what you would do on other [musical] dates. The other thing is that if you are doing a wedding gig you want to mix up the styles of music. You have some people who want to dance this style, some that want to dance that style, and actually the people that are coming are coming as couples and they want to dance with themselves together all night long, and so sometimes your tunes will be a little longer, say give them a little more time, but then again don't go too long because the worst thing is for a dancer to have to leave the floor before the song is done. You want to get as many people up as possible and fill as many needs as possible. And with the swing dancers, although they come with somebody they want to dance with many people, and you don't want to have songs that are really, really long, because they're not dancing with their honey, you know? You don't want long pauses between tunes either.

What players play because the place they're working in requires it enters their repertoire, ready to be activated when needed and even taught to others when necessary. What they play in one place affects what they do in another, so that the music of even serious jazz groups likely shows the influence of other kinds of music they have played somewhere else on some other night. Careful listening usually reveals some traces of all the kinds of music they play and have played, from strip joint to church, in any player's output, most clearly in short musical quotations but also in stylistic features.

As a result, dividing musicians into subgroups—such as jazz players, commercial players, and so on—is a mistake. We might better think of these as ways of playing, ways of doing the job. Some people can sometimes engage in just one form of the activity—perhaps the desired one called "jazz"—without participating in the less-desired versions of the trade, like playing for the weddings and bar mitzvahs and fashion shows and dances that make up the customary employment of someone who makes a living playing popular music. But most players have done it all, and probably will again.

How Musicians Learned Tunes in These Places

Just as playing has to take place somewhere, so does learning. A player of Becker's generation (black, where Becker is white, and an inhabitant of New England, where Becker worked in the Midwest and on the West Coast) describes how he accumulated an immense repertoire on the many jobs he played over the years, from formal and informal teachers he encountered, and from what was available on the air and on records. He says about one particular friend:

> Every week he would buy sheet music. Every job he worked he would buy sheet music. And he would let me have his sheet music and I would use it and then I'd give it back. That was his sheet music, it wasn't mine. So I would learn ... I would copy the line, put the chord [symbols] in, and use my ears.
>
> I had a teacher, a trumpet teacher, and actually he taught me

tunes. He would play tunes, he would take a tune, say, like "Tenderly." That was one of my first tunes, written by Walter Gross (1946). The first record was with Sarah Vaughn. He sat there and would sing part of it and say, "We're in the key of C" and I had to find the changes, and if I didn't find it he would spell it out, "It's C major, the next chord is a G chord, but everybody now plays it in an augmented eleventh," you know, that kind of thing. And the next time I saw him I would say, "Let's do 'Tenderly'" because I had woodshedded [practiced] it. And then he would start in on another key. And after a while I got the message that you have to woodshed those tunes in *all the keys,* you know, to get the feel.

I had to learn tunes, and first of all I had to learn how to play blues, in several keys. The idea was blues in G—sharps fare better with string instruments, especially guitar, so you learn the blues in G, in D, we also had to learn them in Bb and in Eb, because of the horn players. And we had to learn "The St. Louis Blues," and we had to learn the form of the "St. Louis Blues," that portion where it goes minor. And there were a couple of others, there was a tune called "China Boy," I don't know who wrote this tune but it apparently came out of 1920, somewhere around there. "Rose of Rio Grande," some of these tunes are written by these older fellows such as Isham Jones, Gus Kahn, he wrote "I'll See You in My Dreams."

And things like "On the Alamo." And then we had to learn the Ellington tunes. Another friend, I played with him, he taught me so many tunes. He said, "You've got the ears, just listen." We played many things, blues, ragtime, he taught me the form for rag—there was a form involved. We worked on a Cole Porter tune, it must have been 108 measures, "Begin the Beguine." He was teaching me how *to research* and learn about a tune, and the different forms of tunes.

He also taught me to play Ellington, such as "Rockin' in Rhythm."

So I would hear a tune, hear it on the radio, go see a big band, I want to learn the tune, I want to sit and play it, and if I don't play for anybody but myself, I dig it, I dig the tune, I dig myself playing' the tune. Even now I'm ready to learn tunes.

And, of course, the Ink Spots. I liked the Ink Spots. Everybody liked the Ink Spots.

That was another way of learning tunes, from radio and television. Singing groups, like the Four Freshmen, they were with Stan Kenton, and there was a group before them called the Pastels. They used to sing a tune called "After You." It had *great* harmony, *close* harmony, the brass, the reeds together. So that was very important to me. Because then you had these *singers*. And the big bands started to take a back seat to the singers.

That was all so *important* for me and it came from the radio. It was also important for me because it taught me the keyboard. It also helped reinforce my knowledge of chords and chord movement. So that was my learning. Whatever I could hear from the radio, from big bands, and one of the bands that I heard as a little kid, I said I was going to be a musician, was the Jimmy Lunceford band. That band was a bitch, man.

A white player of the same generation and from the same part of the country told a story that varied in some details:

I guess I was around 13, 14, something like that, when I started playing. There were essentially three places you heard tunes then, if you lived where I lived [a smaller New England city]. First of all, there was the *Hit Parade,* I mean you heard that every week and they played all the hit tunes of the day, so you learned them from hearing them over and over on the *Hit Parade.* Then there was another program, *Make Believe Ballroom,* they pretended it was a broadcast from a real ballroom and they played all the big bands, Dorsey, Goodman, Miller, Ellington, so you would hear what they were doing. And then the third thing was the remotes, from different hotels and ballrooms, like [he imitated an announcer] "And now from the Hotel Bradley in Boston, it's the orchestra of Shep Fields and his Rippling Rhythm."

So I learned a lot of music, a lot of tunes, that way, just listening to the radio. And then I began to play in dives in town. I played in these really terrible places, they were cruddy, they smelled terrible, they were full of soldiers and sailors completely drunk and fighting all the time, big fights. We played on a bandstand, it was sort of a crow's nest, about ten or twelve feet up, a little stand, you got to it up a ladder, there was a trap door you had to go through. When the fighting started, we'd pull the piano over the trap door so they couldn't get up there with us. We made two dollars a night, a dollar and a half or two dollars.

[What did you play in these places?] The usual stuff. The leader was a drummer—the bands were all trios, piano, drums, and a horn, never a bass, that was a luxury, so it was pretty sparse. He'd ask me if I knew a tune and if I didn't he'd bring in the music the next night. I could read.

[Were you reading sheet music or lead sheets?] Lead sheets, I had learned the chords so I could read from a lead sheet. This is when I was in high school. We played all the standard tunes of the time, I can still remember what we played: "Jeepers Creepers," "I Don't Want to Set the World on Fire," I hated that one, "You Can Depend on Me," "Satin Doll," and one—to me this tune brings back my entire adolescence, I can remember dancing to it in the high school gym—"I'll Never Smile Again," the one Sinatra sang. That song can bring back all that romantic adolescent feeling. And we played "Body and Soul," of course, "Stardust," "If I Had You,"

"Sentimental Journey," "A Nightingale Sang in Berkeley Square"—or was that later? I think it was around the same time. This was during the war, I was in high school from 1939 to 1943, so we played those tunes from the war, you probably know them too, like "When the Lights Come on Again All over the World." And, of course, we played the blues, mostly in Bb, but in other keys too.

About that time I graduated from the dives and began to play in nicer places, they had floor shows. There'd be a juggler or something like that, an Irish comic, and a girl dancer, who would strip. And some places I played had a chorus line, several girls who danced, but they didn't strip.

That's when I began to play show tunes. I mean, we had been playing Gershwin, Irving Berlin, even maybe Cole Porter, in these other places, along with other things, but this was a better class of club and the music was better. We played tunes like "Blue Room,"

"It Had to Be You," "Confessin,'" "Lover Man," "Deep Purple," "Time on My Hands," "White Cliffs of Dover"—that was another one from the war—"Our Love Is Here to Stay," we were playing some of the great tunes, Gershwin, Porter, Harold Arlen. No, we weren't playing the later Arlen tunes, like "Comes Rain or Comes Shine," but we were playing the ones from [the movie] *Cabin in the Sky,* like "Cabin in the Sky," "Stormy Weather." It's like there were two levels of tunes and we were playing both of them. We played "I've Got a Crush on You," "Night and Day," we played Irving Berlin, "Alexander's Ragtime Band," that's one of the first tunes I ever learned, but also like "Cheek to Cheek," that was more complex with that double bridge and it's quite long. And we played Ellington too. "Sophisticated Lady," "Satin Doll," "Don't Get around Much Any More."

By now I was playing in these better clubs and I was also beginning to play with society bands, in the big hotels, for parties. These were bigger bands, anywhere from six to ten pieces, so they had music, and I learned tunes from the music we played. We played all the standards and a lot of show tunes and then, with these hotel bands, we played novelty tunes, you probably played them, there were always these novelty tunes like "Pistol Packin' Mama," remember that? And "The Three Little Fishies," "Hut-Sut Rawlson on the Rillerah," and we played congas—they would do these dances so you had to play the special music for the dances, for the conga lines, like "The Mexican Hat Dance." There were a lot of them.

I had a band while I was in college. We played everything at the university—fraternity dances and parties, all sorts of stuff—and worked a lot. This was just about the time the bebop revolution hit, and we went crazy for all that. Dizzy, Bird, we listened to all their records, learned to play "Grooving

High'" to the chords of "Whispering," and all those tunes.

Contemporary musicians still learn on the job (as of the last half of the first decade of the twenty-first century) in the same way. One of our interviewees, well known as a rising young avant-garde jazz saxophonist, also learned a lot of much more conventional repertoire, but originally simply in order to play the jobs he was getting when he began making a living playing:

I was playing with older musicians in situations where a lot of the times there were written-out arrangements so there was not a lot of faking, not a lot of me having to know the melodies. There was a lot of reading. Did you ever work in Boston a lot? Society bands and things. When I did do gigs that involved a lot of faking I was playing with my friends, we knew similar tunes. The older guys knew the tunes. But then again I could have been more diligent and learned the tunes I was reading on these society gigs but I didn't. It was more reading and less faking. I haven't played a wedding in so long I can't even think of one, but we played things like Duke Ellington, "Satin Doll," or "Take the 'A' Train." Or "I Can't Get Started." I was starting to work in Boston with society bands.

I didn't listen to a lot of the older players playing *standards.* I didn't listen to Oscar Peterson a lot. I didn't listen to a lot of vocalists. A lot of my background is from Miles [Davis], the more recent Miles quintet with [Col]Trane, Philly Joe Jones, Wayne Shorter. I don't have a background in jazz standards. I came to that later, an appreciation for that music. I didn't understand its place in the repertoire of jazz music. "I Fall in Love Too Easily" was to me the same as "Moanin,'" just another tune. My learning tunes was very disorganized and scattered.

I certainly knew a lot less tunes then than I do now, so my repertoire was pretty limited and I would just say, "I don't know the tune." Hopefully, the other players wouldn't have started already. I didn't learn a lot of tunes until after college, playing weddings. I had to go play weddings to make a living. A majority of the tunes we had to play was dance music from the forties and that whole group of jazz standards. You know, Cole Porter, the Great American Songbook, plus the big band standards too.

[So you would learn those?] Well, I would *not* know them and then after the gig, if I was doing what I should be doing, I would go home and try to learn them.

When I was in college we had a steady jazz gig and we probably didn't play a lot of jazz standards, although sometimes there was a singer, so I'd accompany her, but I still really didn't learn the melodies and learn them well. I was very into Coltrane so I was playing a lot of his tunes and Miles tunes, the tunes that they recorded: "Giant Steps," "Impressions," "Nardis," "Green Dolphin Street," "No Greater Love," easy Cole Porter standards,

"What Is This Thing Called Love," or "I Love You." The Cole Porter tunes that Trane recorded, those I would know.

Younger players also learn more contemporary pop repertoire that older players don't know. Recall Faulkner's discovery of the Stevie Wonder repertoire described earlier in this chapter.

Although musicians learn tunes now just as they did then—from books, records, and listening to the radio—they now learn, too, from a source that wasn't available fifty or sixty years ago. Somewhat to the surprise of older musicians, who don't always approve of this development (even though it provides a good source of income for many of them who teach jazz in high schools or colleges), young musicians increasingly learn jazz in school. They take classes in jazz and improvisation. They play in school ensembles, particularly "stage bands" with the instrumentation of a standard forties or fifties big band—four rhythm (piano, bass, drums, guitar), four or five trumpets, three or four trombones, five saxophones—and play elaborate arrangements by the teacher or one or more students. Teachers lead students through the increasingly complex and arcane melodic, rhythmic, and harmonic experiments that typify contemporary jazz. Bands compete, like school athletic teams, and return with trophies, having placed first or second in a state, regional, or national competition. These young musicians seldom play for dances or parties, in bars or restaurants, or in any of the kinds of places musicians learned the trade forty or fifty years ago. The teachers, usually still playing in the usual range of venues, find a solid base for their musical activities in a teacher's salary.

Because high school and college students of jazz usually do not try to earn a living playing music professionally—not while they are in school anyway—they contentedly learn what the teachers teach and don't learn the more ample repertoire acquired by players who have learned on the job over a period of years. A player who had learned music in such a school found going to work in the world of commercial music, and playing sessions with older musicians, a shock. He didn't have the repertoire these situations called for:

I was going to school for this music [jazz], they were telling me "You've got to memorize these tunes" as I was going along, "you've got to memorize these tunes," and the only capacity I had to do that was my brain. Memory was largely about these chords: a Bb major seventh, an Eb major seventh. I wasn't hearing the Roman numerals, I wasn't hearing the four chord, I just had to memorize that the four chord was, say, G, so I was not listening to the tune in the depth of the ear, the capacity of the ear, as much as I was trying with the brain to just memorize one chord, one lettered-name chord, one after another. So when I got to things like "Stella by Starlight," it was a nightmare. I didn't know what a sharp four minor seven flat five [sic] was, I didn't know what a flat seven dominant sounded like, I just knew this thing was in Bb and I've got to memorize this Ab seven comes before Bb. It was—it was pretty bad, man.

So I had to *read everything.* After I got out of college I still had to tote that book *[The Real Book]* around, had to read everything.

I used to go sit in with the older cats, sit in, you know, these jam sessions on Sunday nights. I figured that getting out of school, I was all ready. They'd start this tune and I'd get lost in the changes, man, I didn't know where I was. The older cats would turn around and look at me reading [the chords to the tune]. "There Will Never Be Another You," something like that, something I should know. "You don't know that tune?" one of the older cats would say. "Well, I know it, I'm reading it," I would say. "You don't know it if you have to read it." And I would feel pretty small. If I got a negative vibe from somebody on the first tune of the night, it would affect the whole evening for me back then. I was so sensitive to all that, temperamental musician and all that, getting ready to break like glass at any minute. I wanted to play jazz so much. I tried *so hard.* I put so much into it that I couldn't do it. It wasn't music anymore to me. It became like a calculus problem. I found out later that all this stuff was just a tune, it's music, and then things begin to open up a lot more.

When I [first] learned how to do this music I did it very technically. This scale fits this chord. You must know this chord. You must know this arpeggio. It really wasn't explained to me that all the scales, the arpeggios, did for you was to prevent you from playing wrong notes. They didn't take the solo for you. The scale doesn't take the solo for you. The arpeggio doesn't take the solo for you. It just prevents you from, you know, it helps you satisfy the craving of the chords. It prevents wrong notes. It's lifeless.

I wasn't doing any singing. I was just looking at a chord and saying, oh, it's G augmented, well, I know I'm going to play a whole tone scale because that's.... It was tuition money taking the solo. I had nothing to do with it. It was a forty-thousand-dollar education taking the solo; I was just a poor bloke holding the guitar. I wasn't involved.

[The teachers at the school were] telling everyone the same information. So when that chord comes along you are going to play out on a Dorian [mode] because that's what they told you to do. You were told to disregard anything that was out of that box that you could have come up with from your own musical reservoir. You didn't even go inside your musical reservoir that had been built since you were a baby. You have this big reservoir of music and tunes, whether it be "Yankee Doodle" or "Mary Had a Little Lamb," that's instilled before I was able to sing. It wasn't until years later that I started to become intellectual about music, but like everyone I had it at birth. I never drew upon that to play music. I always drew upon the blackboard to play music. It wasn't working out, man.

["On Green Dolphin Street," "Blue Bossa"?] All the wedding band jazz, yep. [What does wedding band jazz consist of?] "Black Orpheus," "Blue Bossa." ["In My Solitude?"] That's too abstract. ["Don't Mean a Thing if It Ain't Got That Swing?"] Yeah, probably "Satin Doll" at a reception. ["Woody 'n' You?"] No, not "Woody 'n' You." ["Stablemates"?] No. ["Foggy Day"?] Yeah. ["All the Things You Are"?] Maybe in a pinch. [And would people have the book in front of them?]

When I first started playing *out* on those types of tunes, I played with guys who were older than me, accomplished wedding band commercial players, and they knew *all those tunes.* I was the guy with the music stand that didn't know any songs.

For all its shortcomings in the eyes of players like this, the experience of learning repertoire in school fills the gap, perhaps inadequately, left by the disappearance of the hundreds of clubs in which players like Becker learned. Many fewer bars, restaurants, and other places where musicians worked so many nights and such long hours now present live music. A stubbornly "old-fashioned" piano player, who tells customers that he can play any request written before 1954, told us:

> I had the good fortune to meet a lot of restaurant owners who liked jazz, there are a lot of them here in town. These guys are all about the same age, they grew up on this music, it's their music, and that's what they want to hear in their restaurants, so they hire me. I've got this one and another one [named after a famous early jazz player], you know that place? He likes this music—well, you can tell from the name of the place that he likes it.

He feared what would happen when these restaurants closed or changed hands. And, within two years of this interview, two of the restaurants in the area that had featured piano players during dinner did close. In the same period, some of the clubs where Faulkner's interviewees, and Faulkner himself, had worked cut back on live music, reducing the amount of work available for them.

Still, these older adepts of the standard repertoire find work and, when they do, they seldom experience difficulties analogous to those of younger players who don't know that older material. They find it easy to avoid the newer post-bop repertoire (discussed in the next chapter) and feel no embarrassment when they do. When asked about the newer music like Chick Corea, Wayne Shorter, and Thelonius Monk, one older musician answered:

> You mean jazz compositions. It really doesn't come up for me, mostly it doesn't come up, just doesn't come up. I don't work with guys who play those things. And I don't get asked to play them much, if at all. I know a few things, like I know "Round Midnight," if

someone wants to hear something by Monk, I can do that.

[What about "Blue Monk" (which Becker then sang for him, since he didn't know it by name)?] Yeah, I've heard that but I don't play it, no one asks for that. Or what's that other one? "Ruby, My Dear," I've heard it but I don't know it, I can't play it, if someone asked for it I'd have to say, "Sorry, don't know it." Some things you get asked for a lot. You have to play "Round Midnight," you have to play "Lush Life," but other things, I just don't know them. Like Brubeck, I get asked to do "Take Five" a lot and I can't do it. Someone wanted me to learn it and I said, "Listen, I'd have to work on that for weeks before I felt comfortable playing in 5/4, and frankly, it's not worth the trouble, I don't get asked to do it enough to make it worthwhile to go to all that trouble."

There are fewer jobs for players who know the standard repertoire than there once were because weddings, bar and bat mitzvahs, and other parties, whose participants grew up on rock and roll and other forms of contemporary pop music, no longer require as much familiarity with the standard repertoire as they once did. (Although it is not rare for a wedding band to have to play a first set for the generation of the parents of the bride and groom, consisting of more standard tunes, before the old folks leave and the party gets going with a more contemporary repertoire.) Bruce MacLeod's description of wedding parties circa 1980 (we drew on it in chapter 1) foreshadowed this development (see especially 164–73).

All these changes mean less available work. When Becker told some contemporary players about the forty-two-hour weeks he put in on the bandstand of the 504 Club in 1950, he expected them to respond sympathetically to his tale of being overworked. Instead, they said, enviously, "Gee, we never get to play that much." They envy the opportunity those hours gave him to practice tunes over and over, to train his physical and mental responses in the standard harmonies and patterns, to become accustomed to doing what these jobs demanded of him without having to think about it. Few players have that opportunity today. What Becker and others of his generation learned on the job, contemporary players learn by practicing at home or playing in occasional sessions without pay.

So the places musicians played provided the conditions in which they both performed and learned to perform. The constraints of particular performing situations determined the limits of what could be played and those limits determined what players could learn on the job.

A Note on Time Periods

We haven't put dates on the changes we've described. We haven't said that venues changed in this particular way on this date or even in this general range of dates. What we described didn't change all at once or at the same time or the same rate in every part of the country or local community or even in every part of every small local musical subcommunity.

The worlds and communities in which musicians work and live consist of many small entities: bands, bars, clubs—all the things we've described—each with its own history, its own contingencies affecting its existence, its own twists and turns. This restaurant does well and the owner indulges his taste for jazz by hiring a small group; that one does poorly and gets rid of the music. This college experiments with bringing in jazz groups as part of its concert series and sells a lot of tickets; that one tries the same experiment, loses money, and doesn't try it again. This community suffers a business downturn, affecting expense-account-fueled patronage of bars and other music venues. That one experiences a boom as its major local industry gets some big orders and the local entertainment provides more work for local players than they had before. While such changes are not independent of larger historical shifts, they do not take place in such a precise way as to make it easy to speak of changes that affect all the players in a community in the same way at the same time. There is a lot of slippage.

Individual players likewise have their own histories. This one becomes part of this group of young players and learns from, acquires, and reacts to that experience in a way related to his own development and his own occupational history, while another player arrives at a different place by running into a somewhat different group of age-mates. This one takes lessons from this teacher who requires him to study and learn these tunes, while others learn something a little (or a lot) different from another teacher.

Becker lived and worked in Chicago just before television decimated the tavern business and the places in which he learned repertoire simply disappeared. Faulkner learned to play as a teenager in Los Angeles at a time when a short drive down the California coast to Hermosa Beach took him to the Lighthouse, a legendary site of jazz innovation. Becker played piano, and there was always more need for piano players than for players of other instruments (piano being the instrument hardest for conventional groups to do without at that time), so he remained in Chicago while his age-mates and colleagues who played other instruments went on the road with big bands and made the professional connections that took them into other worlds of playing where other repertoire was important. Faulkner got into the music business when big dance bands appeared less frequently on the radio (and so he heard less of the Tin Pan Alley output than he might have ten years earlier) and when popular music of the kind Becker grew up on was being rapidly replaced by rock and roll and other musical forms.

These multiple and varying influences on what people heard, learned, and had to learn intersected in multiple ways, and simple patterns of covariation will not capture the reality of what happened. What's best, we think, is to recognize the ways people learned and then the ways they put that learning to work in the company of others, without trying tofind simple patterns that would make prediction of outcomes possible. And this is what we have done: no large generalization about how things changed on this or that date.

6

Things Change: The Music

The places players play in shape the content of what's played, but they don't determine the contents of anyone's individual repertoire. Players learn on the job, but they learn off the job as well, as they meet players with similar or intersecting interests, and follow their own ideas of what kinds of music deserve their attention and excite them, what kinds of music they feel they have to learn and play. The kinds of musical ideas young musicians encountered and took seriously changed during the active performing lives of the people we talked and worked with, as players developed new aesthetics and worked out the implications for their own musical performance.

We've seen how musicians learned songs in new ways, and saw too that very few musicians have the luxury of playing just what they want, mostly playing what their jobs require, using their ingenuity to create an effective working compromise between what they find interesting and what the job demands. As the organization of the music business changed, the content of the repertoire musicians played changed too. Most importantly, as the world of available jobs changed, players added original jazz compositions to their repertoire. This music made different demands on them, gave them new things to learn, and left them uncomfortable in new ways. The new forms made trouble for players used to the old ones, but they also opened up new vistas of musical exploration.

Two bodies of material make up the major components of what the jazz repertoire has become. The older repertoire persists. Many situations require playing those tunes: the pop tunes that became standards when players selected them, on the basis of tradition and recordings by well-known jazz players, and are permanently embedded in American musical culture; ethnic music; show tunes and other popular genres; and some popular jazz compositions, which had much the same form as the standards. Most working musicians have learned that repertoire, and its harmonic and rhythmic underpinnings, and feel comfortable playing it. These excerpts from Dick Hyman's lists of "Standard Tunes Everyone Ought to Know" (Hyman 1982a, 1982b) indicate the breadth and eclecticism of that standard repertoire:

After You've Gone
Ain't Misbehavin'
All of Me
All the Things You Are
Almost like Being in Love
April in Paris
As Long as I Live
Autumn Leaves
Back Home Again in Indiana
Bluesette

***

Laura
Lazy River
Let's Fall in Love
L'il Darlin'
Limehouse Blues
Love for Sale

Lover Come Back to Me

***

Spring Can Really Hang You up the Most
Sugar
Take the "A" Train
Tea for Two
Tenderly
That Old Black Magic
That's a-Plenty
Them There Eyes

The songs range from more or less traditional jazz tunes from the teens and twenties ("That's a-Plenty") through the familiar standards of the twenties and thirties ("All of Me" and "Tea for Two") and the popular songs of that era that didn't persist as favorites of jazz players ("Lazy River" and "Sugar") to the more sophisticated tunes of the late thirties, forties, and early fifties ("Laura" and "All the Things You Are"), later compositions in the same style ("Spring Can Really Hang You up the Most"), and jazz compositions like "L'il Darlin'" and "Bluesette." Unless a player plays nothing but contemporary jazz gigs, he needs some familiarity with this broad and varied repertoire, though how much will depend on his particular circumstances.

The second body of material consists of contemporary jazz compositions. The character of these compositions varies so much that no musical label can cover all of them. Some musicians and writers refer to this music as "post-bop," that is, post Dizzy Gillespie and Charlie Parker and their contemporaries. Others use the names of its most well-known practitioners to indicate what they have in mind—"You know, Wayne Shorter, tunes like that"—and they usually add other names: Herbie Hancock, Chick Corea, Joe Henderson, or older players like Thelonius Monk or Charles Mingus. In fact, these names only scratch the surface, because after bebop no single kind of music has dominated the scene as the standard repertoire did in earlier years. And that indicates that what followed bebop did not have a unified character, but rather consisted of a variety of experiments, each based in small groups of collaborators, none of their production achieving the status of what "everyone has to know." That, and the radical character of some of the experiments, has splintered the contemporary jazz repertoire in unprecedented ways. For convenience, we will refer to all these developments as "post-bop," and hope that readers will remember that this is shorthand for a highly differentiated repertoire, little of it known by large numbers of players.

A warning. We can't easily separate players into those who play the old repertoire and those who play the new repertoire. Some play only one or the other. But not many. Players find it impractical to specialize completely in the newer repertoire unless they can make a living playing concerts and in more or less avant-garde jazz clubs. Playing the older repertoire exclusively does not restrict employment and performing opportunities in that way, but it might give such a player a reputation as an "old fart" and decrease the esteem in which people who can do the newer repertoire hold him. So, in fact, most players play some mixture of the two. Some songs from the post-bop repertoire have become "standards," in the sense that many players know them and impromptu groups can play them with little trouble. And even the most avant-garde younger players—those, at least, who work regularly—play some or most of the older repertoire.

The Older "Standard" Repertoire

We described earlier the general character of the three kinds of songs that make up the standard repertoire. Musicians often played the blues, a twelve-bar harmonic pattern (in the most basic form, just three chords) with simple traditional melodies or, at least in the earlier phases, musiciancreated melodies which were themselves quite simple. Players frequently just said, "Lets play some blues," named a key, and counted off a tempo.

Or they played the survivors of a little-understood sifting process that reduced the mass of Tin Pan Alley – produced popular songs to a manageable number by ignoring most of them. Songs remained in the pool of active standards because someone had thought them good enough to play and record, and the recording had become part of an informal canon of good tunes that had been played by Coleman Hawkins ("Body and Soul") or Lester Young ("You Can Depend on Me") or Roy Eldridge ("Rockin' Chair") or tunes that had been sung by Billie Holiday or Ella Fitzgerald or, sometimes, by Frank Sinatra or Mel Tormé. It's a long list. Other songs remained available for incorporation into that body of material because recordings of them by good players existed, and they might be found by an adventurer looking for new things to play. Or they might become standards because they were written by a songwriter universally considered good—the standard list includes George Gershwin, Cole Porter, Irving Berlin, Harold Arlen, Duke Ellington, and Jerome Kern. Songs by many only slightly less well-known composers (Hoagy Carmichael, Harry Warren, Fats Waller) often entered the canon too.

These songs had the traditional character described earlier: thirty-two bars long, divided into eight-bar sections arranged as AABA or ABAB or one of a few minor variants; a range not much over a tenth; no "unusual" skips or notes. Many songs departed from these rules occasionally, more often as players and singers grew older, more secure, and more adventurous.

Other songs jazz players played resembled these popular songs, but had been composed by the players themselves. These "original" compositions embodied the formulaic structures common to standards, often consisting of a new melody composed to fit the harmonic patterns of an already existing song. Most of the first generation of bebop songs belong to this group: "Groovin' High," remember, was based on the chords of "Whispering," and "Hot House" on the chords of "What Is This Thing Called Love?"

This older repertoire is not stable. Older tunes no one plays any more disappear (although they remain potentially available in sheet music and on recordings). And some of those that have disappeared do get discovered and reintroduced into the active repertoire. (Songs Becker learned in his youth—"Smoke Gets in Your Eyes" and "Long Ago [and Far Away]"—have been "discovered" by the middle-aged players Faulkner works with.)

For many years, these three sources—pop tunes, original compositions that closely resembled pop tunes, and blues—made up the jazz repertoire. With the addition of pop tunes of lesser musical interest to the players but often asked for by customers, and ethnic material, this was what players had to know and, for the most part, did know. After the rock-and-roll revolution, and the drastic changes in popular music that entailed, and after the less drastic but similar revolution in the music coming from Broadway and from the still-existing popular-music publishing business, the repertoire musicians knew and had to know became much more varied, as we detailed in the last chapter.

The Post-Bop Canon

But the musical changes that created the most disruption for musicians who had grown up on the older repertoire came from the new kinds of compositions musicians themselves composed. When rock and roll replaced the older, "standard" repertoire for the general public, jazz gradually turned into an art music played to concert and quasi-concert (jazz club) audiences. Freed of its ties to dancing and what audiences not particularly interested in jazz wanted, the music became less conventionally melodic, less conventional in its organization and in the tonalities it used, and more inclined to an avant-garde interest in modes, other scales, and other structural foundations. Listeners had to study more to appreciate it, and some of them found it less emotionally resonant than earlier forms of jazz (that reaction typically diminished with time and increased familiarity). This music has its own repertoire, based largely on the recorded output of the well-known experimenters listed earlier and many other composers less well known.

New experimenters exist everywhere and players can easily discover them and the forms and songs they have pioneered. Some younger musicians treat the music of Shorter, Corea, Coltrane, and their generation as the music of the establishment, looking to a next generation of experimental players as various as Dave Douglas, Dave Holland, John Zorn, Kurt Rosenwinkel, and going back as far as Lennie Tristano's experiments in free improvisation in the early 1950s (Billard 1988, Shim 2007) and Muhal Richard Abrams and the Association for the Advancement of Creative Musicians (AACM) in the 1960s (Lewis 2008). Many players and groups use the full resources of contemporary computers and synthesizers, especially laptops that can be brought to work just like a drum set, amplifiers for guitars and other instruments, or electronic keyboards.

Since no central source produces this newer jazz repertoire—there's no post-bop equivalent to Tin Pan Alley—and since it has no large popular following, many varieties have always coexisted and none has ever dominated the field. Some players find improvising on modal scales interesting. Others, if they can get colleagues to share their interest, as they often can, build a shared repertoire out of the works of particular players or groups. No universal "what everyone knows" can be counted on as a basis for playing together. Some of these experimenters live in the world of clubs and concerts. Some have found homes in the jazz programs of universities or high schools.

So many streams of new music exist, each a choice from many musical possibilities, and few players know all, or even many, of them well. Each presents, as we'll see, distinctive problems for players. Each has a distinctive repertoire, shaped by the people who pioneered it. As a result, players can no longer assume that someone who shows up on the job with them will share their knowledge of any large number of tunes. (See the discussion of the somewhat similar situation in France in Coulangeon 1999, 41–62.)

The Real Book and its clones mitigate, to some extent, the potential chaos this situation can create. In an emergency, anyone who can read those lead sheets can play a great variety of repertoire more or less well. But fake books don't do away with the problem entirely, and many players remain uncomfortable when suddenly confronted by a style of music they barely know.

Feeling Comfortable in Different Repertoires

As we saw earlier, musicians feel comfortable playing a tune when they know they can execute what it and the playing situation they're in call for. We connected that feeling to their knowledge of the underlying patterns of the song they're playing. Now we'll take account of the problems produced by the changing repertoire resulting from post-bop innovations.

Feeling comfortable in the standard repertoire

When musicians perform together, they want to know three things about the tune they're playing. First, where is the beat? Regular rhythmic pulses furnish signposts that help them coordinate what they are doing, and relate what they do to what others do, so that, when the group plays, it plays together. Accents regulate the length of notes, phrases, and sections of the song, marking off divisions within and between bars. A time signature tells players what kind of note (quarter note, eighth note, etc.) receives one beat and how many such beats there are in a bar. Vertical lines divide the staff into bars containing notes whose time value adds up to that number of beats. A 4/4 time signature means that a quarter note gets one beat, and one bar contains four quarter notes (or the equivalent); a 6/8 time signature means that an eighth note gets one beat and one bar contains six of them. Even without written music, musicians use schemes like this to organize their playing. For most of its history, American popular music confined itself to a very few time signatures: 4/4 for most songs, 3/4 for waltzes, and occasionally such variants as 6/8 (which players usually count in two) and 2/4 (counted in two, as 4/4 itself often is).

These numbers convey information about the relative time value of notes. A quarter note is half as long as a half note and twice as long as an eighth note. How long any of these notes lasts depends on the tempo, how close together the beats occur. Some number per minute, as counted by a mechanical or electrical metronome, is the usual mode of calculation, but in playing situations someone communicates time values by "giving a beat." Classical music groups rely on a conductor or one of their members to "give a downbeat," indicating—by the length of time occupied by an upward gesture of the hand, arm, or head followed by a downward movement—the length of one beat. In jazz groups, someone, usually but not necessarily the leader, counts off eight beats (two bars), two beats in the first bar, four in the second. Occasionally, the piano player or another rhythm player, sometimes a horn player, will just start playing, perhaps without warning, alerting the other players that it's time to begin and setting the tempo.

The beat gives players important basic information. Accented beats indicate where the current beat falls in the bar (is it the first? The second? The third?), and the beat's regularity keeps players oriented to the same system of counting, so that they arrive at the same notes, chords, and sections of the song at the same time, rather than straggling in in disorder.

Players, orienting themselves in the music's flow, routinely ask a second question. What key are we playing in? Where is the tonic note or chord, the resting point that closes a cadence and so signals the beginning or end of a section or chorus of the song? Key signatures (the notes at the beginning of a written score telling players which note is the tonic and which will have to be altered in what direction to create a major scale) give them that information in a highly conventionalized language most people learn in school: a five-line staff on which a note's placement indicates its pitch, and a system of signs (sharps, flats, and naturals) indicating the key—which note will be the tonic note, the root note of the chord that creates the feeling of resolution defining a cadence—and allowing the alteration of notes at any point. Most people who can't read music nevertheless recognize the language of "do-re-mi" that teachers use to convey the idea of a key and its associated scale, and know that "do" is its resting point. Listeners, as they follow the music, substitute the idea of tonality for the idea of key, easily identifying the note that is the resting point of "do." They needn't know which particular note is that resting point, which key the music is actually in, to follow its harmonic structure and shape, only the relative position of notes and chords. When you play, of course, you need to know the precise key as well. So, when someone names a tune to play, musicians ask: what key is it in? And when they hear "Bb" or "G," they know what note on their instrument will serve as the resting point of cadences, the tonal "home" of the song, what notes will be sharped (raised a half step) or flatted (lowered a half step), and can deduce a great deal of the additional information they will need to perform the piece.

Finally, and not at all least important, musicians ask: where are we in the tune? Given that the tune has some kind of structure, what is it, and which part of it are we playing at this moment? They want, first, to know the exact structure of the tune. Does it have an AABA structure and, therefore, a bridge? Does it have two similar sixteen-bar sections (ABAB) that differ only in their last few bars, the first one leading into the repetition of the A theme, the second one coming to an end? Is it some variant on those patterns that they can easily grasp? Or is it something "weird," a pattern organized on some other principle, perhaps easily graspable but not common, for which they might need more specific instructions?

With the answers to these three questions, competent players (most players who work have at least this level of competence) know where they are rhythmically, tonally, and in relation to the structure of the tune. When all the players share that information, they can play together easily, even though they have no music and have never rehearsed. That's the solution to the riddle posed at the beginning of our book: how do they play together without music and with little or no preparation?

This general solution usually works, and musicians use it in all kinds of situations. Not only when they play, but also when they listen. Players listening to recordings tap their feet as they find the rhythmic pulse. They hum to establish the tonic note of what they hear. They search for the repetitions of melody or harmony, which reveal the structure of the tune. They analyze what they hear almost automatically, habitually, and as a result can quickly reproduce key elements of the tune when they have to.

If you can't quickly and easily make such an analysis you may feel, and may say, if you aren't embarrassed to admit it, that you're lost. Faulkner describes listening to a contemporary jazz group and finding it impossible to tell where they were in a standard song he knows well and should be able to orient himself to without trouble:

I was at a concert of the Monterey All Stars, with Terence Blanchard, Benny Green, James Moody, and a bass player and percussionist. The first tune they played was Dizzy's "Bebop" at a medium tempo. Moody took the first solo, very bop. Terence's solo started out bop but then moved into the Miles-like, post-Miles of "Miles Smiles" and Wynton [Marsalis] inspired. No problem, I could follow all of it. However, a few tunes later, the band did "Time after Time," in which it was difficult to find a tonic or tonal center and the chord changes that Benny Green was playing were very far out. It was hard to find where they were in the tune's chord structure.

It was beautiful, to be sure, floating very much on top of the original chord changes. I suppose this is what they mean by "re-harmonizing" a tune.

Players who can't find the answers to these questions while they are playing with others suffer—and cause—acute embarrassment and disorientation for themselves and others. In chapter 4, we described David Grazian's adventures when he found himself on the stand of a Chicago blues club, in well over his head. Ingrid Monson (1996), in her analysis of the work rhythm sections do, gives a detailed account of how the pianist, bass player, and drummer ordinarily provide much of this information to the instrumentalists playing melodies and improvisations. She analyzes a specific recording, bar by bar, showing how the rhythm section constructs a background for a soloist's improvisation, indicating tempo, tonality, and place in the structure. The importance of this work stands out when one of them, the bass player, "gets lost." Somehow getting six beats ahead of the pianist and drummer in the simple harmonic structure of the blues the band is playing, he persistently plays "wrong" notes, that don't sound "right" with the chords the others are using as the basis for their improvisation. When he ignores the hints they repeatedly give him, they finally—to avoid the confusion of having the band in two places in the song at the same time—accept his idea of where they are.

Such events occur rarely, and competent players usually find the standard signposts to be all they need to find their way through the musical landscape.

Performance Practice

Actually, it's not as simple as we have made it sound. Barry Kernfeld made us aware that beneath all these things we have focused on lies another phenomenon, which he explained to us in the following way.

All of these popular and ethnic styles (and their extractions, derivations, and re-creations as jazz styles) are permeated by deeply conventionalized agreements regarding musical roles and actions (known in medieval and Renaissance music as "performance practice," a concept that may be applied to any and all musics), and the process of learning to collaborate in live performance in any of these styles is the process of learning to fulfill those conventionalized expectations, to learn the essentials of performance practice (which exist in the face of and despite all the romantic notions of spontaneous creation that surround jazz).

(A good example can be found in Kernfeld's discussion of "swing rhythm" [1995, 12–18], in which he describes just such understandings as they work in the interpretation of what would routinely be notated as straight eight notes, but which are seldom played that way.)

Kernfeld noted that we had mentioned such things from time to time in this text but had not made the phenomenon central to our analysis, even though some of our examples (e.g., the discussion with the bass player about how to play a tune you don't know in chapter 4). But we hadn't had the idea when we did ourfieldwork and did not pursue it systematically or consciously and so don't have the material to allow us to make it as central as it should be. As an example of what that kind of knowledge would consist of, we can't do better than quote the following example Kernfeld gave us.

If you are a jazz string bass player, you learn how to produce a plucked, sustained tone quite different from the classical pizzicato. You learn that it's the bassist, not the drummer, who has the greatest responsibility for maintaining the beat, and at some basic level of near incompetence, it's actually much more important to keep playing boom boom boom at a steady tempo on some indecipherable low note than to get the changes right while dragging the rhythm. You are the rock upon which the band rests, and therefore you have to be secure in all the song forms, so that you may guide the band through its performance, e.g. (on an AABA tune), into the bridge, out of the bridge, and into the beginning of the next chorus, as you proceed chorus-by-chorusby-chorus, doing this in coordination with textural changes supplied by the drummer. You learn appropriate situations in which to use a two-beat (intro to "Bag's Groove"), a four-beat with the root on beats 1 and 2 and the fifth on beats 3 and 4 ("Cherokee," the A section of the head), a walking four-beat ("Cherokee," the A section), a drone ("Lonely Woman," "Bitches Brew"), the bossa nova root and fifth pattern (anything by Jobim), the samba root and fifth pattern ("Nica's Dream," the A section), a calypso pattern ("St. Thomas"), a funk riff ("Chameleon"), and on and on and on. You learn that a ballad for dancing requires an unchangingly slow pattern in the bass (maybe with a 6/8 rhythm-and-blues feel), but a ballad for listening requires the superimposition of double-time and even quadruple-time ornaments that swing. You learn when to come in, when to lay out, how to trade 4s and 8s (if it's modern jazz), how to play stop-time and slap the wooden body of the instrument (if it's Dixieland), and whether any given song or performing situation is or is not appropriate for a bass solo. Maybe you learn that your double bass works really nicely on jazz gigs, but discover that you ought to be playing electric bass with that salsa band, and from there you encounter the Cuban anticipatory bass style of playing ahead of every downbeat and a new set of conventionalized expectations opens up.

I could go further with this, but you get the idea, for the bass. I believe that I could construct similar descriptions of standard performance practice for any instrument involved in popular and jazz styles, and it is this constellation of conventionalized musical behaviors that provides a fuller and more accurate answer to the question of how they play together without music and with little or no preparation.

Feeling comfortable in the post-bop repertoire

The post-bop repertoire varies enormously from one practitioner and group to another, so no generalization about these collections of tunes can be accurate. Still, many, if not most, of the songs post-bop groups play do not use these standard landmarks. Sometimes they do, but not so regularly that players can depend on it. Even when these musicians play pre-postbop songs, they may do it in a way that disguises, complicates, confuses, or otherwise fails to give complete answers to questions about rhythm, tonality, and structure. More often, players dispense with the old landmarks and the kinds of structure they imply, relying on other orienting mechanisms.

Tempos, meters, and keeping the beat. Players accustomed to the standard repertoire feel at home in 4/4 time and, a little less so, 3/4 time. But newer compositions and styles of playing don't restrict themselves to those or the related and essentially similar 2/4 and 6/8 times. Instead, they use a variety of other meters: 5/4, 7/4, and 9/8, among others. Wayne Shorter's compositions often use 3/4 and 6/4 time (e.g., "Miyako" and "Iris," "Wildflower" and "Footprints," respectively).

Unfamiliar meters pose serious problems of orientation for players who have never played them before, or seldom. The accents in 5/4 and 7/4, for instance, do not occur in the same repetitive way they do in more familiar meters. Musicians count 4/4 time like this: *one*-two-*three* -four, a strong accent on one, and a lighter but distinguishable accent on three. They may tap their foot twice in the bar to keep time (jazz players unashamedly keep time with their feet in a way classical players almost never do). The regular accents make clear where the beat is and where the player is in the current bar. You can't keep time so simply in 5/4. Players unfamiliar with this kind of meter often divide the bar into a segment of three beats, with a strong accent on the first, and a segment of two beats, with a similar accent on the first: *one* -two-three, *one* -two. But it can also be divided into two equal segments, each two and a half beats long, or in other ways, and the same sorts of possibilities exist for 7/4 and other less familiar meters.

Unfamiliar meters also make it difficult to use familiar and habitual rhythmic and melodic figures in improvisations. Jazz players routinely use short melodic figures, usually lasting no more than a bar or two, as modules out of which they construct solos. Paul Berliner devotes large sections of *Thinking in Jazz* to the way players consciously "[use] the discrete patterns in their repertory storehouses as vocabulary, ideas, licks, tricks, pet patterns, crips, clichés, and, in the most functional language, things you can do" (102). His chapter "Getting Your Vocabulary Straight" (95–119, and the associated musical examples on 540–43) shows how fundamental to jazz playing these habitual phrases are—players pick them up from live performances and recordings and practice them in every key, so that they can serve the purpose, in improvisation, of conventional phrases in conversational talk.

But these vocabulary fragments typically come from work done in 4/4 time, and players can't easily transpose them to time signatures with a different meter and different patterns of repeated accents. They experience playing in unfamiliar meters as difficult and awkward, and spend long periods of serious practicing to acquire that ability, just like the practicing they did when they first learned jazz. Of course, those players who have done the requisite practicing can feel just as at home in these meters as they do in 4/4, and many players have made that investment. Other musicians who play regularly, equally experienced and competent in other respects, refuse to make the effort (remember the older piano player quoted in the last chapter, who said it wasn't worth the trouble to learn such things because "it doesn't come up" for him).

Another difficulty arises because of changes in the routine way drummers play their part in a rhythm section. In earlier forms of jazz, musicians expected players in the rhythm section to "keep time": establish and maintain a clear and easily heard rhythmic pulse you could orient yourself to as you played, always knowing "where [beat] One was." Pianists through the early thirties, and often later, played "oompah" rhythm: a strong bass note on the first and third beats of a bar, a firm chord in the right hand on two and four. Guitar players played a steady four beats to the bar on unamplified instruments, which could scarcely be heard but could be felt. Bass players have changed their style of playing rhythm less than the others, though they now have to think about playing solos as well as rhythm, and they use a wider range of notes in a chord or scale. Drummers usually kept time with some combination of bass drum accents on the first and third beats of a bar, regular accents on the snare drum, a steady pulse of the high-hat cymbal on the second and fourth beats of a bar, and a repeated eighth note figure on a cymbal. The multiple changes that accompanied the bebop revolution included substantial changes in their conventional practice. They stopped providing a steady beat on the bass drum, instead using it for strong accents (often on the upbeat) that other players sometimes called "dropping bombs," and creating more complex and less repetitive patterns on the other instruments in their set. These changes made rhythmic patterns less clear to other players, potentially leading to confusion about where bar lines were located and where the beat was. A traditional musician's joke repeats the apocryphal utterance of a player lost in a rhythmic confusion created by this kind of drumming: "A One, a One, my kingdom for a One!" (That is, he is looking for a clear indication of where the first beat of a bar is and can't find it.)

Finally, playing very fast tempos may be beyond the capabilities of some players who may lose track of where they are in the song or where they are in the measure, though they can play the same pieces easily at slower tempos. Alternatively (not common, since most players try playing faster rather than slower) a piece played very slowly may fall apart as players can no longer discern where the beat is. This happened to Becker in a seven-piece band he worked with. It had an arrangement of Neil Hefti's "L'il Darlin'," which they kept playing slower and slower, just to see what would happen. Eventually, it happened. The piece lost all its momentum and just died. The band stopped playing, having lost all sense of where the beat was.

Scales and cadences. Some post-bop tunes do not rely on a conventional tonal structure that immediately makes clear a definite tonality (that is, one that tells players what key they're in) and the typical harmonic patterns associated with it. Even when they use the well-known II-V-I cadence, they do it in ways that don't let players make use of their familiarity with those patterns. And often they don't use such cadences at all, relying instead on scales as organizing principles of a song, around which improvisations can be built.

John Coltrane's 1960 composition "Giant Steps" creates just such a problem for players accustomed to II-V-I sequences because, though its harmonic structure builds on the same II-V-I sequences, it does so in an unfamiliar way. Consider the first three bars of "Giant Steps":

B Maj   D7   G Maj   B♭7   E♭Maj

The first harmonic move, from a tonic chord to a dominant seventh chord a minor third above it (B to D7 here), is not unknown in standard tunes, though not very common. (The move to the dominant seventh a major third above, leading to a circle-of-fifths sequence arriving at a conventional final cadence in the original key, occurs more frequently.) The second move, from D7 to Gmaj, completely conventional in itself, however, doesn't end on a dominant seventh, leaving the cadence unresolved. Instead, ending on a major chord, it firmly changes the key to Gmaj, and then immediately repeats this move, going up a minor third to Bb7, and changing keys again, V-I, to Eb.

Such abrupt key changes occasionally occur in the standard repertoire. "My Old Flame" and "Here's That Rainy Day" change keys repeatedly in similar ways. In "Giant Steps," happening repeatedly, it becomes the tune's fundamental building block. The cadence is so unusual and such a distinctive feature that musicians familiar with it treat it as a name whose meaning everyone will know. To say, "It's 'Giant Steps' chords" communicates as much to initiates as saying, "It's 'I Got Rhythm' changes" communicates to players of the conventional repertoire.

Not only are the changes somewhat unfamiliar, they take place rapidly. (The difficulty only gets worse when the tune is played at a very fast tempo, as it usually is.) The chord changes every two beats in several of the measures, so that you have very little time to get settled in it before the next chord arrives. Vocabulary patterns, the small phrases players routinely rely on to fill out measures, ordinarily stay in the same key for large parts of a song, and the same chord for at least a bar and usually more. "Giant Steps" changes key ten times in sixteen bars. So players have to construct, practice, and learn new ways of thinking about the harmony, and new vocabulary pieces to use in dealing with it. Otherwise, they can get as lost and as at a loss for what to do as David Grazian described himself being when a member of the blues-club band pushed him into the spotlight. Without extensive practicing and experience, you cannot play this material at all.

Many post-bop tunes differ from conventional standards in other ways. Some songs have, essentially, no chord changes at all. Miles Davis's "So What," based on the Dorian mode (a scale beginning on D and using only the white keys on the piano is an easy way to understand what this is) has a conventional AABA structure. The A section consists of eight bars in that mode (with a Dm chord as the harmony) and the B section consists of eight bars in the same mode raised half a step (with an Ebm chord as the harmony). Conventional players wouldn't find this difficult to understand or play, but they have trouble thinking of what to play without the stimulus of changing chords to provoke their imaginations.

The modal model opened the door to further experimentation with music based on scales rather than harmonic patterns. Organizing music around scales rather than sequential harmonic structures has often appeared in other kinds of music, and players sometimes encountered it in pre-bop times. Becker remembers:

When the band was playing a Latin tune, someone might say to the piano player, "Play a montuno for a while," and then everyone else would light a cigarette and the pianist, bassist, and drummer would take off on an extended improvisation on two chords, always dominant seventh chords: D7, say, and Eb7, a half step above it. That was the entire structure. You invented melodies and rhythmic figures, alternating, more or less, between the two chords. This kind of improvisation could get very lengthy and complex, though not when I was doing it, because I got bored quickly, but I could see how it could be interesting.

(Becker may misremember this, or he may have run into a diluted and distorted version of a well-known Afro-Cuban musical practice.)

Another variation appeared in American jazz following Coltrane's innovations. Nicolas Slonimsky, a music theoretician, defined a scale as any upward-moving sequence of notes between the two notes of an octave; such scales could have any number of notes up to twelve. He compiled an almost thousand page book (Slonimsky 1947) showing all the logically possible scales, beginning with scales made up of two notes, and complicated with one or more "interpolated" above or below the scale notes. (For instance, a "tritone" scale, consisting of the two notes of that interval—say C and F#—and notes a half step above them—C# and G.) Some jazz players, hearing that John Coltrane studied this book, go through it looking for possible variations on what they now do. In addition, some players have begun to use scales from other musical traditions (for instance, klezmer, played by John Zorn, and Hungarian, played by Uri Caine) as the basis for their improvisations.

Structural variations. Instead of a formulaic thirty-two-bars strain divided into eightbar sections (and these usually divided further into regular two-and four-bar phrases), post-bop songs can, though they often follow regular patterns, consist of sections made up of other combinations of numbers of bars put together in other ways. Tom Harrell's "Sail Away" consists of a twenty-four-bar A section divided into three eight-bar phrases, the second a slight variation of the first, the third a transposition of the theme a minor third higher; a sixteen-bar B section, divided into two eight-bar phrases, the first a paraphrase of the A theme, the second a further variation of that theme; and a sixteen-bar C section, a shortened version of the A theme.

Wayne Shorter (whose name musicians often used in talking to us as shorthand for the entire body of post-bop composition, as in, "You know, the Wayne Shorter stuff") has often used unfamiliar formats. "Speak No Evil" consists of a fourteen-bar A section (repeated once), an eight-bar B section, and a fourteen-bar C section, which is a slight variation on the A theme. "Yes or No" has a fourteen-bar A section, repeated once, a sixteen-bar B section, followed by a fourteen-bar repeat of A. (The B sections of both tunes play the role of the bridge in conventional standards.) "El Gaucho" and "Pinocchio" have eighteen-bar themes. "Miyako" has three eight-bar phrases followed by four bars during which one note is held while the harmony beneath it changes four times (altogether, twenty-eight bars). "Mahjong" begins with an eight-bar melody over two chords that alternate, one per bar, followed by the same melody (with different chords), eight bars of a new theme, and four bars of changing chords over a sustained note. The sixteen-bar theme of "Nefertiti," according to the score, is played without solos ("melody is repeated many times; fade on cue to end"). Twenty-eight bar "Toy Tune" has a sixteen-bar A section, a four-bar B section, and an eight-bar C section.

The recorded repertoire musicians refer to when they learn these tunes contains many similar departures from the thrity-two-bar AABA structure. The sixteen-bar A section of Joe Henderson's "Inner Urge" consists of four four-bar segments in each of which melodic fragments are repeated over a different major seventh chord. The chords, fully resolved, do not provide a sense of "logical" harmonic movement. The eight-bar B section's chords are similarly static. These twenty-four bars, repeated once, make a forty-eight-bar song, on which soloists improvise. Freddie Hubbard's "Intrepid Fox" is twenty-two bars long. Chick Corea's "Friends" contains a twelve-bar A section, a fifteen-bar B section made up of three five-bar phrases, and an eleven-bar C section—thirty-eight bars in total. Kenny Dorham's "La Mesha" is twenty bars long.

The Real Book contains dozens of songs that build on similarly different structural patterns than those of the older repertoire. These unfamiliar formats make it hard for players accustomed to thirty-two-bar songs to orient themselves, to know where they are in the song, without (at least at first) consciously counting bars and sections.

For all these reasons, players unfamiliar with the conventions of postbop playing can find it difficult to play the music and often try to avoid it.

How Players Deal with Multiple Repertoires

Many players feel at home with a variety of kinds of music: conventional standards tonight, post-bop formats the next night, perhaps even ethnic music (polkas, for instance) on a third night. But many sometimes find themselves in situations that make them uncomfortable because they, or one or more of their colleagues, don't know the music the playing situation requires.

They solve, or sometimes just live through, these contretemps in various ways. Sometimes players familiar with the post-bop repertoire find themselves in situations where they have to play an older repertoire with which they aren't very familiar. Less frequently, but it happens often enough for players to take it seriously, someone at home in the standard repertoire finds it necessary to play post-bop tunes he doesn't know and has trouble with. We hear about these dilemmas from both sides of the divide.

Older players have been in the business long enough to have learned material from several eras, just from playing jobs that required them to learn it. A bass player in his sixties told us:

When we were younger, American standard repertoire was in the air. It was around. This is before fusion, when jazz was still based on popular tunes, and you heard those kinds of tunes, popular tunes, everywhere, even in movie scores and TV scores, you heard tunes based on diatonic changes, that swung, and that kind of music was in the air. Younger musicians growing up today, by the time they are old enough to be conscious of music, that kind of music is really not in the air anymore. So for them to learn tunes they actually have to go find tunes and learn them. We got them a lot by osmosis, tunes were in the air, in the air; today, music is not melodic, and so it's harder. I had a kid from where I teach a couple of years ago, a trumpet player, very talented, who asked me, "Well, how do you learn standard tunes?" And I gave him that lecture that I just gave you. I said, "It's harder for you guys because you are not surrounded by them the way we were." For younger players today it's harder for them to learn the standard repertoire. They really have to make an effort, I think.

As he says, younger players often haven't learned standard tunes that way. They began playing seriously in the 1960s, when that repertoire was no longer "in the air." References that feel obvious to an older player may be meaningless to someone who grew up in a later era. Talking with a younger saxophonist (perhaps in his thirties), Faulkner ran into this:

I mentioned that one of his arrangements sounded like Dave Pell and the Dave Pell Octet, and, in my words, "Very West Coast, Dave Pell–like." He looked at me and said, "I don't know that." I also said to him as we drove by a local blues and rock-and-roll joint, which occasionally has jazz groups, that "That is where I saw Bud Shank and Bill Mays last year, great concert, great duo, they did a lot of West Coast tunes, like Russ Freeman's The Wind." He said, "I don't know Bud Shank's playing."

What these younger players heard instead was, for instance, Miles Davis's early post-bop experiments, on records, and those tunes were often the first music they ever learned, as this bass player in his early thirties, who grew up in that era explained:

The first tune I learned to play was "ESP" by Wayne Shorter. [And you were totally comfortable with the tune?] No, I didn't know any better that I wasn't. You know, I wasn't learning rhythm changes [the chords to "I Got Rhythm"] first. "ESP," "Nefertiti," those were the first batch of tunes we learned to play together. [That was your "Alone Together" and "Funny Valentine"?] Well, I didn't know "Alone Together" or "Funny Valentine." I thought jazz began and ended with mid-sixties Miles [Davis], and then playing with other players I had to learn standards for club dates and whatnot. Then I got the repertoire from Nick Brignola. He was gigging in the mid-fifties when the old repertoire was still important. Nick never embraced any of the Wayne Shorter tunes. He played a few Herbie Hancock tunes.

My friends and I, we were all trying to figure it out, that music, so here we are going for this music that is as advanced as jazz ever got, and not having any kind of a background other than we just tried to figure it out and play what they were playing. That's when we got started, trying to play like that. Later I became a broader-based musician, and it worked. I learned a lot of tunes.

Players who entered music this way soon found that they didn't know the standard repertoire the older players they worked with (and who were usually the ones who hired them for jobs) wanted them to know. The same player tells us:

I started to play with this guy, Nick [a well-known baritone saxophone player]. He's a bebopper and a standards [repertoire] man. He knows every song in the book. He came up through the really strong bebop era. He's a strong bebop player. There's a certain quality to his playing that I would describe as what the white jazz players were playing, there's a certain quality to the way they put together the notes in their solos, the selection of riffs, really close to the changes [type of] playing.

These guys knew all these tunes, they'd been doing them for years, so when I got on the gigs I was learning the tunes on the gig. I'll never forget a concert with this bebop trumpet player. He called "Stardust." I'd heard it. I heard it on a Herb Alpert album, but I hadn't played it. I got through it and I played it right, just totally by ear. You know, you're playing a ballad from memory and now you're playing it by ear. My hands are going in the right places. I knew it but didn't know I knew it.

Nick was really a standards guy and played a lot of club dates. And on the club date there's the jazz book with all the jazz tunes that everybody has, and that's generational, that generation had a different batch of tunes that they loved playing on. There's a set of tunes that seems to transcend the whole history of jazz, like "All the Things You Are." Everybody knows it, everybody plays on it, and everybody likes the challenge of the tune. But then there are tunes like some of those Wayne Shorter tunes or Herbie Hancock tunes, which are specifically jazz standards. They're not from the Great American Songbook.

Players experience difficulties and problems learning the standard repertoire, but soon can rely on the knowledge they have acquired of all the standardized features of those songs discussed earlier in this chapter: the formulaic structures, the harmonic patterns built on the II-V-I cadence, the easily found rhythmic markers. Learning the post-bop repertoire requires players to become familiar in that same intuitive way with a variety of different basic structures. (See a player's description of learning the "Giant Steps" progression in chapter 4.)

A player who does not run into an equivalent of Nick, who does not eventually learn some of the older repertoire, finds himself in situations like this one, described by an older guitar player who does know it:

I'm on my way to perform a freelance gig with a vocalist, bass player, drummer, and myself on guitar. I hit some traffic so I arrived a little late, just enough time to set up and be ready at start time. I noticed that on the bandstand the equipment of the bassist was different than it had been in the previous weeks I had played this gig, but I didn't see the bass player. I usually open up the sets with a couple of trio tunes before the vocalist, who is the leader on the gig, comes up to sing. It's time to start, and around the corner comes a young man whom I hadn't met before. He picks up the bass, adjusts his tuning and the controls on his amp, and looks at me.

So I said to him, "Let's start with 'I Remember You' in F." He said he didn't know it so I suggested "Just Friends" in G. He didn't know that either. I said, "How about 'Satin Doll' in C?" He said he didn't really know that one either. It's time to start so I didn't have time to look for a fake book in my bag, so I said, "Okay, let's just do a blues in G." I don't know how someone can call themselves a jazz bassist and not know any jazz standards.

For the next tune I asked him to suggest something he knew and he said, "How about 'Mr. P.C.'?" which is a minor blues by John Coltrane. Even through we had just played a blues I said, "Sure, fine, but let's play it a little faster than the last one." After that tune the vocalist comes up to sing. She has a book with all of her tunes in it so she calls "Exactly Like You." Some of the chord changes she has in her book are strange, so when I work with the usual bassist, who is experienced, and we get to a strange chord, we just look at each other and smile and play the "right chord." With the bassist on this night I had to play all the strange, wrong chords because he didn't know any of the tunes. Needless to say it was a very frustrating evening. I think it is so important for working jazz musicians to have many, many jazz standards committed to memory, but it seems there are many players, younger and older, that don't think this is important.

Musical Morality

Some musicians' remarks already quoted hint at what we eventually recognized as a major theme: how musicians occasionally turn questions of repertoire and its performance into moral issues. A classical example of this occurred when Faulkner heard an older (late fifties), very experienced (had worked with many well-known jazz names) bass player explode because someone he was working with had to consult a fake book before playing the well-known standard "All the Things You Are":

Dave started in on a piano player, who "doesn't know any tunes and has to have the music in front of him to play blues in F." He was very heated about this. I said to Paul [the piano player], "Let's do 'Alone Together,'" I think that was the tune I suggested. Paul said "I don't know it but Dave can tell me the changes [as we play]." Dave's response was, "I don't want to do that. I have to do that with a piano player who doesn't know any tunes who should remain nameless, he doesn't know tunes and I have to tell him through the entire gig, this change, that change. It's a drag. If I get a call to do 'Rite of Spring' then I won't take that kind of gig, you get someone who can do that, someone who can read that kind of music. You call me to do a gig with standards, tunes.... But if you call someone to do a gig and he doesn't know any tunes, then he shouldn't take the gig in the first place. Don't take the gig if you don't know tunes, so I end up having to tell him the chord changes on every tune because he doesn't know them."

Why would such a minor lapse provoke such anger? At the most local and intimate level, we see the playing out of a moral point of view that showed up most clearly in relation to the historical shift we described earlier, but which applies much more widely: the emphasis on competent performance as a sign of an appropriately professional character and attitude.

Ingrid Monson (1996, 183–84) makes the general point:

Since musicians most typically improvise within the context of a particular tune, a prerequisite to successful participation within a jazz group is a repertoire of tunes that may be called by other musicians—and the ability to play them in more than one key. While musicians do use collections of lead sheets known as fake books and can be seen reading these tunes from them, there are certain standard jazz compositions that musicians are expected to be able to play without their aid. In fact, a significant loss of face occurs if a player has to read a tune that everyone else in the band knows. Older musicians generally know a lot more repertoire than younger musicians and can embarrass younger players by calling a tune they don't expect.

The bassist we quoted above expressed this as a moral principle: musicians should be able to do what needs to be done at the time of performance. They should know what they ought to know in order to play the job as it has been defined to them, which in turn means that they should have the basic knowledge any competent player should have, or the ability to pick up what needs to be known quickly and efficiently, so that the performance can proceed smoothly and satisfy the people who need to be satisfied. That's a very long-winded definition of competence and its moral value.

The lapse provoking a sanction need not be anything spectacularly incompetent or noticeable, but players, acutely sensitive to the possibility, cannot forget these embarrassing situations and the scorn of others. Faulkner recalls:

> I was playing a commercial dance gig at the wedding palace, Chez Josef, and the piano player called, for the last tune, "The Party's Over." I knew that I knew the first part of this tune, but was not totally familiar with the second part of the tune. Well, everything goes fine: he plays the introduction

and I played the first eight bars correctly. At the ninth bar, where the words go "It's time to wind up ... the masquerade," now we are at bars 9–14, I realized that I did not know the tune from bar 9 to bar 16. I fumbled around trying to play something, anything. Then at bar 17 the tune that I DO know returns and from there on I played the whole tune correctly, but bars 9–14 were not correctly and accurately played. The piano player, a stickler for detail, and quick to point out others' lack of musical knowledge, almost exploded. He glared at me and said, "Jeez!" He bounced up, got red in the face, scowled at me, and then turned away, and didn't speak to me for weeks after the gig. I had made the mistake of looking over at him when I got to the part I didn't know.

I was embarrassed and went home and started to learn "The Party's Over." For this to happen again on a gig with these perfectionists would be a disaster for me. He would never hire me.

We didn't often hear these moral principles expressed openly and directly, nor did we hear many stories of such openly hostile reactions on the stand. We heard, rather, players talking about how they knew that others would judge them negatively if they failed to know or to learn what they should know, how they had been so judged in the past, and about the steps they took to avoid such sanctions. Another musician, talking about his experiences with a group of very competent musicians, said:

> They knew a lot of songs, they played great, and for some reason they welcomed me into their fold. They would just start songs on jobs, assuming that I knew everything. You know the embarrassment of not knowing the tune is a very great motivator to know the tune for the next time.

He described another musician he played with who, he said, could hear anything and play anything after hearing it once, and the pressure this put on him to learn new tunes quickly and thoroughly:

When he started hiring me on jobs he'd call a song and I wouldn't know it. And so I realized very quickly that it is better that I just told him that I don't know it but let's play it anyway. And in those days he would sort of very quickly hum the melody, play the chords, and I'd look at his fingers and hear the root motion of what he was playing on the guitar.

And then I had a teacher who had said, "Whenever that happens to you, go home and go through your record collection until you find that song, and sit down and use it as an ear-training experience." And so I wasn't learning melodies then as much as I was learning chord changes. Melodies came later. That was another phase of things, 'cause being a bass player in 1981 and 1982, it wasn't as important, at least as it seems today, to play interesting solos. I knew some standards when I met him, I knew "A Nightingale Sang in Berkeley

Square" and some off-the-beaten-path ballads, "Love Is a Many-Splendored Thing," "It's Magic," tunes like that.

I also realized that he'd show you once, in a great mood, with a great attitude, second time a little less of an attitude, and the third time you didn't really want to ask him, so it really behooved me to learn the tunes as quickly as possible on my own, if I didn't pick them up there.

More experienced players usually forgive ignorance of some tunes as long as the player takes the exposure of his ignorance as a warning and learns what's necessary.

Similarly, experienced players treat knowing tunes, and especially knowing many tunes, as a positive virtue, something to cultivate in the spirit of self-improvement. A seasoned piano player described his approach to working with a trumpet player who was a tune hound:

I'll say to him "Hey, what tunes do you want to play tonight?" Because oftentimes he has an idea, but I don't like to refer to sheet music when I'm playing with him. It's more fun [without the music], and you own the tune when you have it memorized rather than reading it out of a fake book or whatever. I much prefer, if it's like a tune that I don't really know, I don't want to read a fake book, then I'll go to the fake book or a version of it that I know or I'll ask him "What are the changes that you use?" And we'll talk through the tune over the phone or whatever, and I'll go practice it and learn it.

Finally, experienced players sometimes use highly moral language to voice their irritation with younger players whose familiarity with newer repertoire (mainly post-bop), the scores for which give them more guidance, does not (for these critics) make up for their inability to play older material easily. According to a reed player in his fifties who leads his own quartet and quintet (talking about musicians of his own age):

We are constantly haggling over repertoire. My philosophy is to choose great songs, both from the jazz and standards traditions, especially those that are not played often. Two other players [in the group] have much less affinity for the standards, many of which in aggregate are typically referred to as the Great American Songbook. They prefer the more complex jazz pieces, probably because these are usually self-structured with respect to rhythm and harmony. Standards on the other hand often require imposing altered harmonies and rhythmically interesting "hits" on relatively simpler structures to make them sound more in the jazz tradition (which is how most of the great jazz groups alter standards). I believe the preference for "pre-made" jazz tunes reflects both a lack of imagination or experience with how to treat the standards in the repertoire and also a lack of familiarity with the GAS [Great American Song Book] in the first place. Often these players are unfamiliar with standard tunes that are brought in to a rehearsal, or think that standards are the very often played tunes recorded by important jazz groups.

We should make clear what this player means by "self-structured." The lead sheets of older jazz standards typically contain simple, unaltered harmonies and give no specific directions for how the tune should be played. Experienced players routinely complicate the harmony with interpolated modulations that don't appear in the printed music, and add altered notes to the indicated chords (raised and lowered fifths, ninths, and thirteenths). Bass players improvise foundational lines and drummers likewise improvise ornamentation. This leader's colleagues, however, typically play many parts of the tunes they want to play just as they were played on the recording made by its originators. From his point of view, playing this way loses the spontaneity so important in the older style of playing:

Arrangements like these can be found in Jamie Aebersold's books; for instance, an arrangement of "Nica's Dream" will have the whole

Horace Silver arrangement from the original album laid out for the horns and the rhythm section. Another Horace Silver tune, "Filthy McNasty," had a similar layout with horn riffs, breaks, and blowing sections on the chord changes. It was all very organized. The piano player had the hip changes all spelled out for him and the percussion player had his road map before him so he could read just what the drummer played on the original Jazz Messengers album. The tunes from the Great American Songbook require alterations on the chord changes to turn them into something magical, and that is why Dick Hyman wrote a book designed to introduce piano players to that music while simultaneously introducing them to altered chord changes and a more modern style of solo piano playing and, not incidentally, for "comping" or accompanying behind the horn players.

Of course, players in all traditions have often played tunes (or parts of them) just as they heard them on records they admired, although they seldom had the accurate transcriptions now available. Most players play parts of "'Round Midnight" as they appear on the Miles Davis recording, and most players who play Ellington's "Take the 'A' Train" incorporate several of the improvised solos (or parts of them) into their performance of the tune.

These differences in the idea of what constitutes a "standard" and which parts of it are "standard" leads to serious misunderstandings and disagreements:

> Some of these guys think that if you call a standard (from the GAS [Great American Song Book]) that you are playing tunes you would play on a wedding gig. They treat these as commercial tunes, something like that. They want to do what they think are hip "jazz tunes," and that "Have You Met Miss Jones?" or "I Love You" or something like that, those are not jazz tunes.

All the matters described in this chapter bring us to the point where we can finally answer these questions: What happens when a number of players, each with his own background and individual repertoire, find themselves on the bandstand, ready to play? How do they decide what to play? What do they play? The list of songs they eventually play does not arise mechanically out of what they each know, or what they know collectively. It comes out of a process of give and take on the stand, which we turn to now.

7

On the Stand: Putting Repertoire to Work

Negotiating and Enacting the Repertoire

It's taken this long to get to what we set out to explain: how do people who may not even know each other or have ever played together, and who have no written music in front of them, play together competently in front of an audience for several hours? We know now what they have listened to and learned earlier and elsewhere in their musical lives. We know the kinds of places in which they play. We know how their tastes and knowledge vary depending on historical circumstances. We're ready to understand what happens when all that converges and they actually play together, climb on to the bandstand, adjust their instruments, and the leader (if there is one) says, as a leader Becker worked for long ago liked to say, "OK, gentlemen. Show time!"

We gave a provisional answer to the problem of how a group of musicians solves this problem of coordination many pages ago: we said they can play together because they all know the same tunes. But now we know that's not exactly true. Sort of true, but not true enough that anyone (either the players involved or we as analysts) can depend on it. Because often enough they don't all know the same tune and, handled the wrong way, that situation can lead to disaster. Faulkner recalls:

> I was at a gig, listening to the band, a wedding gig, and someone in the band called "Skylark." The tenor player had a rep as the man who knew every tune, but that afternoon at the wedding he didn't know the bridge to "Skylark," and the band's rendition of it came off the rails at the bridge. It was awful, as in wrong note after wrong note with the piano player then getting

sucked into the vortex of wrong notes, and mistakes after mistakes. Fortunately, after those eight bars of misery, the band jerked back into the last A section.

Players sometimes refer to an event like this, evocatively, as a "trainwreck," which no one wants to cause or be involved with.

In that mythical first moment we described, then, in order to avoid the difficulties that might result if they started to play something and one or more of the others didn't know it, they don't just name a tune and start playing it. Instead, as we heard over and over again, one player turns to another, and says, "Do you know...?" and then names a tune, hoping that the other player will know it. He can't be certain the other player knows it. Remember the musician who said to a bass player he hadn't met before, "Let's start with 'I Remember You' in F"? And the bass player didn't know it. Nor did he know "Just Friends" or "Satin Doll," tunes any player of a certain generation would almost certainly know. No one likes it when that happens, but everyone knows it can happen. So they usually try to discover what their colleagues can do by asking, "Do you know...?" Which is why we gave this book that title.

What follows from this initial inquiry varies. In the simplest case, the other player says he does know it, and perhaps asks what key they'll play it in. Musicians almost always play tunes in the "original" key, the key of the original sheet music or some other key that "everyone always plays it in." Or sometimes a player suggests an alternative but will also accept the original. (To give you the idea, the original key of "Sunny Side of the Street" is C; the original key of "'Round Midnight" is Eb; and the original key of "You Can Depend on Me" is F. if nothing else is said, any randomly assembled group of musicians will play those tunes in those keys.) Musicians negotiate keys quickly and unobtrusively, in what don't *look* like negotiations because they occur rapidly, since the parties involved are re-ratifying an agreement reached somewhere else some other time.

Faulkner's field notes describe such mini-events:

The bass player, a woman in her thirties who was the leader, said, "What would you like to do?" I said to the piano player, "Stardust," played the first few notes, and said, "Key of C." He raised his hand in the shape of the letter *C* and I counted off eight beats, two bars of four each, coming in on the pickup notes in the last bar.

Later on that evening, the leader said, "Anyone want to play a tune?" I said, immediately, "'Body and Soul' and as a bossa" and counted it off. I didn't worry that anyone in the rhythm section, piano and bass, wouldn't know what key I was going to do the tune in, I knew that they knew what key I was going to do it in.

Many possibilities, other than the simple answer yes, follow the initial "Do you know...?" What happens if the answer is "No, I don't know it"? At one extreme, the person who made the suggestion may ignore the confession of ignorance, even treat it as a weakness not to be indulged, and play the tune anyway, creating the possibility of a trainwreck. A female bass player in her early thirties gives us an example:

> The leader called this tune that I'd never heard of and I turned to the guitar player—now this is in a concert, [there's] no music [arrangements, lead sheets written out, no music stands], and I turned to him and I said, "I don't know this tune." The leader was already getting into it and what did this guitar player do? He turned his guitar and his back to me so that I couldn't see his fingers, because I play guitar [and could have seen what the chords were], and, basically, he wouldn't help me out. And that's a drag. [I just] used my ear to get through it, to get through the tune. It was really terrible. I thought that was mean.

She then produces a counterexample, describing a better way things could be done:

A lot of times everybody else [on the bandstand] may know a tune, but if you're inexperienced maybe you just don't know it. For a bass player it's a little easier if you have a piano player who works well for you. I read [the piano player's] fingers, read the chord change, following the pinky in the left hand. I learned many, many tunes from Ralph that way, I mean he's great because he has no attitude and he would just be helpful. I like really like working with musicians like that that are kind of a team that will help each other out.

We were playing a concert and I wasn't near the piano so I couldn't see the piano player's fingers. The leader called some kind of strange tune, something real old, I don't know what it was, I can't even remember. And I looked at the piano player and [said] "I don't know this tune." Here we've got this full house filled with people for this concert. I hadn't been playing bass that long. I don't know all these tunes. So the piano player [is] mouthing the chord changes and throwing down bass notes so I can hear them and, by the end of the first chorus, I had the tune down, and I was able to take a solo on it, you know it was wonderful because you know people like that are comfortable, they don't mind, they want to help, and they are thinking about the audience and they want to have the best musical experience possible.

At the other extreme, after getting a negative answer to the question "Do you know...?" the person making the suggestion tries again, looking for something everyone does know or at least thinks they can play (whether they know it or not). What happens next can take many different paths, depending on the resources of the individual players, their reasons for knowing and playing what they do, the nature of the playing situation, and the many other things talked about earlier.

Whatever the musicians do, it never follows automatically—from the givens of their background, knowledge, the venue, the audience they are playing for, and the power relations within the group—that they will or won't play any particular tune. These givens create possibilities and constraints. But what the players do depends on the negotiation that follows. Each player enters that negotiation perhaps wanting to play something, perhaps wanting to please the leader and other players, capable of doing some things and not others. We use the term "negotiation" because the group doesn't simply add up what each one wants or take a vote. They bargain, responding to each other in a waltz of maybes and let's try this ones—what we can call the dynamic of the bandstand—and the result may be something no one had in mind or even particularly wanted. As we will see, these negotiations take place almost imperceptibly. A nod, a glance, or a one-word remark register desires, rejections, and agreements.

We can say that the players "enact" the repertoire as they make their collective choice and play it, turn it from what might happen into what did happen. The common use of the word "canon" to describe the conventionally sanctified collection of works everyone knows and respects doesn't accurately describe what we observed and heard of these negotiations. Musicians don't choose what they play from such a list, nor are their choices the same from one performance to the next. Each night presents them, potentially and often in fact, with a new situation: an audience that wants something not just like what any other audience has ever wanted; a new member of the group who may or may not share the other players' ideas about what would be good to play; a new venue or bar owner to please. And they respond to the situation by making a choice from what they collectively have available. But they never know for sure what they have available, since players often reveal unexpected gaps in their knowledge or, on the other hand, are willing to attempt songs they don't know; or are ready to at least read the proposed song from a lead sheet in *The Real Book.* Performances lack the consistency and stability more standardized and well-distributed forms of knowledge might make possible.

Performances thus exhibit neither the regularities of a highly formalized system of knowledge and behavior nor the chaos a total lack of shared knowledge would produce. The musicians we saw gave highly variable performances, seldom the same from night to night, but which nevertheless shared much material. We aim to understand and explain both the stability and the variability of what they played from one night to the next, looking at what happens from two angles: on the one hand, what players are thinking about when they respond to suggestions and, on the other, some routinized methods they use to deal with the problems that inevitably arise. Throughout, we focus on the fact of negotiation: how agreement arrives in steps, as players try to satisfy their own desires and criteria of judgment while producing an acceptable and appropriate product for others.

What Players Are Thinking About

When a tune arrives on the bandstand, complete with the sponsor who "called" it, the other players accept or reject the idea in a rapid, barely noticeable, negotiation. Each of the people engaging in the negotiation is thinking about what he'd like to accomplish, and what he'd like to avoid. A lot of thinking lies behind the split-second decisions that lead the players to say yes or no to a suggestion. What are they thinking about? We'll focus on the extreme situation, when they have to decide whether to play something new, something they haven't tried before. That makes the calculus that players use to decide the question more obvious.

Until now we've treated the agreement to learn new tunes as the default response, the choice players make unless they have a reason not to. We've accepted the ideas that knowing tunes is a good thing, that a competent player will know many, and that the more they know, the more competent they are. If we look at these questions as players sometimes do, and consider what good it does anyone to learn a new song, we'll see why they often treat these premises as not so obvious. For them, it may not always be a good thing to know a lot of tunes and learn still more; time spent learning new tunes is, after all, time they could spend, perhaps more profitably, practicing scales or long tones, improving facility or endurance or some other equally valuable quality. When players think about these questions, they debate with themselves, setting the advantages against the disadvantages and weighing the consequences of what they might do. They bring these arguments to the negotiation. We could even say, though this makes the process seem more conscious and deliberate than its casual and brief character warrants, that these thoughts can represent a player's bargaining position in the negotiation that takes place. Here are the arguments they give themselves when someone proposes a new tune they don't know on the stand during a performance.

Everybody else knows it. A player on a job, hearing someone call tune *x* and seeing everyone else nod agreement, will likely conclude that he should know it too. If he doesn't, he will look less competent than he wants to look, and other players will wonder what's wrong with him that he doesn't know it (this is the generalized statement of the standard at work in the complaint we quoted earlier about a player who didn't know the chords to "All the Things You Are" without consulting *The Real Book)*. The calculus here is: "I don't want to look incompetent."

Novices frequently reason their way to this conclusion, learning from the early jobs they play what they should know in order to exhibit the competence that will lead to them being asked back to play more jobs. Knowing tunes is the due you pay to be a player. The Dick Hyman list of "150 Tunes Every Piano Player Should Know" implies this criterion, the "should" arising from the idea that everyone else will know them and, if you want to play with everyone else, you should know them too.

In general, if everyone in your musical community knows a song and feels that it can be called without fear of causing anyone any problems, each individual player will feel he should know it, because he will look foolish if he doesn't. If some people in the community know it but others don't, and audiences don't demand it, players who don't know it or don't like it, can refuse to bother with it, and not suffer as a result.

Someone else in the band wants to play this tune. I've heard it before, thought it was nice or at least OK, good enough to learn, and now that someone has called it, I might as well learn it. If the opportunity hadn't arisen in just this way, that would have been alright too, and I wouldn't have learned it. But since it has, I will. This often occurs in a situation we'll discuss in more detail below, where players feel an immediate pressure to play something, experiencing a silent moment they know they must fill with a tune, but what tune will it be? If this immediate impetus to play involves learning a new tune, that gives them sufficient reason to make the effort.

When musicians play together over some period of time, the desire to please probably grows stronger. A player might reason, "This group that I work with will be better equipped to do its job if I learn this tune, and my doing so will add something useful to the group repertoire."

I heard a recording of this by a well-known musician whose playing I respect, and it interests me. The tune would encourage me to play well and make me sound good, so even though there will be some upfront cost in learning it, I'll make the effort. What aspects of a tune does a typical player find "interesting"? We have little direct explicit evidence about this, but can guess that they are aspects that present solvable puzzles. That is, the tune gives the player a puzzle, something he realizes he doesn't quite know how to do and would like to learn how to do, partly just because it's there. We've already met an example: the player who wants to learn how to get from the last two bars of the second A section of "Smoke Gets in Your Eyes" into the bridge (the B section), which presents him with a problem in enharmonic thinking. (The A section, remember, ends on an Eb, the tonic note of the key, but then, without changing pitch the note becomes D#, the third note of the B-major scale, B major being the key of the bridge. The player wants to make that change of key clear melodically in a way that makes harmonic sense.) He knows he can solve this problem because other people, especially respected players on available recordings, have evidently solved it before him. Playing it now will help him solve it for himself, which inclines him to agree to a suggestion to play it. (Solving problems like this goes far toward putting players at ease in playing situations, and providing them with the feeling of comfort described in chapter 6, which makes playing a pleasure rather than a terror.)

Players who find, from time to time, that they have to play unfamiliar chord progressions might welcome the opportunity to get that problem, and all its cognates, solved so that when the next new embodiment of it comes up they are ready for it. Or they may just admire the person who made the recording so much that they want to learn what that person knows by imitating it, playing the tune and the solo that excited their admiration. If Don Fagerquist makes a recording of "Give Me the Simple Life" that makes apparent the ease with which he negotiates those "interesting" changes, a player might feel that learning that tune would teach him something that will be useful in situations that haven't come up yet but probably will. (Sociologists will recognize here a version of Thomas Kuhn's [1970] description of "normal science" as providing solvable puzzles for scientists, and thus making it possible for scientific work to go on.)

The leader or the person who has hired the band wants us to play this tune. I personally don't like it, but we have to play it or suffer some unpleasant consequences (up to and including being fired), so, what the hell, learn it and play it. Every musician who has played professionally for very long has had to learn some despised pop tune for such a reason. Generations of players learned "Night Train" or "How Much Is That Doggie in the Window?" or a hundred other such songs. The list depends on what years are involved and the specifics of the work situation. For instance:

A company hires the trio every Christmas holiday. His and his wife's favorite tune is "Unchained Melody." Neither of the others knew it, so we couldn't play it, and the owner of the firm reminded us that he asked us to play it last year and we couldn't because they didn't know it. I knew it and played a couple of bars for the owner and promised that we would learn it for next year. He said, "That's good. My wife and I met when we were listening to that song and we really like it and it would be nice if you could play it for her." I agreed. And I told the others, "We better get the music to this tune and learn for next year's Christmas party."

The tunes you have to play needn't be despised pieces of uninteresting dreck. Players begin to find anything boring when they've played it too often. A piano player who often works with another musician (sometimes one of them is leader, sometimes the other) says:

> I don't like having to be in front of them [the audience] and having to play shit I don't want to play at the moment. [Like what kind of tune?] Like a tune that I've done, been there, done that. I have nothing left to say, there's nothing left to say on that tune. Like "Moonlight in Vermont." I've played it a million times and I'm sick of playing it. There is nothing left to say on that tune. Yet you have to play it, he wants to play it and I have to go through the same routine, figure out what to play here because its pointless anyway, having to go through that process in front of an audience.
>
> When I'm leading the gig it seems that it is entirely different, the motivation to play a song

comes from a different place. I mean he's a wonderful player, he's a wonderful musician, he has big ears, he can blend when his chops are up, blend nicely, good intonation, and he can back up. But he does remain in control of the gig constantly [in terms of the tunes he calls]. You know, I like to play a bop tune occasionally, or a "free" or a "funk" tune. He doesn't like bop, he doesn't seem to want to do bop. I mean I've called "Donna Lee" and we'll do that, I can't say that, we've done some bop. It's original tunes he shies away from: my tunes.

If I learn this tune, no one else I work with knows it. But I might be able to teach it to them, in which case the group's repertoire will reflect my personal taste a little more, and I will be able to play this tune, and tunes like it, more often. Players have many idiosyncratic likes and dislikes. If they could do just as they liked they might play material quite different from what they ordinarily play. Having heard something they like, they look for ways to get others to try it. Band leaders have more power than other players and, when they want to play a new tune, they might give the other players the lead sheet and tell them to play it right then, or to practice it and be ready to play it Saturday night, or just tell the other players to listen to the tune on some recording and "know it by Saturday, because we're going to play it," thus taking advantage of the ability most musicians can be expected to have to learn a song by hearing it. Players who lack that organizational power rely on their ability to be persuasive, which sometimes, but not always, works.

When new forms of jazz arise and become fashionable, the content of what "everyone knows" changes too. What must be known and what needn't be known doesn't reflect a song's innate quality, but rather the judgments people make about it, and are thus specific to a particular occasion or venue, and to an era or generation of taste. The rise of big band swing produced tunes, synonymous with certain bands, that everyone had to know, because audiences frequently requested them: Glenn Miller's "In the Mood" and his (borrowed from Erskine Hawkins) "Tuxedo Junction"; Duke Ellington's "Take the 'A' Train," "Solitude," "Mood Indigo," and many others; Count Basie's "One O'Clock Jump." All those became part of the standard repertoire. When someone called one of these tunes, players wanted to be ready to play it, because it had to be played. Others from the same or similar sources (e.g., Basie's "Taps Miller," Miller's "I Dreamt I Dwelt in Harlem," Benny Goodman's "Benny Rides Again," or Woody Herman's "Buck Dance") never became widely known or played.

In more recent times, other tunes achieved this kind of status: the canonic tunes of bebop—associated with Dizzy Gillespie, Charlie Parker, and others—and post-bop—the repertoire created by Thelonius Monk, Wayne Shorter, Chick Corea, Herbie Hancock, and others—have, for some players in some communities, achieved such recognition and become part of what "everybody" knows and, therefore, what everybody must know (as we saw earlier).

Songs in the reservoir from which players choose what to call carry a time stamp, belonging to one or another era in the development of American popular music. Musicians feel more open to playing a tune from an era with whose general style they already feel familiar. Venues and occasions sometimes specialize in music of an era, and the agreements players make about what to play reflect the pressures arising from that fact.

What players must know on one job may not be necessary anywhere else. Here is a communication from a leader/singer in her fifties to the people who will be playing a job with her:

> Per requests to me, I've made a list of possible tunes for tomorrow's gig for ya'll to take a look at. This gig is advertised as a Roaring 20's party with dance instruction in the swing dances as well. We got the swing and the standards covered, no prob, but the following tunes are specific to the 20's and 30's so they will be my

first choices when I'm asked to call a tune. Anyone can nix any choice they're not comfortable with.

There followed a list of twenty-six songs, dated from 1918 to 1934, with the keys in which she would sing them, which were not the standard keys but rather a fourth higher, as is common for female singers.

Unsuccessful attempts to get players to add new material to a repertoire. Every suggestion of what to play next creates the opportunity for the other players to make one of the responses we've just considered. Seen from the point of view of the tune suggested, every rejection is a failure to move it along the track to being something "everyone knows." These events deserve special consideration, but we don't have many cases to work from. Becker, a confirmed tunehound with a preference for melodic tunes with interesting harmonies, can testify to the difficulty of getting others to learn new material that is esoteric in the strict sense of being known by very few audiences and very few other players:

I have had this experience repeatedly over the years. Tunes that I like a lot, that have the cachet that comes from being recorded by players whose name often lends respectability and interest to a song, tunes with "interesting" changes and constructions—have failed to arouse the interest of my colleagues. Try as I might, I could never get people I played with to take up tunes like "Suddenly It's Spring" (though it was recorded by Stan Getz) or "Let's Get Lost" (recorded by Chet Baker).

The piano player we quoted earlier about being bored playing the same old tunes speaks of the difficulty of teaching a leader new tunes he doesn't want to play. When asked about the leader's willingness to learn the tune "Invitation," he replied:

> Nope, I'd have to write it out and work on him for several weeks before we would do that tune, rehearse it. I've called it many times. He's very comfortable with some other [modern jazz

compositions] that he's put his stamp on. He feels like he owns them. We'll play those tunes with regularity; they are part of our "set list." I get the feeling that he's a little insecure on stage, because he's the leader of the gig and he feels like he needs to keep it going rather than being open. For me, it stops the flow.

Forms of Negotiation

Musicians do not enter negotiations about what they're going to play unprepared. Certain problems come up repeatedly and they make plans for dealing with them. Players responsible to bosses and clients for the performance—mainly the leader—know that they have to produce an evening of satisfactory entertainment in the form of a string of competently played tunes, and these responsible parties often make "set lists"—preplanned selections of what the members of their group will do to meet this demand. In a more abstract way, most players carry with them short lists of things they know they can do without having to think much about it, to help them meet the moments when they have to choose a tune on the spur of the moment and can't think of anything. These lists create elements of stability in a situation of possible chaos and trainwrecks.

Seen abstractly, the players select, or someone selects for them, elements from a pool of available resources. Considering all the tunes that, between them, they know and can play, they pick some of them, put them in an order, and enact that as their performance. If they haven't preplanned their set and evening, they make their choices at the beginning of the set or from moment to moment, choosing the second tune after they finish the first, and so on. Throughout, they take into account all the other people whose opinions will matter, engaging in the inconspicuous acts of negotiation we've described. (Becker [1982, 192–225] calls this process of continual choice that shapes the art work "editing.")

In the least complicated version of repertoire enactment, the group plays the set list they, or the leader, constructed before they got on the stand. The negotiations that produced that result have happened already and the musicians just play what's already been decided.

Many people, leaders but sidemen as well, follow some simple rules when they make these lists, and the similarity of the resulting lists smooths their acceptance by the musicians who enact them. A leader explains his formula, one most players would consider reasonable and sensible:

A set should be arranged like a record album, a medium up tune to start, a slower tune, then a ballad, maybe a bossa or Latin tune, and then an up tune to end, something on that order. That makes the set interesting to the players and to the people who are listening or dancing. I've found this to be a good idea.

Set-list makers follow some general rules of thumb. Vary keys and tempos from one tune to the next. Don't do all up-tempo tunes in Bb, instead stick something slow in G between them. Pay attention to what you know about the desires of important other actors. Musicians complain about music that is "all the same." A local audience may want to hear certain tunes they have heard the group play before or tunes for which the band is known. The person who hired the band may have told the leader or one or more of the players what he wants to hear. Owners of bars and restaurants usually keep an eye on audience response and tell the musicians to do what the customers seem to want. An experienced player and leader in his forties described what he thinks about when he thinks about this mixture of demands and constraints, and makes the set lists he carries to jobs. His systematic approach probably goes further than most leaders would bother with:

> You are trying to reach people other than the would-be jazz aficionados, strict bebop lovers, you're trying to reach an audience that would like some variance in what they hear. It goes back to something my wife said after I brought her to a few jazz shows

where they play mostly notey bebop most of the night. "You know," she said, "it sounds the same to me after about the second or third song of the night." And I realized that for a somewhat uneducated listener, but someone still interested in listening, the nonvariance of texture from song to song made it boring and made it also the same song. It was important to make one tune different from another tune, and then, in thinking that way, how do you go from tune to tune?

[What are the things that make a tune different from other tunes?] You want to pick a tune so that you follow it with a tune that is interesting and different from the previous tune. The things that we think about are texture, meaning rhythm, such as in a bossa nova, straight-ahead swing, a ballad tempo, waltz. Everyone is different; everyone likes different things so you need to make things varied in a way that lets you reach a greater number of people with your music.

So I developed this little chart. What similarities do tunes have, and what differences do they have? So I would make a column: what's the tempo, say 140, a half note equals 140 on this particular song, a half note equals 86 on that particular song. I would write the tempo of the tune whether it was a bossa or Latin, what key was it in, not only what key but whether it was a major sound or a minor sound, you know, those are colors, major are happier, minor compositions more melancholy or dark. So you don't want to follow a minor melancholy dark tune with another melancholy one. You don't want to follow a slow ballad with obviously another slow ballad. You will put people to sleep and bore them to death.

[So you developed this chart for tempo, texture, style of tune?] Key signature, major or minor. I wouldn't want to follow a tune that was in Ab with another tune that was in Ab, or one that was essentially centered around the same key. And you have so many rhythms in the jazz idiom to draw from, why get stuck with a swing tune followed by a swing tune, followed by a swing tune? Even if the tempos varied a little bit, to me it is too similar. So why not take a samba at that point? After playing a nice ballad, take a nice samba that is going to be different from the previous two tunes. You play a ballad and then you play a fast bebop tune.

He doesn't forget that he must also satisfy, in some way, the desires of his professional constituency, keeping the players in the group interested:

You are always trying to find a new tune. You are always trying to make things fresh. It's exciting for the players to have a fresh tune, a tune they really like, and consequently the audience can hear the players' excitement about the tune in their playing and it becomes a piece that's exciting for them.

A group about to play a series of similar performances for a succession of similar audiences (on a concert tour, for example) may create such a list and play it in the same order at every appearance for two weeks. On a longer tour, they may avoid boredom by having a longer list of tunes everyone knows, which they draw on for each performance. In either case, they know what they're going to play before they arrive on the bandstand:

We would always start off with a blues, and here ... that tempo. [He counted off a tempo, slapping his hand on his leg.] That tempo, a kind of [the leader's trademark] tempo. And then he would call a handful of tunes that we usually did, and it varied. If we were in a club, it was one thing. If we were doing a concert, it would be put together from another point of view. Everybody got a solo piece. I usually did "Oleo." You know, I'd play the head on "Oleo" with him. Then he'd take a long solo. It was my feature and he'd take a long solo. And the other one I got as a feature was "Triste." He'd play the tune but I usually got a long solo, two or three choruses, sometimes four, he didn't push you out, if you were done you were done, if you wanted to go for another one, even if you were having trouble, you would still get it.

For many jobs the players neither make nor need a set list. Instead, they collectively decide, or the leader (if there is one) decides, from moment to moment, song to song, what they're going to play. They negotiate the set list as the event proceeds. In a big band, which has a book of written arrangements, the leader may just call out a series of numbers, and every player digs through his pile of music to find his parts for the short list of three or four tunes the leader has just put together. Leaders vary in how far ahead of time they make their choices, sometimes waiting until the last minute so that they can respond immediately to the way the crowd has reacted to their previous choices. (The leaders that Bruce MacLeod described in chapter 1 usually worked this way.)

The set list constructed from moment to moment looks like preselected set lists whose construction we described earlier, and similarly depends on the ideas and capabilities of the players involved, differing only in exposing those features more clearly. Instead of knowing from earlier encounters whether or not this or that player knows this or that song, and putting it on the preselected list, the person calling the tune finds it expedient to ask, "Do you know...?" In either case, the list maker has to consider the possibility that the answer to that question is "No, I don't."

Often the person who got the job, the one who must satisfy the people paying for the music, finally decides what to play, tells the others what to do, and expects them to be able and willing to do it. On occasion, a strongminded or impatient player (often a pianist) just starts playing something and expects everyone to fall in behind him.

But one or more of the others may not want to play what's been called because they don't know it well or at all. They may nevertheless be willing to use the skills described earlier and play it from a written or printed lead sheet, or play it if someone else plays the first chorus, relying on their ability to reproduce it after one hearing. Other players may balk at playing something at a tempo they know they will have difficulty with, or something they do know but in another key. All these situations lead to negotiations that, seldom taking more than a few seconds, determine what's played. Faulkner recalls:

I was playing a gig at Castle Street with Alan Simon and Bob Weiner (drums), and Dave Santoro (bass) wanted to play "Iris," a Wayne Shorter tune. Thank goodness Alan said, "I don't know it well enough to play it. I know it but not that much." Dave wanted to play it, and sort of urged Alan to give it a try, and Bob was nodding enthusiastically, but Alan was insistent and there was a pause and I said, "Let's do 'Nica's Dream.'" "Okay," Alan said, and Dave nodded his head in approval and Bob was ready to go as I counted the tune off. It didn't take more than forty-five seconds but boy was this a big event for me.

As I said, thank goodness Alan Simon said he didn't know the Wayne Shorter tune "well enough to play it" right then. (Bob and Alan are in their late forties, Dave in his fifties.)

This negotiation was over in an instant, and an inattentive observer might not notice that anything had actually been negotiated.

But it's worth lingering over this trivial incident. Ordinarily, sociological analyses focus on moments of tension and conflict, because that's when unexpected events interrupt collective activities that ordinarily go unnoticed, and make us aware of everything that is going on at a moment when people would usually say "nothing is happening" (Becker 1998, 95–98). In this case, a player suggests that the group play a song they haven't, as a group, played before. Some of them know it, but others don't, and there is a possibility of serious difficulty, perhaps leading to a prolonged pause in the music as the group works through the conflict. But one player says forthrightly that, though he knows the tune, he doesn't know it well enough to play it. Other players think he probably could play it and urge him to try. Another player who himself doesn't know it watches nervously. The first refuser insists that he won't play it, and that settles the matter. The one who hadn't said anything proposes another tune, which everyone accepts, and the evening goes on. Why did our informant say "Thank goodness"? Because he didn't know the tune very well, if at all, but was reluctant to confess that to these players he respected, because he did understand how his refusal or inability to play it might lead others to think he was a little less good than he wanted to be thought.

As the informant says, the whole event lasted perhaps forty-five seconds. Microevents like this occur all night long, mininegotiations over every choice, some of them shorter than this one, perhaps a few of greater length. An evening's performance, the enacted set list, consists of a long series of just such mininegotiations, each contributing a small step to the process of set and repertoire construction, each intensely meaningful to the participants. Even more microscopic negotiations take place via looks, small gestures, and fragments of what's played that communicate an opinion on or attitude toward what's being discussed or has been decided. We seldom heard anyone speak directly about these negotiations. They go by too quickly, seldom holding up a performance, and then only when it really "doesn't matter," that is, when no one is paying any attention to the music or cares much whether there is music or not.

If the players don't know each other well, some additional unknowns enter the equation governing what they play next. One player calls a tune but perhaps the other players don't know it (always a possibility). This player recalls trying to choose a tune without being sure the other players can follow his lead; he knows them but doesn't know how far their abilities extend:

> I wasn't sure what the others knew. You call the tunes and forge ahead and hope that "All the Things You Are" will work. I wanted to do "Have You Met Miss Jones?" but

wasn't sure they knew it. ["Miss Jones" is known to have unfamiliar, and therefore difficult, chord changes in the bridge; not everyone knows it and it's hard to pick up on the fly.] This was a "musicians meet on the bandstand and have to decide what to play" moment. I have been on gigs with these guys, but not like this.

Coordination by Gesture

Players can indicate a tempo by snapping their fingers and counting, traditionally counting one bar in two—two beats to the bar—and a second bar in four. Everyone begins at the appropriate moment at the end of that bar or the beginning of the next one. They indicate an ending by nodding their heads "meaningfully," the meaning arising from the context—that it is, for instance, the last few bars of the song—or, more rarely, by drawing a finger across the throat. They may indicate a tune by naming it verbally or by just beginning to play it, in either case indicating the key by holding one or more fingers up or down to indicate the number of sharps or flats in the key signature—twofingers down means two flats (the key of Bb, whose signature contains two flats) and onefinger up means one sharp (the key of G). A trumpet player can raise his horn to indicate a ritard or a cadenza, which he will play over sustained chords by the others. Tapping the top of your head can indicate that it's time to go back to the start of the tune ("the head").

A tune may have well-known backgroundfigures someone can play while someone else plays the melody, or a well-known introduction, such as the quotation from Rachmaninoff's Prelude in C# Minor that Charlie Parker started "All the Things You Are" with. The soloist may want to add a four-or eight-bar "tag" to his choruses on a tune, have the rhythm stop completely for a "break" on the last two bars of a chorus, add several bars at the end of the tune, or slow down for an out-of-tempo ending. All these can be accomplished with a nod, a small hand gesture, or meaningful look whose meaning arises contextually.

"What Do We Play Now?" (The Little Pieces-of-Paper Puzzle)

Small items of behavior often betray the existence of a larger phenomenon of collective action. The puzzle of the small item's existence shows us where a larger issue lies, and how the people we're observing handle it so routinely that no one notices that there is a problem. One such small item made us aware of the performance pressures that confront musicians every time they climb on the bandstand and how they influence the choice of tunes during a performance.

Players often bring lists of songs, handwritten or typed on small frayed pieces of paper, to the job. Many told us that they carry such lists in their instrument cases. Not set lists, constructed to be played as written for that evening's job, these lists usually contain no more than the title, standard key, and first note of a song's melody. Alternatively, players may have a printed "little fake book," an alphabetized and much longer list of song titles with keys and starting notes (as opposed to the bigger fake books containing melodies and chords discussed in chapter 3). In either case, the titles remind them of a melody and its accompanying harmonies. The key and first note give them, and the people they are playing with, the minimal knowledge they need to play the tune together. These lists don't give them information they don't know, as the larger fake books do. Instead, they serve as reminders of what they do know and have available as instant repertoire. Faulkner collected such lists from a number of people he knew and worked with:

> I have a list of tunes that Bob Sheperd and Dick DiNicola work from. You know, "You Stepped out of a Dream," "Ain't Misbehavin'," "Day by Day," "Bluesette," "Love for Sale," and about seventy tunes

on little pieces of paper. I also have my own list on little pieces of paper that I wrote out in anticipation of playing a gig in Rome two years ago. Then I have Steve's New Year's Eve rotation schedule on paper. I also have the little green book I made up in Rome last time in anticipation of playing at the Alexanderplatz jazz club, and another sheet of all "weather tunes" that I was going to play as a goof on a gig one night ("Stormy Weather," "I've Got My Love to Keep Me Warm," "Here's That Rainy Day," etc.).

On the little 3×3-inch piece of paper from Dick the drummer, I find the following titles: "It Could Happen to You," "Just Friends," "Just in Time," "Making Whoopee," "The More I See You," "My Romance," "Chicago," "Crazy Rhythm," "Don't Be That Way," "I Get a Kick out of You," "Jeepers Creepers," "Just One of Those Things." Flip side: "I Remember You," "Stormy Weather," "Summertime," "That Old Feeling,"

"Time after Time," "When Sunny Gets Blue," "Got the World on a String," "St. Louis Blues," "Our Love Is Here to Stay," "I'll Take Romance," "Can't Get Started," "Slow Boat to China," "I'll Never Smile Again," "I Should Care," "I Didn't Know What Time It Was," "It's Magic."

Why do musicians carry these items around in their cases? What do they do with them? What problems of collective performance produce this behavior?

Players often find themselves in a situation where they have to decide what to play and have to decide *now*. It's time to start, the audience is waiting, the players are ready. But they haven't chosen the first tune and can't begin playing until they do. These moments differ from the situation of choosing tunes in general in being more intense. With greater pressure on the players to do something *now,* the problems and processes of tune choice become more visible.

At such moments a kind of collective indecision sometimes takes over, as individual players think about what they know and would like to play, add to their consideration what the other players may know and want to play or may want to avoid, and find that these thoughts generate a large and bewildering number of possibilities. As they privately go through this review, the musicians realize that other people are waiting for them to start. That creates a small moment of intense anxiety, eventually dispelled when someone makes a choice and they begin to play.

Similar moments of choice occur throughout the evening, every time the players finish one song and enter a moment of silence before they start another. Once they start playing, they cued whatever audience is paying attention to expect more music. When the music stops, the audience (presumably, though not necessarily in fact) waits more or less patiently for it to resume. The musicians again experience an immediate and intense pressure to play.

A band playing for dancing wants the dancers they have lured on to the floor to keep dancing. That will please the people who hired the band, which, in turn, will be good for getting future work. So the musicians want to continue playing at the same danceable, crowd-pleasing tempo. But they want to change the tune, to avoid boring themselves and the listeners. Here's a typical situation, as Faulkner experienced it:

The trombone player has just finished playing the theme song of Tommy Dorsey (the well-known trombonist-bandleader of the thirties), "I'm Getting Sentimental Over You." The band wants to continue that mood and keep the dancers on the floor, so the tenor saxophone player plays a second chorus of "Getting Sentimental." The crowd is still dancing, but the trumpet player, whose turn it is to play, has heard enough of that tune and thinks the audience might have too. He wants to play something at the same tempo, in the same mood, and knows many songs fitting this description. But which one to play? He has to decide right now, as the saxophone player reaches the last bar of his chorus and the piano player looks for a cue as to what the next tune will be and what key he should therefore modulate to. This creates a miniversion of the tension that arises over what to play as the first tune of the night.

Here's how it's resolved. The trumpet player decided to play "East of the Sun," and mouthed the title, not giving a key because he assumed the piano player would know it and would pass it on to the bass player, and then started playing, while the others fell in behind him without any problems. (A preselected set list, of course, disposes of the need for even this small negotiation—which is why leaders make them.)

Players typically resolve the problem in seconds, though it often seems like forever to the players who "can't think of anything" or can't make up their collective mind. That's when they reach for those "little pieces of paper." Here's Faulkner's recollection of his first look at one of these resources being used:

I went into a jazz club in Hollywood in 1968. The alto player was a B-list player, meaning he was very good but not as recognized as one of the monsters in the business. There is the rhythm section, and the lights are on him and he is looking at a little black book, and he quickly turns around to the bass player first and then the piano player and calls a tune, presumably from the little black book. Say the tune is "I Love You" or, better, "I'm Old Fashioned."

Looking at the list reminds the player of possible choices for the next tune. But it doesn't fully answer his question about "What do I play now?" He inspects the possibilities in the light of a number of the other problems we identified as arising in the playing situation, all of them affecting his choice. Most importantly, he wonders if, when he chooses a tune from his little piece of paper, the others will know it and be able to play it. And he will therefore ask "Do you know...?" As we've also seen, some situations make it likely that the answer to his question will be yes, to the point where he may not feel it necessary to ask.

Do the other players know the tunes from which the player consulting the list chooses? When the members of a group assembled ad hoc for one night have often played together in the past, perhaps in a variety of similar ad hoc groups, they can choose easily, drawing on the contents of their shared performing past. At its best, such a situation produces a feeling of ease and euphoria. Everyone feels comfortable. A pianist describes how working with players he knows well produces this feeling:

> Hoo boy, what tunes did we do during the first two hours? Nope, they weren't off the list, but came up as I thought of them. With Dick and Steve, I'm able to say I spoke not a word but went straight to my next tune through the entire two hours. After all these years, these guys are great at following me if I suddenly slow down after a final bridge for a rubato ending—or whatever harebrained stunt I might pull at the very last second. Some

of the tunes were "Ya Gotta Try" (a Hefti tune suggested by Dick), a samba I wrote a few years ago called "Gigi's Samba," because it's based on the changes to "Goody, Goody," "Where or When," and some tune I launched as a waltz that morphed into a half-time 4 and then back to 3 later on. I'm sure there were others because we played continuously, but durned if I can remember what they were.

When you work with people you've often played with before, you feel sure that they not only know the basic elements of the tune—the melody and harmony—but also a variety of other elements that help the players do what they want to do: sound professional, "together," like they know what they're doing. One player starts playing a tune, the others recognize what he has started and immediately fall in behind him. In this situation, the choice of what to play next is relatively simple (though other complications arise when you consider the audience side of the equation). Becker describes his experience working with the same players for a year:

> We often began to "run out of tunes" late in the evening. As we considered, interminably it sometimes seemed, what to do next, I would occasionally just start playing something that had "popped into my head," something I felt like playing, knowing the drummer would begin to accompany me and the saxophone player would either continue the tune when I finished a chorus, or name something else he had thought of after I started.

Why are the lists players consult written on little pieces of paper? Faulkner found the answer when he looked in his trumpet case and saw that he had put together his lists for specific occasions using whatever fragmentary writing surface he had available at the moment:

> I have just rummaged through my instrument case and found the little green book I put together for the Rome gig. It is a tiny 1.5×1.5 Fort Mason Officers Club booklet. I also found a list of tunes on a

single sheet of lined engineering paper, with "Stella by Starlight" at the top, and some kind of priority given to Chet Baker tunes ("Alone Together," "Stella"), I think something like that was at work. I cannot remember when I made up the lined-paper list or for what gig or gigs. I was making a list of tunes that I am comfortable with, that's what's important.

Any musician can buy, and many have, the small printed fake book of tunes with keys and starting notes described earlier. But people who have those books continue to make lists on little pieces of paper, in little notebooks like the one Faulkner describes. Why isn't the printed book good enough for all these specific occasions?

Little pieces of paper differ from printed books by being far less permanent, and thus more likely to have been made to use *now,* for this job, this place, these people. Occasions differ in what you may have to play, and what you may find it possible to play, for a very specific audience: the family and friends attending a bar mitzvah party or a wedding; the employees eating, drinking, and dancing at a company-hosted party; New Year's Eve at the Officers' Club at a military base; the people who have come to this bar or restaurant for years; the swing dancers who can tell you the exact metronome marking for the tempos they want to dance to. Each of these groups wants different songs, perhaps played in a distinctive style; or, since it may not be paying close attention, a group might pay attention only when it hears something it don't like. Occasions differ, too, in terms of whom you will be playing with, what they like to play, and what they know or don't know, so the list made for the particular occasion will also reflect the specificities of the band's makeup. If the list proves useful on the particular occasion for which it was made, the player might keep it, maybe in his instrument case, for use on the next similar occasion. It doesn't take up much room, so why throw it away?

When you know before you arrive at the job what constellation of audience, players, and other contingencies will be waiting for you, you can prepare—taking audience tastes and player competences into account—a list of what you might play when you have to make the kind of quick choice we've described.

But jobs also provide the occasion to try new things, so you might put on the list tunes you have recently learned, or recently heard and would like to try out, as well as those you know well. Since you don't know if you will ever run into just this constellation of audience, players, and place again, the list may be useless after the immediately upcoming performance, so you don't make it in a more lasting way, intended for continuing use. You make it for tonight. The list needn't be very long because, even on the seven-hour jobs Becker worked, you would play no more than forty or fifty tunes and, on the much more common three-or four-hour jobs, as few as fifteen. In either case, those fit without trouble on a small piece of paper. You can write it in pencil for the same reasons. If any aspect of this set-up changes, the list you need changes too.

When conditions create less pressure for the players, they feel more at ease, more able to experiment, and they enlarge the list of potentially playable tunes accordingly. Recall the details of Becker's experience in Chicago (described in earlier chapters). This band, playing for similar audiences every night, didn't need little pieces of paper because tonight was just like the night before, and what worked one night would work on any other night, with predictable and easily prepared-for variations:

> We needed a fake book, a big one with the melody, chords, and words, because occasionally someone would show up at the bar, drunk and aggressive, wanting to hear a tune we didn't know or didn't ordinarily play and could not just start in on in a simple, routine way. We couldn't plan for these random requests and, when we got them, we turned to the fake book, looked it up, spread the book out on the piano, and, Bob reading and transposing over my shoulder, we played the request.

Audience members can shape the performance by making requests. When players know the tune, they play it. Requesters often don't know the correct name of the tune, creating a problem. This example comes from Becker's experience playing in a club in Kansas City:

> A drunk came up to the stand and asked us, belligerently, to play "Keys in the Mailbox." None of us knew a song by that name (in fact, there is a country-and-western tune with that title, but at the time of this event it hadn't been written yet) and we couldn't find one in the fake book. I asked the guy to sing it and he began to sing: "The key's in the mailbox, the same as before..." He didn't need to go any further because now we could all identify the tune as "A Cottage for Sale," whose first line he had mistaken for the title. We played it and everyone was happy.

Faulkner had a similar experience:

> We were asked to play "Memories." "Memories"? Did they mean "Memories of You"? "How

does it go?" I asked. "Memories, from the corner of my mind..." He meant "The Way We Were."

Did I tell you the story about "Send in the Clowns" and the high-paying gig I did for some millionaire at his summer castle on the mountain he owned in New Hampshire? So the millionaire says to the band leader, "Will you play 'Send in the Clowns'?" The bandleader says he doesn't know it and then looks around at the lead line—alto, trumpet—and says "Do you guys know it?" I said, "Not really"—a very bad reply, meaning I probably could play some of it, like the line "send in the clowns" (the notes are B-C-D-A, and that's about all I knew)—but what I really meant was, "No, I don't know it." The alto player is a pure jazzer and didn't even reply. I looked at the bass player, who I thought knew plenty of tunes, and "Send in the Clowns" was a big New York favorite at the time with Sondheim's show on Broadway and every singer singing it on every television show.

Now the guy was in my face, saying, "Will you play 'Send in the Clowns'?," as if to say, "If you don't, I won't be happy, and I get my way." Considering the castle on the mountain was his summer retreat, I was not arguing with him on that one. So I counted off four and "Send in the Clowns" starts up, sort of. Now remember, no one knows this tune, but if they know just a little bit of it then we can, fingers crossed, get through this and get Mr. Rich Guy out of our hair. Well, we get through the first four notes, the "send in the clowns" part, and I play it again. You have to remember, Sondheim's tunes all sound like the second alto part in a big band chart, don't they? After repeating this line, I decided to take it down to F#, back up to G, back to F#. I look at the bass player, as if to say, "Do you know where we go next?" I'm not getting any help from the bass player. The piano player didn't even try. None of us had any interest in ever learning this song.

After stumbling around on this—and having no clue about the bridge, or whether or not there was a bridge—the requester of the tune looked at us and, mercifully, turned away and rejoined his guests.

Boredom and New Repertoire: Bringing in Tunes and Their Fate

How and why do players inject new material into what they know and play and suggest to others while they're on the stand?

Playing the same material over and over, night after night, with the same people, bores most players. Boredom leads some of them to search out new songs, and other players sometimes refer to these explorers as "tunehounds" (we even have one among us: Becker) and depend on them to create innovation by recommending new songs. Other players, perhaps content with the tunes they and their colleagues already know, will nevertheless usually agree to try out new suggestions. Similarly, some players like to experiment with new ways of playing old material: playing "Body and Soul" as a bossa nova, or trying old tunes in unfamiliar keys or time signatures. Leaders, concerned with developing their group's style and distinctiveness, often ask the players who work with them to learn new material, either songs or arrangements of already known songs. Musicians often refer to the first of these activities as "bringing in" tunes: bringing unfamiliar tunes to the attention of other players and recommending that they add them to their repertoires, at least for the job they're currently playing.

Comparing two histories of the introduction of the same tune—"Time on My Hands"—shows the variety of dynamics involved in such an event. Becker remembers playing this tune in his youth, but not when or how or where he learned it:

> By the time I was playing with Bobby Laine in working-class bars, it was part of my working repertoire, a song I knew so well that you just had to say "Time on My Hands," and I would go into a

four-bar intro in the key of F (the standard key).

I had picked up a lot of tunes because I wanted, for whatever reason, to learn new tunes; many other players made do with a smaller repertoire. Bobby had a limited repertoire, and playing it seven hours a night bored me, especially late in the evening. I tried to remedy that by introducing new material, picking things I thought he would go for and teaching them to him on the stand. Our repertoire grew as I kept bringing new tunes in over the year or two we worked together. In the end we had a lot of stuff one or the other of us could just call, or not even call but just start playing.

Faulkner learned the same song in a different version of the "bringing in" process. Rob first saw it in when Jay, the guitarist/leader of a group Faulkner played in, brought it to the gig and wanted the trio to work on it and be ready to play it on the job. He'd found the tune on a recording by Pepper Adams and taken that version off the record. Rob, quite taken with it, remarked on the interesting harmonies (from the Adams recording) Jay had given them for it. The original chords are:

Fmaj7 / / / | / / / / | F dim / / / | / / / / | Gmin7 / / / | / / / / | C7 / / / | / / / /

The Adams version is:

Fdim / / / | / / / / | Fmaj7 / / / | / / / / | Bmin7b5 / / / | E7b9 / / / | Gm7 / / / | C7 / / /

Rob thought this version definitely cuter, more hip, and more modern, and thought that it didn't do violence to the feel of the tune. He also remarked on the augmented fifth in the melody in first bar of the bridge, and the b5 later on in the bridge, which together make this a tune that appeals to a modern jazz player's sensibility.

Tunes don't always migrate from their origin in someone's head to becoming something well enough known to be playable by a large number of players on request as simply as that. Not everything gets recorded by Pepper Adams or his analogues—that is, recorded by some jazz player whose CD will come into the hands of and be listened to by someone like Jay, who is looking for new material.

Vincent Youman's "Time on My Hands" made the giant step from the composer's head to the printed page, to dozens of recordings, which continue to be made to this day. The song has been recorded over two hundred times, beginning in 1931 and going at least up to 2004, Adams's recording having been made in 1981.

Conversely, "Forgetful," a tune written by the well-known jazz composer Tad Dameron, which Becker likes a lot and has often introduced to other players, has only been recorded fifteen times, several times by Chet Baker, and more than once by Boyd Raeburn, who led an avant-garde but not well-known band from Chicago, and by a few not very well-known singers and instrumentalists. Most of the recordings come from the '40s and '50s, though Baker recorded it (again) as late as 1980. If you don't know Chet Baker's version(s), and few musicians do, you would probably never know it existed.

But "Forgetful" has at least been recorded. A player Faulkner knows has written some original tunes and recorded them on a homemade CD. He gives his CD to people so that they can hear the songs and learn them. It's only perhaps since the turn of the century that you could make a CD easily and at no great expense, and be able to give it to people so that they could learn your tunes, which might then become part of more people's repertoire. In earlier years, no one heard or knew these orphan compositions unless they heard the composer himself play them.

Coda

Songs get played as the result of on-the-spot negotiations between players at the moment of public performance. All the pressures and constraints of prior learning, present occupational situation, and the organizational context of the performance focused on these players push their negotiations one way or another, resulting in what actually gets played on any given occasion.

We can't identify any body of material as the definitive and canonical list of The Repertoire. We can only acknowledge a large, amorphous, shifting body of musical materials players can and may choose from, when the time comes to play, recognizing that what they finally play will not result from the inherent musical merit of the tunes nor from the combined expert judgment of generations of experienced players, but as a vector reflecting all the influences and pressures we have described.

8

The Results of Bandstand Dynamics

When performers, who have learned some but not all of the possible songs they might have learned, come together in situations where they have to play for a certain amount of time for whoever is there, what they play is their repertoire for that occasion. The payoff for such a vacuous general statement lies in what you get when you specify each of the inputs. *These* players playing in *this* place with *its* demands and using *the* repertoire that is, one way or another and at one level or another, available to them individually and collectively, create, on the spot and perhaps for this one time only, a repertoire, *the specific list* of songs they play on that occasion.

In the most general case, a working repertoire exists for just that one occasion. In the last chapter, we considered the situation of musicians who have never played together and have not agreed on a repertoire, and we described how they work out what to play and how to play it while they are on the stand. But, of course, musicians who assemble for a job often have played together before and now we look at two common forms that takes and see how these prior experiences create specialized repertoires they can rely on to create an evening's performance: on the one hand, the working repertoire of a semistable group and, on the other, the generalized repertoire that characterizes what we might call a playing region or musical community, a geographic area whose resident musicians work together often enough, even if not in stable combinations, to develop a repertoire in common.

All these variations on the way songs become repertoire and the way players use repertoire show how the workings of the relatively small number of mechanisms and elements we have described can produce highly variable results from one time and place to another. This chapter describes some of the relatively (only relatively) more permanent features of the constantly changing repertoire landscape.

The Working Repertoires of Semistable Groups

When musicians play together in the same situation (or the same kind of situation) for weeks or months, they work out many of the routine problems of repertoire. They find things they can play together, and want to play together, and so develop a more or less stable working repertoire: programs of material they can play easily, without much forethought, in the kinds of places they usually play. Working repertoires vary in how many tunes they contain, how much variety exists among them (whether the group plays the same tunes, or types of tunes, night after night), and how much room the material offers for improvisation. They play in this kind of bar or restaurant, or for that sort of party (weddings, bar mitzvahs, holiday parties), and the working repertoire they develop becomes a resource they can call on again and again. They know what they jointly know, what the situations demand or will tolerate, and have a list of tunes they only need to select from and arrange sequentially to produce an evening's performance.

The amount of time people play together, during which they can develop a working repertoire, has diminished substantially since the late 1940s and early '50s. Becker, working with small groups in the 1950s, regularly played six nights (forty-three hours) a week. Musicians today feel lucky if they play two or three jobs a weekend, three or four hours a night. A Chicago drummer Becker discussed this with said:

> Six nights a week working (and seven hours) I can't imagine. People always talk that way about playing clubs in the '30s and '40s. There's no place to play these days, really. In Chicago, at least, there are a few places you can hang out to play jam sessions. But real gigs are pretty few and far between. On the other hand, there are offshoots of academic or quasi-academic music programs that involve big-name jazz

guys as mentors, who encourage the youngsters.

Contemporary players, with so little playing time in public, have no time to get bored and start looking for new material. More importantly, they don't have time to learn anything new on the bandstand, and instead need written music or recordings to learn from at home. In the older period, musicians experienced jobs in bars as a *routine,* not to say a grind. When the number of such jobs decreased, that kind of gig became rarer, an *event,* and everything that happened on the job required more preparation. As a result, developing a working repertoire no longer happens "naturally," the inevitable consequence of spending many hours together on the stand. Players who learned tunes by playing long hours barely recognized that they were learning new material or the skills they exercised to do it. A guitar player describes the process:

> Somebody would half know the tune a little bit. We would get through it, we'd find the right harmonies ... all of a sudden, we have a new tune. This would

improve your skills as far as listening and hearing, hearing a bass line, trying to hear what the chord was without having any music.

In such groups, "bringing in" new tunes occurred (and for some players still occurs) routinely and over a period of weeks or months, and their repertoire grows in a way that seems natural and unremarkable. Faulkner explains:

Jay brought in "Pensativa," the Claire Fisher tune, and "Never Let Me Go," and we did both of them on a recent gig at the Italian *ristorante* in Springfield. Jay is like that, he will hear a tune and like it and then bring it in to play. I told Paul about "Prelude to a Kiss" and the treatment I had heard Paul Bley do on the local jazz show. Bley had done it as a bossa and it worked, so I called it on the gig with Jay and Dave Shapiro at Egremont Inn. It worked and we seem to have now added it to the regular set of tunes we do in the trio.

Such groups still find themselves in what some of them experience as ruts, many complaining about the same old things from *The Real Book.* A saxophonist/leader said:

> They brought in "Serenity" by Joe Henderson, a fourteen-bar tune ... and also "Speedball." All were very hip and I loved them from the first time we played them.

> This was way different from the usual *Real Book 1,* you know, the overplayed, dated, or uninteresting stuff they suggest, like "Green Dolphin" ["On Green Dolphin Street"], "Fever," "Softly" ["Softly as in a Morning Sunrise"], "Bye Bye Blackbird," "All the Things You Are," "All Blues."

Musicians who play in groups like these add new songs to their own individual repertoires, as one or another brings in new tunes the others then acquire. Faulkner explains:

> There is no substitute for steady playing. It may be one of those clichés but, at the best of times, it's as if you have been taken over by some other power and you just

relax and let it go. Last night at Castle Street in the Berkshires—I was down with a mild flu and had no energy—but once on the band stand everything changed, no force, nice and easy, just play the room. Jay is introducing Benny Carter tunes into the sets now and it's "Key Largo," "Blues in My Heart," and more. Also "Never Let Me Go" with great changes. Sidney Bechet wrote some very hip stuff and we did it last night also.

As we've seen, they also learn new ways of playing old songs, in Latin rhythms or different meters or, most commonly, by extensively reharmonizing standard tunes. Contemporary texts containing "modern chords" for standard tunes by Dick Hyman, Jamey Aebersold, and others, include more modern harmonies and voicings than the original sheet music. (We discussed these kinds of harmonic substitutions—adding sixths, ninths, raised and lowered fifths and ninths, and raised elevenths to the chords or substituting chords based on a different root for the originals—in chapter 2.) Players of earlier generations made such substitutions freely and considered many of the common ones (e.g., a tritone substitution of a IIb7 chord for a V7) more or less interchangeable—as, in fact, they usually were. What a soloist might play over a dominant seventh chord in a turnaround will almost always sound appropriate over that common substitution.) Contemporary players often replace this informal and unsystematic practice with written substitutions, "reharmonizations."

Such substitutions once created controversy. Becker's early experience (circa 1950) puts this practice in historical perspective:

> I was hired for a night to play in a trio in a bar, replacing the regular piano player. We played the first set, which consisted of tunes like "My Blue Heaven," to give you the flavor, and when we took an intermission, the tenor player (who was the leader) offered to buy me a beer. Something in his demeanor warned me that I was going to get a talking to, though I couldn't imagine for what, since I wasn't

aware of having done anything terrible.

He started the conversation by asking if I was married. I said I was, and he wanted to know if I had any children. I said I did, and he asked how many children I had. I told him one, and he nodded, with an air of "I knew it!" and said, "Well, if you had three kids to support like I do you wouldn't be playing those far-out chords. Cut it out! I want to keep this job."

What he was expecting was the harmonization that appeared on the standard lead sheet, without sixths, ninths, and other added notes. He took that harmonization seriously, to be played as is; I took it as a sketch of the fundamentals to be improved on. I treated it like one of Bach's harpsichord players would have treated a continuo part.

Harmonic substitutions seldom create controversy among contemporary players, except when they produce serious discords, such as might happen when a piano player plays one set of chromatic descending chords and the guitar player plays a different set. Competent players playing together regularly can quickly find agreement about harmonic patterns.

Over months and years, groups that work together steadily, and the jobs they play that make their longevity possible, disappear: a bar closes, a leader retires or moves away, the style of music they play no longer appeals to people. Similarly, players move away, join other groups, or stop playing professionally. So the lifespan of a working group varies considerably, some groups remaining together more or less for years, while others last no more than a few weeks.

These working groups often consist of players from different musical generations, who bring different musical sensibilities, different skills, and (most importantly) different tunes to the job. A veteran bass player Faulkner has worked with explained, "I am not a bebopper. Not in the sense that you are. My interests are in later Miles [Davis], not the Miles of the Prestige years with Paul Chambers, Philly Joe Jones, and Red Garland." The Miles

Davis group that is a reference for him is the band of Ron Carter, Tony Williams, and Herbie Hancock. In his field notes, Faulkner comments:

> He is a big fan of Chick Corea and Dave Holland. I know this, he knows I know this. He also knows that I don't know many of the Corea/Holland tunes, and other tunes of that period. He's asked me, "Do you know [a tune by Chick Corea]?" I never heard of it and told him so. I said I knew "Tones for Joan's Bones" off one of my favorite Corea albums, *Now He Sings, Now He Sobs,* something like that, and I had seen the tune written out by someone in my circle of playing friends. He also asked me, "Do you know 'Eye of the Hurricane'?" This is a tune by Herbie Hancock on *Maiden Voyage.* I had heard it and played a big band arrangement of it but I would never call it on a gig and I was uninterested in learning it too.

When they work together on a job, the bass player picks up tunes from Faulkner's repertoire as Faulkner picks up tunes from him. That experience occurs frequently, as the uncertainties of hiring and finding work bring together people whose repertoires vary significantly.

Players learn different things as a result of working with different groups, and thus more or less continuously add to their own personal repertoires. What they know reflects what they have learned playing all these jobs as well as what they learn because they heard something on a recording or saw a piece of music and thought it looked interesting enough to practice and become comfortable with. They teach songs from their own somewhat idiosyncratic repertoires to others on the job, and learn from those players' equally idiosyncratic repertoires.

Types of Working Repertoires

The working repertoires groups develop in this way, consisting of a more or less stable number of tunes they all know and are prepared to play, and a disposition (variable from group to group, maybe from night to night) to learn new things and try them out in the work situation, can be classified according at least to four characteristics:

1. Size. The number of tunes available as resources (the pool)
2. Diversity. The variety of tunes the group is prepared to play, or how different the songs are that are selected from the pool
3. Capaciousness. The amount of improvisation players can engage in as opposed to having to play things as written or rehearsed
4. Variability of set and performance night after night

We have classified working repertoires into eight types, using four criteria of difference (each divided, for analytic simplicity, into "high" or "low," though real examples would exhibit continuous variation).

"Size" refers to the number of tunes the repertoire contains. This number changes all the time, as the group acquires new tunes and drops others. But some groups operate with a very small repertoire (a group assembled for the purpose of a concert tour, for example) while others (a band playing in the same bar over a period of months or years) will accumulate a very large number of tunes they can play without trouble.

"Diversity" refers to the musical variety of tunes the repertoire contains. At an extreme, a band specializing in Polish American social events might play nothing but polkas, and a Latin band might play nothing but mambos, cha-chas, and bossa novas. At another extreme, a band might play nothing but post-bop material, tunes by Wayne Shorter, Charlie Mingus, or Chick Corea. Other bands might restrict themselves to the Great American Songbook or to recent pop tunes. Still other bands will be ready to play all of these kinds of music and almost anything else that might become necessary.

"Capaciousness" refers to the amount of room the band's routine ways of playing leave for players to improvise and experiment with what they do play. In some bands, players choose styles and improvise freely. Others require imitation and repetition. The repertoire of a "ghost band" exemplifies this possibility, as when a "Glenn Miller" big band plays the Miller arrangements as the band recorded them, with the soloists repeating the solos from the original recording (as tenor saxophone players still play Tex Beneke's solos on Miller's "In the Mood").

"Variability" refers to how much each night's selection of tunes differs from that of preceding and succeeding nights. Four dimensions of variation, each divided into high and low, yield eight types of repertoires:

Type	Size	Diversity	Capacious-ness	Variability
1	H	H	H	H
2	H	L	H	H
3	H	L	L	H
4	H	L	H	L
5	H	L	L	L
6	L	L	L	L
Etc.				

Here are some of these possibilities as they appear in real life, embodied in some of the groups we have been using as examples throughout (and whose names we have somewhat whimsically used for the types).

1. The "Bobby Laine": Many tunes, lots of improvising on the chord changes, continual novelty and, once introduced the tunes will probably be repeated now and then over the life of the group. (HHHH)

2. The "Tristano" (named for Becker's piano teacher Lennie Tristano, who followed this pattern strictly): A very few tunes (in Tristano's case, perhaps no more than a dozen standards, including "Ghost of A Chance," "What Is This Thing Called Love?" and other tunes well known to jazz players of his era) make up the core set, played in no particular order. Everyone in the group knows them. This repertoire is characterized by low turnover in tunes selected, and few new tunes introduced; the old ones are sufficient to learn and improvise on. The players improvise as long as they like, as many as eight or ten choruses. (LLHL)

3. The "Pinardi" (named for a bandleader Faulkner worked with, mentioned elsewhere in the text): The leader continually introduces new tunes, in a variety of styles, into the group's repertoire, and then makes a constantly changing selection from this variety. The group might play a tune one week during several performances and then not play it again for months. The players take two or, at most, three choruses on a tune. The set list varies greatly from night to night, with the constant introduction of new material. (HLLH)

4. The "MacLeod" (or club date; named for Bruce MacLeod, who describes it in chapter 1 of this book): A leader intent on pleasing the clients who have hired him for their party organizes a great variety of songs to fill an entire evening. (HHLH)

Each kind of repertoire works in a specific kind of playing situation. The "Bobby Laine" works best in places like the Chicago clubs Becker worked in with him, where the band played long hours for an uninterested audience, and where it was likely the performers got bored and looked for variety.

The Local Musical Community

Among players who don't ordinarily play in the same group (or who may never have played together at all), living and working in the same musical community produces similarities and overlaps in individual repertoires that operate, just like the shared repertoire of a group that does play together frequently, to provide a basis for the quick and easy preparation of an evening's performance.

A musical community grows up around a network of jobs players can comfortably get to and from in an evening of driving. Some find it easy to stick close to home, perhaps most especially in larger cities, but most players in smaller centers have to travel to get to a larger number of jobs and opportunities to play. The Amherst Valley, where Faulkner makes his professional home, typifies this kind of community. Players will drive to nearby towns (Springfield, Massachusetts, 23 miles) and cities (Boston, 87 miles), to neighboring states and, for a good job, will go as far as New York City (157 miles). Because the Valley has many small towns and cities, players from a variety of places all make themselves available for work in the general area, and players from many places find themselves playing together, not regularly but now and then. Not necessarily neighbors in everyday life, patterns of work create a sort of community among them, as reputations travel and occasional performances together create some at least minimal acquaintance with each other's knowledge and abilities.

We became aware of this phenomenon when we realized that tunes had histories in such communities, passing from one player to another on the stand in the course of a performance involving people who may not know each other well, if at all. In that way, a community-wide repertoire grows up over a period of years, some of it known in common (everyone, let's say, will know "All the Things You Are"), some of it known by a large number (though not all) of the players in the community (as many would know, for instance, "Blue Bossa"), and some known by a few (as in the more esoteric compositions of the post-bop composers or out-of-the-way pop tunes of the kind Becker specializes in). The least widespread will be songs created by local players, which they have taught to a few people willing to go to the trouble of learning them.

Tracing the origins of specific tunes uncovers the patterns of incorporation of a tune into a community repertoire. A full investigation of the process would discover each step in the tune's movement through the community by gathering detailed information on the occasions of its playing over time. We didn't do that, but saw enough steps here and there to know that the process occurs and takes many forms. Here are some examples we noted, all taken from Faulkner's experience on the job. P1, etc., refer to players in the community;

the arrows indicate the movement of the tune from player to player.

Adoption and incorporation. "Moon and Sand," composed by Alec Wilder. P1□P2□P3□P4. P2, P3, and P4 did not know the tune before P1 showed it to them. They liked it, learned it, and incorporated it into their personal repertoire of tunes. Specifically, Becker (a Wilder fan) showed the tune to Faulkner, and they played it together. Faulkner showed it to Messer, who recalled that Pinardi showed it to him, although he later forgot about it. Messer (a leader) then put the tune into the set list for his group and it became part of their "book," and Lieberman thus learned it.

Rejection. "The Scene Is Clean," composed by Tadd Dameron. P1□P2□P3. P1 showed P2 a tune, P2 showed P3, and P3 did not want to play it or learn it. The piano player in Dominic's group introduced him to the tune. Dominic liked it, downloaded it from the Internet, printed a copy, and then showed it to Faulkner one night. Faulkner already knew it, because Clifford Brown and Max Roach had recorded it. Faulkner remembers: "Dominic and I played it along with a music-minus-one rhythm section [a recorded background]. I'm reading the tune and its chord changes, and I decided I didn't want to solo on it. It is too difficult for me and I don't want to spend the time and effort to learn it. I'd rather spend my time on other tunes." The tune gets stuck at P3 (Faulkner), who does not transmit it to any P4s: "Dominic wanted to play this tune and have me play it with him at an upcoming concert with his group at Amherst College, where I would be the guest soloist. But I said no, and the tune was not incorporated into the set list and learned by the other players on that gig."

Adoption, Rejection, and Abandonment. "Sky Dive," composed by Freddy Hubbard. P1□P2. P1, Jay (leader of a group Faulkner plays with), wants to play Freddy Hubbard's "Sky Dive." Faulkner relates the sequel:

> He urges me to learn it. I tell him I'm reluctant to play it because I don't feel comfortable with the chord changes. Jay insists, and we

play it at several concerts. I can see that Jay wants to record this tune, or put it on the set list as one of the tunes to be considered for the upcoming recording session. I keep playing it, being a good soldier in the group, but, despite being complimented on my solos, I don't feel I am getting into the heart of the tune and am beginning to see my soloing on this as just another Freddy clone type of stylistic imitation. Jay and I keep up a friendly banter about the tune and my reluctance to play on it, and after five months and six or seven gigs in which he has called it, "Sky Dive" disappears from the set list. At least for now, we have not played it. When I asked Jay where he got it, he said he'd heard Hubbard's recording and liked the chord changes and thought it worked for our quintet. It does work for the trumpet and tenor line, and this is something he is sensitive to, the texture of the sound on certain tunes that Rob and Paul, trumpet and tenor respectively, achieve. "Sky Dive" was in heavy use for a short period of time, and then Jay removed it from the active list, at least so far. I will play it for him, but under duress.

Adoption. "Dream Dancing," composed by Cole Porter. P1☐P2☐P3☐P4. Faulkner explains:

I heard this on a Ruby Braff tape someone made for me, most likely Frank Laidlaw in 1980 for a gig I played with him in Bermuda. I loved it, and four years later played the tape again. I told Jay that I love the tune. He found the sheet music for it and a couple of years later wrote out a chart for guitar and flugelhorn. He continued to work on this tune and a year ago wrote out a duo bop line for the two of us and called it "Dream Line." The tune was incorporated into the group repertoire, Dave Shapiro (bass player) already knew it, of course, but Paul Lieberman learned and apparently liked it because he takes some beautiful solos on it. Unlike "Sky Dive," "Dream Dancing" has had a long history in this group, generating lots of activity for Jay: several arrangements of it, a written and rewritten duo line, heavy and continued use on gigs.

Adoption. "Jean de Fleur," composed by Grant Green. P1☐P2☐P3. Faulkner: A bebop tune with the nice chord changes. There was no negotiation over this one. Jay passed it out on a college gig and the quintet read it down. While the A section is repetitive and, in my opinion, too long and tedious, I chose to shut up and play it, having expended energy and options when I complained about "Sky Dive." Besides, Paul sounded great on this during the gig, eating up the chord changes and setting the performance bar high for the rest of us. Jay learned this tune by listening to a Grant Green CD reissue, wrote it out, and then wrote out harmony parts for trumpet and tenor, and it quickly became part of the working set list. He said, "It's a little awkward, harmonically, I like to play on it, it's different." We didn't do the tune at Castle Street due to the problems I was having with the flugelhorn's sheered-off spit valve. Nevertheless, we play "Jean de Fleur" on nearly every gig we do—two choruses on the solo sections, you could take three choruses if you wanted, and a likely candidate for the planned record date.

Rejection. P1☐P2. Faulkner:

Dominic says that Bill, the drummer, brings in many ideas for tunes. Most of those tunes are of the Monk persuasion. "I have to reject two out of three of Bill's suggestions. Most of what he and the other members of the band want to play is in the *Real Book 1.* He wanted to do this Monk tune, I can't remember which one, and it just didn't work, it sounded like all the other Monk tunes we play, and yet these guys want to play these Monk tunes. I was away on a trip during one rehearsal and when I came back they had been working on a new tune, and what's the tune? It's a Monk-like tune written by someone. I mean, come on, give me a break. I had to tell them, nicely, that we can't do only these kinds of tunes, if we do we'll sound like every other group of musicians who get together in the Valley and play tunes. There are some great players, wonderful players, in the Valley. If we are going to be distinctive and set ourselves apart from those players, we have to play a wide variety of tunes, and be eclectic about our tastes and what we play. Every tune can't end up sounding like a Monk tune."

(Note that these players are all around fifty; it is not a case of an older player being dismissive of the tastes of younger players.)

Adoption, Incorporation, and Potential Incorporation. "La Mesha," composed by Kenny Dorahm. P1□P2□P3□P4 and P5, and P2□P3. A bass player had been doing this tune with Jerry Bergonzi, a well-known saxophonist he sometimes worked with. He told Faulkner that Dorham was his favorite trumpet player, and asked if he had heard this tune. Faulkner said no, and the next time they worked together Dave gave him a copy of the lead sheet.

I transposed the lead sheet into my key (Bb) and told Poccia about it, whereupon he immediately found it and downloaded it and passed it out to Ken and Bill before our next rehearsal with his quintet. It was added to the group's set list. Incidentally, Jay got a copy of the tune from either Dave or me around the time of the Egremont gig. He worked on it for a couple of weeks and told me, "I found that the tune at its original slow tempo was not too interesting for me I tried it as a bossa at a slow tempo and the chord changes really worked, it is quite beautiful." "La Mesha" may or may not become a tune on the set list of the trio of Jay, Dave, and Rob.

The detailed descriptions our field notes contain show the kind of difficulties a systematic study would entail, and the kind of fruitful results we might expect from it. We see, in these fragmentary histories of songs in this musical community, how everything that has come before in the book coalesces in the paths songs follow as some players learn them and like them, feel comfortable with them, persuade others to try them, and try to work them into the ongoing repertoire of specific groups they work with, while others reject the tunes and block their inclusion into working repertoires. And we see further the negotiations between players that decide the songs' fates. But we also see the kind of close detailed observation necessary to get at the relevant details, and can imagine the difficulties that would be involved in mounting a full-scale research on the problem, central as it is.

The Fragmentation of the Repertoire

In the world of post-bop and beyond, the repertoire of jazz has increasingly become fragmented in a way that resembles the repertoire of contemporary pop music, in which every band plays their own compositions (this is what distinguishes them from one another). Each musical group develops its own material, its own songs, and its own ways of playing them. No two groups develop the same songs or play songs in the same way. You can't use what you learn playing with one group when you play with another group, because you have only learned their unique repertoire, which shares little or nothing with the repertoire of other groups. (This situation is described, somewhat, in Stith Bennett's pioneering *On Becoming a Rock Musician* [1980].) As a result, when people from different groups meet to play together, they find that they know little in common, and have difficulty negotiating anything at all to play. This seldom occurs in real life in the world of commercial musicians, because they have to be able to find repertoire in common in order to play the jobs they play. That is not the case, however, with jam sessions, where no external constraints impinge on what players choose to play. An adventurous guitar player says:

> My friend who occasionally plays in New York tells me it's difficult to

go to a jam session down there because nobody knows any tunes. That's the other side of it. There's very little of a balance. Like my friend, who has this incredible background of the Great American Songbook and the [jazz] classics, jazz tunes, has simply taken that as an influence and come up with his own music. So he can go to a jam session up here and play with us and there's a common language. And according to him there is not that common language in Brooklyn, let us say.

[So playing "Have You Met Miss Jones" or "End of a Love Affair"?] It's not going to happen, they're not interested in it. [Are they interested in Wayne Shorter tunes?] Probably. ["Fee Fi Foe Fum," which is based on Coltrane's "Giant Steps"?] Probably. [What do they play?] I don't know, I would be interested to know. But my friend has turned me onto music that, well, like he has turned me on to this tabla player, he's got me interested in Indian music, Indian classic music, and polyrhythmic wedding music, multiple key signatures, complex time signatures, which is a big thing in New York now—absolutely. That is what's happening right now. This is spearheaded by Dave Holland's work with his band, very multimeter rhythms.

Young musicians, studying jazz in specialized jazz programs in schools, can approach this sort of hermeticism because they seldom play commercial jobs. For the most part, they perform in the school setting, playing informally with other students, giving recitals before an audience of friends and relatives, and not having to respond to the requests and demands of club owners, fathers of the bride, and similar outsiders. Whatever they play, within limits, pleases their select audience and they develop a repertoire that is potentially unique, especially when it includes their own compositions. These compositions can't be described in a simple shorthand, because they are too complex to be described by their resemblance to already known tunes.

Nor can anyone learn them from a recording, since often enough no recordings exist, or at least none that are available from anyone other than the composer.

The best description we have of this kind of repertoire at work appears in Marc Perrenoud's *Les musicos* (2007), an ethnography of young French players whom he calls "ordinary musicians": players who play jazz, often very avant-garde, but who also play in bars, for parties, and a range of settings similar to (though not identical to) the variety experienced by the North American musicians we have been writing about. His description of a rehearsal by one of these groups that he played with makes clear that only a musician who had rehearsed with them as he had could possibly play in a way that would mesh with what the other players were doing. Cri du caillou, a trio made up of Claude (clarinets and saxophone), Hervé (percussion), and Marc (bass)—all of them experienced players who worked full time in music—"maintained a deliberately and explicitly non-idiomatic relation to conventional musical forms." They rehearsed a full day each week, working on scores written by Claude, "themes for the clarinet or saxophone for which he had a more or less clear idea of what the bass and percussion would play" (Perrenoud 2007, 64, 69).

Since our rehearsal last week Claude had finished writing the second part of *The Child of Silence.* We had spent most of the time in that rehearsal working on the principal theme (an unorthodox counterpoint between bass clarinet and pizzicato bass) and Hervé had finally found a part for percussion by discussing Claude's suggestions (he had at first wanted "rubato, something very airborne"), mixing passages that were lightheartedly rough (cowbells, etc.) at the beginning with brief hits on the snare drum on the accents in the fast phrases of the rest of the theme.

Claude began by showing us the second part of the piece (unlike the first part, he had not written my part in the bass clef), very dynamic, "a parody of circus music or something like that," he said. The bass and the bass clarinet play in unison, and it took fifteen minutes for us to get down with it. The phrases begin, stop, start up again, I hesitated over the placement of an accent, looked at Claude's part to see if he was really playing what was written; at the same time, Hervé tried some things: hitting the accents like at the end of the first part to find a pattern that would work with what we were playing. He tried to make sense of it: "So that's really two measures in 9/4 and four measures in 4/4 which repeat twice, right?" Claude wasn't sure, he hadn't written any bar lines in, he counted it out, "No, it's not that simple, at the end it shifts." Whatever, what he'd written seemed to us "a little heavy." Hesitation. Hervé suggested that he could just lay out. "Let's take it from the top, with the first part and the improv in the same mood as the last time and we'll see how to connect the two."

The first part of the theme came out right the second time, it finished on a C minor chord, out of tempo, that I played on three strings like a guitar player, which linked the end of what was written and the beginning of the improv, with its harmonic color. The percussion laid out. I kept this thing of three strings going for a while (two or three minutes), progressively sliding down and finally arriving a whole tone lower (Bb minor), having passed through some particularly unstable microintervals. Claude improvised around C minor and, while I was sliding down from the first chord, he began to include more notes that weren't part of the scale. Hervé waited for this atmosphere to evolve enough for him to get into it, and he "entered" with a series of chops on a bunch of metallic objects (ash trays, plates, glasses, small dishes) while I ended the chord, so that I could arpeggiate its notes in a purposefully confused way, and

Claude created a first moment of exacerbation after having increased the tension to a maximum by altering the "color" of C minor, which had been stable at the beginning. During this chaotic moment, which lasted less than a minute, I let the sound of the bass disappear behind the percussion which now reinforced the strident clarinet with cymbals, then I grabbed the bow in order to rejoin Claude with high treble notes, which I got thanks to the harmonics which sound when you rub the strings sufficiently close to the bridge. The tension subsided quickly as the hits were spaced out on the drums and the notes "staggered" down (glissandos on the bass, false fingerings on the clarinet), changing into a kind of out-of-breath "death rattle" in order to return to a decadent version of the first theme, in which all the notes slide, not quite in tune, and die in a pianissimo which, by anticipation, reinforced the contrast with the next part, which we had worked on at the beginning of the rehearsal. Claude and I played the weird dynamic unison (no drums) and, in the middle of the third phrase, Hervé played a solo on the mélodica [a sort of hybrid harmonica/accordion with a small piano-like keyboard] which, largely by chance (since Hervé isn't a pianist), seemed wonderful to us. Hervé pursued his idea through the rest of the second written part, placing (with the science of a percussionist) bunches of notes he hadn't quite mastered, until the organ point of the second theme let him take up his sticks again as he put down the mélodica. The second sequence of collective improvisation began with a drum/clarinet duet.... After an hour of intensive work on our interpretation of *The Child of Silence* in its so-far complete version (which as of now only lasted ten minutes), we had done only half of a piece which will certainly be one of the longest in our repertoire and won't really be ready to perform for some weeks yet. My fingers hurt and I suggested a break. (Perrenoud 2007, 71–73)

Players like these also perform in more conventional settings—bars, restaurants, parties, and (in one memorable description) at eight in the morning for a banquet of people in the fishing industry, where their entire performance consisted of thirty seconds here and there, playing anything at all (the organizers of the event didn't care) as background when people in the audience who received awards walked up to the podium to get them. For these events, they do need some material in common to draw on (because the personnel who will play for these events is never completely fixed), although in the French case it includes elements no American would know: popular French tunes of the last fifty years or Gypsy music, for instance.

When we look at the situation of contemporary jazz, we see similar kinds of experiments. The remarkable pianist and leader Uri Caine, for example, produces programs for a small group based, for instance, on Hungarian folk songs or the symphonic works of Gustav Mahler. If you have not rehearsed with Uri Caine you will almost surely not know these songs, or the way he wants them played. The same thing is true of the musician quoted above who was learning Indian classical music compositions. To play them in company with others, he will have to seek out people with his special experience, and there aren't many.

On the other hand, few people can make a living or, what's more to the point, find it possible to play very often with others when their repertoire consists of such esoteric material. To play with others, in the kinds of settings in which musicians ordinarily play, requires knowing things in common, things that will suit the venue in which the performance occurs, and the penalty for not knowing that kind of material is to not be asked to play with those people again. A saxophonist tells this story:

> You'd be amazed at how many guys, some, you know, really big guys that I know, who say, "No, I can't play that without a chart." You

know I've done a gig with these guys, I don't want to mention his name, a pretty well-known trumpet player, very successful in New York right now, and so I said let's do "Cheek to Cheek," and this is fifteen minutes before the gig. And he said, "Do me a favor, write me out a copy of the chart." I said, "Come on, I can't write you a chart." He goes, "I'm not joking. I'm serious. I need a copy of the chart." It's got a tricky bridge, so I said "Just play what you think is right on the A section and I'll take the rest of it." It wasn't good enough for him, I had to write out a chart.

And the punishment comes quickly enough: "I had to now think twice about it if I was going to hire him for a gig. I was really surprised."

9

Playing the Repertoire Game: What We Wanted to Know and How We Learned to Ask a Better Question

We wanted to understand how musicians who work ordinary jobs in bars and at parties—in other words, jobs where they find that they have to play a variety of music, which they can't always fully anticipate—can play together with little or no rehearsal, and with a minimum of written music to guide them. We thought we had a simple and effective answer: they could do that because they all already knew the same music, the same songs. But that wasn't right; they didn't all know the same songs. A lot of them knew a lot of the same songs, but enough didn't know this song or that one, and players who assumed that everyone could play anything risked making a bad mistake.

How could players create a performance, then, since they couldn't rely on everyone knowing a shared repertoire? We focused not on the execution of a shared, already known routine, but rather on the collective creation of a performance, some of whose elements had to be invented on the spot, with such coherence as the performance had coming as much from what was invented as from what was already known. We turned our attention to the continuous process of mutual adjustment through which partial knowledge is shared on the fly and combined, step by step, to produce a performance that is good enough for the occasion and its participants.

Like every other kind of activity people undertake together, what jazz musicians do is neither random and disjointed nor totally fixed and predictable. The proportions of the two vary from time to time and place to place, but performances always mix the two, the terms of the mixture not a simple application of known ways of reaching agreement, but rather an on-the-spot creation.

We didn't come to this position through some kind of theoretical reasoning or as a deduction from prior aesthetic, philosophical, or sociological commitments. Far from it. We came to this way of seeing, hearing, and talking about what musicians do as a result of direct observation. What we have described isn't what we think they ought to do or wish they would do or what they would do if they were doing things right according to some standard. Instead, we've described what they do, as we were able to see, record, and understand that.

So the question that we have, finally, answered is not the one we started with, but the one we learned was the right one to ask as we went on with our work: How do players combine partial knowledge to create a collective activity that is good enough for the variety of people involved in the event?

What individual performers know varies from player to player. No one knows everything there is to know. And no wonder, because the potential repertoire—all the already existing songs that could be performed—contains a large number. Remember the estimate that some three hundred thousand popular songs were published between 1900 and 1950, a low estimate for today since it doesn't include everything written since 1950, the songs written by jazz players that could never have been part of a canon of "popular music," or the ephemeral tunes musicians composed and played on some occasion, which no one ever recorded or published, but which existed at least enough to have potentially been part of some group's repertoire.

Some players know many of these potential repertoire units and others less. What they know will vary, especially historically. Over the years in which the American traditions of popular music—intersecting and overlapping, but not identical—have come into being and developed, musicians and composers have invented many kinds of music and many ways of playing. Some of these traditions are more or less continuous, others distinctly discontinuous. If you know the music of one tradition—show tunes of the '20s and '30s—you can easily learn the very similar tunes (constructed on the same structural and harmonic models) of other *Hit Parade* tunes of those years. But knowing songs composed in that tradition may not help you much if you want to learn compositions of jazz composers since 1960.

Even when a group does know each other and has played together before, often, or even routinely, unexpected events occur, which prevent them from simply running through some of what they all already know how to do together. A new player replaces the one they have developed their well-learned programs with, and all or many of the agreements on which their routinized performances rest require renegotiation. The substitute saxophonist doesn't know a song the rest of them have played as a standard part of their work for years. One member of the established group gets some new ideas of what to play or how to play what they usually play, and everyone has to change what they do as a result. They all know how to play "Body and Soul," but now the trumpet player wants to play it as a bossa nova, which requires the rhythm section to accompany him in a way they might not be familiar with. The people they are playing for want the band to do something they haven't done before—the bride's father, having had a little too much to drink, wants to hear a song they aren't sure any of them know—and they have to consult one another to see who knows it, and how they should play it.

So, instead of being the routine execution of a program all participants know perfectly well, constructing an evening's performance requires constant attention from every participant. Everyone has to be alert to what the others are doing, and continually adjust what he does in the light of what he hears (and, occasionally, sees) them doing.

Since no two performances are ever identical, participants continually learn new material, which becomes part of their personal repertoire, which they add to what they already know along with what they hear from other sources and decide to learn because they think it worth knowing or think that it will at least come in handy sometime. Since bands often change personnel, and many bands are ephemeral, put together for a single occasion, players have many chances to suggest new material to others and similarly have much new material suggested to them. In that way, individual and group repertoires change more or less continually.

What we wanted to explain and understand centers on two interlocking phenomena. On the one hand, when musicians participated in musical performances, they routinely did a competent job of playing together. The bands we observed, participated in, and heard about didn't disgrace themselves. They did just fine. On the other hand, the competent performances they gave didn't come into being without problems, conflicts, slip-ups, and all the other kinds of messes, large and small, that occur when people try to do things together.

So we wanted to understand how competent musical events happen, given all the possible troubles that can and do occur. And we also wanted to understand how these events come to vary in the way they do, from trainwrecks and near trainwrecks to the kinds of highly routinized, repetitive performances Bruce McLeod described.

The most general answer is that it depends, not surprisingly, on how often the players involved play together, how often they play the same kind of job, which calls for roughly the same kind of performance of the same kind of music, and, finally, a version of our original thought, how much they already know in common (though they have to discover that as the evening progresses).

Remember that all sorts of things affect the mostly ephemeral events that underlie musical performances, making them alike in some ways and different in others. All wedding parties have a kind of generic similarity, as do all bar mitzvah parties, or all organizational holiday parties. In each case, the people who hire the band want roughly the same kinds of music, because the events and the people who attend them resemble each other a lot. This makes performances of these kinds resemble each other.

But each event has unique features as well, and these produce unique constraints and pressures for the players. Every couple getting married has a "special song," related to an important moment in their romantic history. The band that can't play this particular couple's special song for them will ruin their wedding. And it may happen that the band doesn't know it and can't play it. But, as we saw, they will probably play it anyway.

The bar mitzvah boy's parents and their friends will probably want to dance to pop tunes of their youth (perhaps the sixties or seventies) while the boy and his friends will want to dance to contemporary, and quite different, pop music. Will the band be able to play in a way that satisfies both the kids and the old-timers? And how will they manage the similar disparity presented by the next bar mitzvah, where what the two generations want varies in the same way, but with different specifics, calling for other songs?

Similarly, playing in most bars and restaurants requires much the same kind of music: not loud or obtrusive, to some degree recognizable by the patrons (who, just the same, will not be paying very close attention, because they did not come there to listen to music), and catering to the ideas and prejudices of the owner of the establishment, who generally has a full set of complicated theories about how the music affects his gross. But what the patrons of the 504 Club, where Becker played with Bobby Laine, wanted (when they expressed such wants, which they seldom did) and the amount of noise they tolerated from the band differed considerably from what the customers of the Egremont Inn in the Berkshires fifty years later wanted and would tolerate from Faulkner and his colleagues. The owner/manager of that club had very different kinds of musical ideas from those of the Mafiosi who ran the 504 Club, though both worried about how the music would affect their gross. And what works at the Egremont Inn may well be wrong for the slightly different crowd at another restaurant in the next town. Each venue presents the players with overlapping but somewhat different requirements from those nearby.

So players can sound like they have rehearsed, though they haven't, because the vagaries of the hiring process eventually bring many of them together repeatedly in the same kind of situation requiring roughly the same kind of music. Groups of players who don't always play together nevertheless eventually acquire a shared repertoire. They may not have rehearsed, but they have played the same things together many times, in various combinations, and thus have developed what might be called network-specific repertoires, bodies of material they can expect others in the group to know and be ready to play, because they have done it often in the past. That's why trainwrecks, annoying the people who hired the band and making the players who create them so unhappy and uncomfortable, happen so seldom.

But, because the bands haven't rehearsed and not all the players have necessarily performed together before and not all of them know all the tunes that all or most of the others they are playing with that night know, and they may not collectively be aware of what will and won't work, trainwrecks do occur. And so do more frequently, less extreme failures to make competent music, which the audience and the people who hired them may not even notice, but which they and their colleagues do notice and which make them uncomfortable and unhappy.

The same kinds of processes take place on a larger geographic scale as well. Geographic areas develop community-wide musical repertoires as, over the years, the local players work with one another and come to know substantial amounts of material in common.

When players share substantial amounts of repertoire, they can go to work expecting that what comes up that night will lie in the range of activity they feel comfortable with. They feel that they will know what to do when the time comes to do something, that they will know where they are in the ongoing flow of the music, that what they play will mesh satisfactorily with what their colleagues are playing, that they won't make mistakes but rather will have appropriate ideas of what to play, and will be able to execute them. They will thus not embarrass themselves with colleagues they respect, not let down the side vis-à-vis the audience and/or boss, and maintain a professional position that will allow them to continue playing what they want to play with the people they want to play with.

Where Else Can You Find Things like This?

Collective action and the musical metaphor

Because sociology is, after all, a generalizing business, what you learn in one place—what we learned about musicians—should, in principle and in fact, illuminate other areas of collective activity, other places where people do things together. One of us has described (Becker 1998, 125–28) seeking this illumination by describing the situation you've studied but forbidding yourself to use any of its specifics. In this case, what can we say we found out if we describe our results, but don't use the words "musician," "song," "job," "boss," and so on?

We could say, for instance, that we learned that when people act together in pursuit of a common goal, they don't act randomly, nor do they respond thoughtlessly to the situation—"Oh, this is situation x so I'll do what everyone always does in that situation," which is a vulgar version of an explanation that appeals to a common culture—but rather they operate in the mode of negotiation. Because they do what they do together, as a group, they never just enact the plans of one person, or the decisions already made by some group. They work out what they do in steps: someone suggests something, someone else doesn't like it but perhaps can't think of anything better, another participant offers a possible compromise, and finally they hit on something everyone is willing and able to do. And our research showed us, too, that a lot of people who aren't the main actors (from some point of view) also involve themselves in these negotiations, directly or otherwise, most especially the people who pay the bills, but, also the people who provide the foundation of raw materials and paraphernalia that make the collective enterprise possible. Solutions to the problem of coordinating the activity of many people, in fact, constitute the subject matter of sociology.

Sociologists have proposed many answers to the family of questions this problem generates. Perhaps most commonly, they attribute successful collective action to the existence of culture, what Sumner (1906) wrote of as the folkways and the mores, what Robert Redfield (1941, 132; 1956) defined as "shared understandings, made manifest in act and artifact." Whatever the term, whatever fancy definitions people give, the underlying idea is that the members of a society (or, to avoid unnecessary definitional problems, some interacting group) all understand situations in the same way, and have similar ideas about what they should do under particular circumstances. When they jointly recognize a situation as being "one of those," they know that what they should do is what they have all earlier learned and accepted as the way to take care of that particular problem.

The classical anthropological understandings of culture treat it as something that exists before any particular participant in the group arrives, so that each person entering the group finds these understandings already in place, difficult to change, and ultimately quite coercive. What choice do you have when everyone else knows what's going on and what to do about it? If I am a young man of an age to get married, and the society I live in says that I must marry my mother's brother's daughter, well, that's what I have to do, nothing to think or argue about. If I have any other idea, no one else will accept it (Alfred Kroeber [1917] called this "the superorganic").

This simple and straightforward answer to the question of how collective action occurs creates problems, because the world is seldom—maybe never—that simple. Situations don't fall so neatly into categories. The solutions that are supposed to be found in shared cultural understandings almost never provide sufficiently clear and unambiguous guidelines for what everyone should do to solve whatever problem they think confronts them. Even if the situation were to be so clear, it seldom happens that all the participants know what they are to do.

Herbert Blumer (1937) criticized the idea of culture for its assumption that human action, when culture governs it, occurs automatically. In his view, the idea suggested that, once a situation had been defined as "one of those," people responded like machines whose buttons have been pushed, without any intervening process of interpretation. For Blumer, this constituted a major heresy vis-à-vis the scripture according to George Herbert Mead—since Mead insisted that an act of interpretation intervened between the recognition of a communication and the response to it—and Blumer would have none of it. (See also Becker 2004a and 2004b, and Tarde 1999, which proposes an unexpectedly similar point of view.)

But Blumer didn't do much to fill that gap other than insist that it had to be filled. We began our study with the intuition that musicians could play together successfully without rehearsal or written scores because they all shared a repertoire of songs, "repertoire" serving as a specific instance of the idea of culture. We almost immediately realized that "repertoire" wasn't strong enough to carry the weight we were putting on it. Everything about it was more complicated than that. What we observed when we watched musicians playing, and when we ourselves played with others, was actually the intervening process Mead and Blumer had talked about, a gradual fitting together of individual lines of action into a coherent collective act.

Some scholars have seen music as the embodiment of this sort of Meadian process. William McNeill (1995) has described, on a larger historical scale, the importance of music and its characteristic feature of "keeping time" in the formation of patterns of collective action. And Alfred Schutz (1964), in his essay "Making Music Together," similarly used the phenomenon of music as the model for the process of "mutual tuning-in upon which alone all communication is founded" (161), and through which people fit their activities together. His suggestive philosophical analysis doesn't, of course, give specific pointers to researchers on music, but it suggests a path we arrived at empirically:

> This social relationship [of people making music together] is founded upon the partaking in common of different dimensions of time simultaneously lived through by the participants. On the one hand, there is the inner time in which the flux of the musical events unfolds, a dimension in which each performer re-creates in polythetic steps the musical thought of the (possibly anonymous) composer and by which he is also connected with

the listener. On the other hand, making music together is an event in outer time, presupposing also a face-to-face relationship, that is, a community of space, and it is this dimension which unifies the fluxes of inner time and warrants their synchronization into a vivid present. (177)

(He also notes, for anyone who might think otherwise, that "there is no difference in principle between the performance of a string quartet and the improvisations at a jam session of accomplished jazz players.")

No one has made the musical metaphor do this conceptual work so well and so clearly as David Antin, in an essay with the provocative title "tuning." Readers will forgive Antin his stylistic quirks (evident in the long quotation below) because of the depth and persuasiveness of his analysis. He says that when people do things together, the togetherness of their actions does not arise because they "understand" one another, but rather from the continual adjustment and readjustment of each participant to what

the other party does. He takes as an example two people walking together: but as it is we have feet two of them and one foot goes forward and that's odd and when the other one comes to meet it they are paired and that's even and so were inventing number now but this regularly recurrent action one foot and then the other were going somewhere and were going somewhere by managing this set of periodically recurrent actions and someone else is going somewhere in the same way though probably at another pace and we have to do something together in this situation to accomplish anything together at all we have to find out what the other persons pace is we have to find what our pace and the easiest way for me to do this is for me to try to adjust my pace to his pace or her pace and for her to adjust her pace to mine we have to adjust our paces each to the other so that we can come more or less into step
now how do we do this? by watching my step and her step i can tell that she's walking slower than i am and at a different angle and I can slow down

or she could speed up and she might
have speeded up too much while i was
slowing down so that she would have
to slow down again while I was
speeding up a bit to catch up and all
the time we would have before us our
ongoing acts that we could compare
because they were still going on in front
of us and we would have some idea
based on our notion of going together
what we would like or require demand
or desire from going together for a
while and we could try for this in our
practice which could all change in a
while but it is this kind of negotiation
I would like to call "tuning"
because that's pretty much like what
youre doing when youre trying to sing
together whether your idea of together
is in unison or fifths or thirds or in
whatever makes a kind of common
sense for your common practice which
may have just become common and
may cease to be common to the two
of you the three of you or the whole
barbershop quartet in a minute or two
or a week or year and I like this idea
of tuning because it depends on an idea
of going for there will be no knowing

without going and no common knowing without some kind of going together for a while (Antin 1984, 130–31)

The specific metaphor of repertoire

We see the construction of repertoire, as described in the body of this book, as the kind of process Antin described, carried out over and over, hundreds and thousands of times, by hundreds and thousands of musicians in a similar number of venues. Out of all that, repertoire comes into existence as the continually changing body of musical material players refer to when they have to perform in public: the reservoir of all those hundreds of thousands of songs they might play during an evening's performance, and as the specific choices they made from that reservoir on this occasion. That is a specific version of the idea of repertoire as it appears in worlds of music. We speak of the repertoire of opera singers, meaning the roles that they have learned and prepared and are ready to perform with whatever opera company engages their services. Or of the repertoire of solo pianists, who similarly have prepared some number of concerti they are ready to perform with symphony orchestras, or the instrumental literature they have studied and practiced and are ready to play for recitals. These are nonmetaphoric uses of the idea of a repertoire.

Sociologists of culture have increasingly adapted the idea of repertoire for use as a core concept of their field (Hannerz 1969; Swidler 1986). Others have made it central to the sociological and historical study of collective action (Tilly 1977, 1995; Traugott 1995). They mean thus to repair some of the flaws of the concept of culture, using "repertoire" to indicate that people acting in specific situations do not find that, because "the culture" has dictated what they must do, they have no choices, but rather that they can choose what they do from a selection of alternatives the society or culture makes available. This introduces the element of choice Blumer required and also makes analyses more realistic, since observation usually shows us that in most situations people do have choices and are not constrained to do what "the culture" requires.

Like many core concepts of social science, "repertoire" is more analogy and image than well-defined concept. The idea of repertoire, even as described by its users, functions more as a "metaphor than a precise analytical tool" (Traugott 1995, 3). Whether as the "items of culture" (Hannerz 1969, 191), the constitutive "tools" for action (Swidler 1986, 275–76), the limited "set of routines" (Tilly 1995, 26) or, more broadly, a "discourse" (Steinberg 1995, 58), a "scenario" (Traugott 1995, 4), or a "language" (Tilly 1995, 30), repertoire simply delimits a "set of routines" (Tilly 1995, 26) available to actors as they assemble and choose a list of possible behaviors.

Ironically, few scholars have explored the concept in the area of social activity from which it came, the sociology of the arts, where we might have expected thick description and rich analysis. The empirical study of such arenas as dance, opera, painting, or jazz provides exemplary settings for discovery and understanding repertoire as its practitioners perform it. The Merriam-Webster dictionary defines repertoire as "a list or supply of dramas, operas, pieces, or parts that a company or person is prepared to perform." Scholars analyzing collective action often invoke artistic work as an example of the interaction in which repertoires are embedded. They refer to jazz ensembles and theater groups when framing a conception of "contentious repertoires" (Tilly 1995, 27; Traugott 1995, 43). Charles Tilly, the creator of the repertoire concept, used improvisation on a delimited list of routines as a foundational image. In an important essay, he wrote, "By analogy with a jazz musician's improvisations or the impromptu skits of a troupe of strolling players ... people in a given place and time learn to carry out a limited number of alternative collective-action routines, adapting each one to the immediate circumstances...." He compares this loose improvisational style with "the more confining written music interpreted by a string quartet." Moving from metaphor to measurement, he says that cultural repertoires identify "a limited set of routines that are learned, shared, acted out through a relatively deliberate process of choice" (Tilly 1995, 27). Tilly was mainly interested, we think, in the conditions under which repertoires came into existence and use and the consequences of using this or that repertoire item.

Our suggestions for the improvement of such ideas come out of our research experience. Collecting observations in the course of our own activity as working musicians, as well as interviews with players which often focused on the kind of details those observations had shown us were important, we have seen another layer of repertoire-building activity. To ask about details of such ordinarily unmarked activity requires that you know they are there to ask about. Without that level of knowledge, you can miss the flow of trivial, ordinary interaction in which the minute-to-minute decisions that create an individual or a group repertoire happen. Our observations and interviewing went hand in hand, working with the mundane interactions of ordinary performance.

These small details open up the workings of the repertoire-building and repertoire-maintenance processes to investigation. When one musician asks another if he knows this or that tune, and the other answers yes or no, this fundamental piece of interaction and collective decision making creates, for the moment and for those two, a fragment of repertoire. Making a list of possible tunes to perform, asking another player what he wants to play, deciding (before or during a performance) what to play and when—those activities constitute repertoire at work. We saw repertoires embedded in action, talked about, argued over, enacted, and evaluated retrospectively. Learning, knowing, memorizing, describing, evaluating, selecting, and playing tunes—doing those things together constitutes repertoire, the culture of working musicians as it is constituted and reconstituted in the daily activities that make up the music business (Faulkner 2006).

The mundane activities that together create and maintain repertoire constitute *enactment.* Enactment links individual and shared knowledge to specific situations, each with its own demand characteristics emanating from audiences, employers, physical surroundings, and the assortment of players who have assembled for that gig. Players learn tunes and use what they have learned working jointly with others who have similarly learned tunes, to create, at least for that one time and often for longer periods, shared knowledge that enables them to perform together adequately (adequately enough for the situation).

We can generalize these features of the enactment process to other kinds of collective action. Generalized roles enacted into positions or generalized conceptions of social behavior appear in a variety of occupations—in religion, politics, business, medicine, and law, among others—as well as in such ubiquitous arenas of behavior as sex. Enactment processes occur in worlds of decision making in crime and policing, medicine, religion, and sports. As examples, consider the way sentencing guidelines constrain the ordering and prioritizing of judicial decisions in the criminal justice system; the way government regulations affect the diagnostic and treatment decisions of physicians; and the way general managers of professional baseball teams decide which players to hire, which to let go.

Repertoire, considered in this way as process, as something continuously made and remade as people acquire, exchange, learn, and teach the relevant elements, gives us a flexible tool for understanding forms of collective action.

Appendix

How We Did the Research

Sociologists routinely explain how they gathered the data on which their story rests. Here's our explanation. Faulkner, who continues to play professionally, kept extensive notes in 2005, 2006, and 2007 on many of the jobs he played and on his other contacts with musicians in the extended community of working musicians in Massachusetts's Amherst Valley and surrounding New England areas. He used those contacts, as well, to arrange extended interviews on topics of mutual interest (easily arranged because the musicians he interviewed found the topics as engrossing as he did). Becker, who no longer works professionally, used personal contacts to conduct a number of lengthy interviews with musicians in the San Francisco Bay area. The material from the two sites did not differ in any substantial way.

Between us, we interviewed fifty musicians, forty-seven men and three women, reflecting the very skewed gender distribution of the business (see Buscatto 2007 for observations on the similar situation in France). The people we interviewed played a variety of instruments: bass, drums, piano, guitar, tenor and baritone saxophone (the saxophone players usually doubled on other saxophones and flute), trumpet, and trombone. Twenty interviews were conducted informally. We conducted thirty more formal interviews, some recorded (twenty-six hours of recorded interviews were transcribed) with the permission of the people interviewed. Otherwise, we typed the interviews from memory shortly after they were done. Interviews lasted between one and three hours. On the five occasions where the opportunity arose, we showed people transcripts of their interviews and asked them to comment.

The ages of interviewees and of the people we observed ranged from 24 to the late 80s. Their musical tastes covered a wide range, from players who primarily played and liked older styles to strong advocates of very up-to-date contemporary jazz styles, and most of the possibilities between: players who identified as beboppers, as players in an older swing style, as post-boppers, and many unpredictable combinations of these. You could not guess or predict a player's musical allegiances and interests from his age, as we have remarked here and there in the text.

The formal interviews focused on what tunes interviewees knew, where and from whom they had learned them, who they had played them with, and similar matters. Sometimes we based our discussion on observations of the musicians playing that we had made earlier, sometimes shortly before our discussions. We avoided general questions about opinions and tastes as much as we could, and took full advantage of any possibility to focus questions and discussion on specific incidents we had observed or participated in while playing. We also took advantage of our own musical knowledge and experience to ask very specific questions about how and why people did what they did musically. We sometimes engaged interviewees in a mutual exploration of something they and we recognized as an interesting question, as in Becker's discussion with a bass player, detailed in chapter 4 as an example of deploying our own knowledge for datagathering purposes. The extensive quotations in the text usually make the nature of the interviews and observations clear. We have made some further remarks on this aspect of our data gathering elsewhere (Faulkner and Becker 2008).

We have made extensive use of our own experiences, both contemporary and autobiographical. That creates problems, since it's clear that we could tell the same story in different ways to make different points. At the same time, that's an advantage, since we can bring many years of experience to bear on the questions we're discussing. There is a vast literature of jazz biography, autobiography, and extended interviews (e.g., Gibbs 2003, Balliet 1986, Hinton and Berger, 1991, to pick a few off our shelves) in which other testimonies can be found. As they each tell an individual story, none of them is exactly like Becker's or Faulkner's, each reflecting the specificities of place and time, of temperament and experience, of the contingencies and accidents of history. But the underlying similarities are such that musicians recognize what they have in common despite those differences. In any event, in writing the autobiographical sections, we have tried to keep the reporting of what happened separate from the analytic ideas we then use those stories to illustrate.

We have not followed the practice of most books about jazz, by naming the people whose testimony furnishes the bulk of the evidence for what we have to say. We did this for several reasons. For the most part, these musicians are not so famous that their names would mean anything to anyone outside their immediate geographical area. Beyond that, because on occasion they say critical things about other players, some of them told us that they didn't want to be identified in the text, a request we honored. Furthermore, while the tradition of jazz studies routinely identifies people quoted and discussed, the tradition of sociology typically doesn't. To be sure, this is a disputed area of sociological practice, as what isn't? Some researchers feel strongly that identifying the people who have helped them by furnishing data serves several important purposes, among them honoring that contribution and also keeping the researcher honest by making it easier to check up on them. (See the discussion and the very different way of handling this problem in Duneier 1999, especially 347–52.) Finally, what sociology wants to do (and this is a great oversimplification, but we think justifiable in context) is not to tell the stories of individuals, but rather to tell the story of kinds of people, in this case of "ordinary musicians." To that end, we have, in the tradition of many great sociological researches based on fieldwork, not identified people or have changed their names when we thought it important.

We haven't produced what is now called an "ethnography" of the music scene in the Amherst Valley or in San Francisco or in the Chicago of the 1940s and 1950s. We aimed, instead, to use the descriptions we collected of incidents and events, of careers and situations, to bring to light the commonplace mechanisms through which musicians create and maintain the repertoire that supports their collective endeavors. We don't expect that every place where musicians work (or, for that matter, any particular place) will operate in this way. We do expect that the general dimensions of the processes involved will, when given values appropriate to specific situations, allow for understanding of the variety of results they produce. Since we have not tried to characterize a particular time and place, conventional criticism of our sampling would be beside the point.

References

Antin, David. 1984. *tuning*. New York: New Directions.

Balliet, Whitney. 1986. *American Musicians: 56 Portraits in Jazz*. New York: Oxford University Press.

Becker, Howard S. 1973. *Outsiders: Studies in the Sociology of Deviance*. New York: Free Press.

—. 1982. *Art Worlds*. Berkeley: University of California Press.

—. 1998. *Tricks of the Trade: How to Think about Your Research While You're Doing It*. Chicago: University of Chicago Press.

—. 2004a. "Interaction: Some Ideas." http://home.earthlink.net/~hsbecker/articles/interaction.html.

—. 2004b. "Quelques ideés sur l'interaction." In *L'art du terrain: Mélanges offerts à Howard S. Becker*, ed. Alain Blanc and Alain Pessin, 245–55. Paris: L'Harmattan.

Bennett, H. Stith. 1980. *On Becoming a Rock Musician.* Amherst: University of Massachusetts Press.

Berliner, Paul F. 1994. *Thinking in Jazz: The Infinite Art of Improvisation.* Chicago: University of Chicago Press.

Billard, François. 1988. *Lennie Tristano.* Montpellier: Éditions du Limon.

Blumer, Herbert. 1937. "Social Psychology." In *Man and Society,* ed. Emerson P. Schmidt, 144–98. New York: Prentice-Hall.

Buscatto, Marie. 2007. *Les femmes du jazz: Séduction, féminité(s), marginalisation.* Paris: CNRS Editions.

Coulangeon, Philippe. 1999. *Les musiciens de jazz en France.* Paris: L'Harmattan.

DeVeaux, Scott. 1989. "The Emergence of the Jazz Concert, 1935–1945." *American Music* 7:6–29.

Duneier, Mitchell. 1999. *Sidewalk.* New York: Farrar, Straus and Giroux.

Faulkner, Robert B. 2006. "Shedding Culture." In *Art from Start to Finish: Jazz, Painting, Writing, and Other Improvisations,* ed. Howard S. Becker, Robert R. Faulkner, and Barbara Kirshenblatt-Gimblett, 91–117. Chicago: University of Chicago Press.

Faulkner, Robert R., and Howard S. Becker. 2008. "Studying Something You Are Part Of: The View from the Bandstand." *Ethnologie française* XXXVIII:15–21.

Gibbs, Terry. 2003. *Good Vibes: A Life in Jazz.* With Cary Ginell. Lanham, MD: Scarecrow Press, 2003

Grazian, David. 2003. *Blue Chicago: The Search for Authenticity in Urban Blues Clubs.* Chicago: University of Chicago Press.

—. 2008. "The Jazzman's True Academy: Ethnography, Artistic Work and the Chicago Blues Scene," *Ethnologie française* 38:49–57.

Hall, Fred M. 1996. *It's About Time: The Dave Brubeck Story.* Fayetteville: University of Arkansas Press.

Hannerz, Ulf. 1969. *Soulside: Inquiries into Ghetto Culture and Community.* New York: Columbia University Press.

Hennion, Antoine. 1988. *Comment la musique vient aux enfants: Une anthropologie de l'enseignement musical.* Paris: Anthropos.

Hentoff, Nat. 1956. "Pres." *Down Beat* 23:9–11.

Hinton, Milt, and David G. Berger. 1991. *Bass Line: The Stories and Photographs of Milt Hinton.* Philadelphia: Temple University Press.

Hyman, Dick. 1982a. "150 More Tunes Everyone Ought to Know." *Keyboard* 8:57.

—. 1982b. "150 Standard Tunes Everyone Ought to Know." *Keyboard* 8.

Jenness, David, and Don Velsey. 2006. *Classic American Popular Song: The Second Half-Century, 1950–2000*. New York: Routledge.

Kernfeld, Barry. 1995. *What to Listen For in Jazz.* New Haven: Yale University Press.

—. 2003. "Pop Song Piracy, Fake Books, and a Pre-History of Sampling." In *Copyright and the Networked Computer: A Stakeholder's Congress.* University of California Washington Center: Washington, DC.

—. 2006. *The Story of Fake Books: Bootlegging Songs to Musicians.* Lanham, MD: Scarecrow Press.

Kroeber, Alfred D. 1917. "The Superorganic." *American Anthropologist* 19:163–213.

Kuhn, Thomas. 1970. *The Structure of Scientific Revolutions.* Chicago: University of Chicago Press.

Lewis, George E. 2000. "Teaching Improvised Music: An Ethnographic Memoir." In *Arcana: Musicians on Music,* ed. John Zorn, 78–109. New York: Granary Books.

—. 2008. *A Power Stronger Than Itself: The AACM and American Experimental Music.* Chicago: University of Chicago Press.

MacLeod, Bruce. 1993. *Club Date Musicians: Playing the New York Party Circuit.* Urbana: University of Illinois Press.

McNeill, William H. 1995. *Keeping Together in Time: Dance and Drill in Human History.* Cambridge: Harvard University Press.

Monson, Ingrid. 1996. *Saying Something: Jazz Improvisation and Interaction.* Chicago: University of Chicago Press.

Pearson, Nathan W., Jr. 1987. *Goin' to Kansas City.* Urbana: University of Illinois Press.

Perrenoud, Marc. 2007. *Les musicos: Enquête sur des musiciens ordinaires.* Paris: La Découverte.

Redfield, Robert. 1941. *The Folk Culture of Yucatan.* Chicago: University of Chicago Press.

—. 1956. *The Little Community.* Chicago: University of Chicago Press.

Schutz, Alfred. 1964. "Making Music Together: A Study in Social Relationship." In *Collected Papers: Studies in Social Theory,* ed. Arvid Broderson, 159–78. The Hague, Netherlands: Martinus Nijhoff.

Shim, Eunmi. 2007. *Lennie Tristano: His Life in Music.* Ann Arbor: University of Michigan Press.

Slonimsky, Nicolas. 1947. *Thesaurus of Scales and Melodic Patterns.* New York: Charles Scribner's Sons.

Steinberg, Marc W. 1995. "The Roar of the Crowd: Repertoires of Discourse and Collective Action among the Spitalfields Silk Weavers in Nineteenth-Century London." In *Repertoires and Cycles of Collective Action,* ed. Mark Traugott, 57–87. Durham: Duke University Press.

Sudnow, David. 1978. *Ways of the Hand: The Organization of Improvised Conduct.* Cambridge, MA: Harvard University Press.

Sumner, William Graham. 1906. *Folkways.* Boston: Ginn and Co.

Swidler, Ann. 1986. "Culture in Action." *American Sociological Review* 51:273–86.

Tarde, Gabriel. 1999 (1901). *Les lois sociales.* Paris: Institut Synthélabo.

Thomas, Robert McG., Jr. 1996. "Harold Fox, Who Took Credit for the Zoot Suit, Dies at 86." *New York Times,* August 1.

Tilly, Charles. 1977. "Getting it Together in Burgundy." *Theory and Society* 4:479–504.

—. 1995. "Contentious Repertoires in Great Britain, 1758–1835." In *Repertoires and Cycles of Collective Action,* ed. Mark Traugott, 15–42. Durham: Duke University Press.

—. 2006. *Regimes and Repertoires.* Chicago: University of Chicago Press.

Traugott, Mark. 1995. "Barricades as Repertoire: Continuities and Discontinuities in the History of French Contention." In *Repertoires and Cycles of Collective Action,* 43–63. Durham: Duke University Press.

Wilder, Alec. 1972. *American Popular Song: The Great Innovators, 1900–1950.* New York: Oxford University Press.

Front Cover Flap

Every night, somewhere in the world, three or four musicians will climb on stage together. Whether the gig is at a jazz club, a bar, or a bar mitzvah, the performance never begins with a note, but with a question. The trumpet player might turn to the bassist and ask, "Do you know 'Body and Soul'?"—and from there the subtle craft of playing the jazz repertoire is tested in front of a live audience. These ordinary musicians may never have played together—they may never have met—so how do they smoothly put on a show without getting booed offstage?

In *"Do You Know...?"* Robert R. Faulkner and Howard S. Becker—both jazz musicians with decades of experience performing—present the view from the bandstand, revealing the array of skills necessary for working musicians to do their jobs. While learning songs from sheet music or by ear helps, the jobbing musician's lexicon is dauntingly massive: hundreds of thousands of tunes from jazz classics and pop standards to more exotic fare. Since it is impossible for anyone to memorize all of these songs, Faulkner and Becker show that musicians collectively negotiate and improvise their way to a successful performance. Players must explore each others' areas of expertise, develop an ability to fake their way through unfamiliar territory, and respond to the unpredictable demands of their audience—whether an unexpected gang of polka fanatics or a tipsy father of the bride with an obscure favorite song.

"Do You Know...?" dishes out entertaining stories and sharp insights drawn from the authors' own experiences and observations as well as interviews with a range of musicians. Faulkner and Becker's vivid, detailed portrait of the musician at work holds valuable lessons for anyone who has to think on the spot or under a spotlight.

Back Cover Flap

ROBERT R. FAULKNER is professor of sociology at the University of Massachusetts and the author of *Hollywood Studio Musicians* and *Music on Demand: Composers and Careers in the Hollywood Film Industry*.

HOWARD S. BECKER is the author of several books, including *Telling About Society*, *Tricks of the Trade*, and *Art Worlds*. Together, with Barbara Kirshenblatt-Gimblett, they are coeditors of *Art from Start to Finish: Jazz, Painting, Writing, and Other Improvisations*.

Back Cover Material

"This book consists of a seamless blend of anecdotes and analysis, filled with delight and insight. Faulkner and Becker, writing from their twin perspectives of professional jazz players and renowned scholars, offer an unprecedented understanding of the interpersonal dynamics of jazz performance and the implications of using jazz as a model for understanding negotiations in other realms of human interaction."

BARRY KERNFELD, editor of *The New Grove Dictionary of Jazz*

"Faulkner and Becker's argument that repertoire is a process has broad implications for understanding collective action in different fields of endeavor and for rethinking the place of the art work in music studies. Writing with characteristic skill and wit, the authors illuminate the vital interplay between the factors shaping repertories and the cultivation of individual artistic voices. They take readers on an exacting

journey through jazz musicians' daily challenges as they prepare for performances and create music on the bandstand. Analyzing musical triumphs and failures, the authors illuminate the deep aural knowledge and skills of 'ordinary' musicians. This is a book that will inspire readers to listen with new admiration and attention."
PAUL BERLINER, author of *Thinking in Jazz: The Infinite Art of Improvisation*

"Splendidly well crafted, *'Do You Know...?'* transfuses the intertwining social and cultural realities of performance practice into social science, for use by all of us. This is an utterly lucid and convincing duet between very different yet complementary dual player/scholars built from four decades of nighttime gigs across the continent. Dense and locally contingent, Faulkner and Becker displace grand claims with deeply detailed and interactive memoir and gossip that magically evokes an era, singing both dirge and triumph."
HARRISON C. WHITE, Giddings Professor of Sociology, Columbia University